Eternity in Time

Eternity in Time

A Study of Karl Rahner's Eschatology

Peter C. Phan

Selinsgrove: Susquehanna University Press
London and Toronto: Associated University Presses

Associated University Presses
440 Forsgate Drive
Cranbury, NJ 08512

Associated University Presses
25 Sicilian Avenue
London WCIA 2QH, England

Associated University Presses
P.O. Box 488, Port Credit
Mississauga, Ontario
Canada L5G 4M2

The paper used in this publication meets the requirements
of the American National Standard for Permanence of Paper
for Printed Library Materials Z39.48–1984.

Library of Congress Cataloging-in-Publication Data

Phan, Peter C., 1943–
  Eternity in time.

  Bibliography: p.
  Includes index.
  1. Eschatology—History of doctrines—20th
century. 2. Rahner, Karl, 1904– . I. Title.
BT821.2.P48   1988   236′.092′4   86-43217
ISBN 0-941664-83-X (alk. paper)

PRINTED IN THE UNITED STATES OF AMERICA

In memory of Felix
whose sense of wonder was contagious
and to Ed and Syble
with love and gratitude

Contents

Preface

Most religious traditions have maintained a keen interest in the life beyond; indeed one of their functions is to provide answers to questions regarding the ultimate and transcendent destiny both of the individual human being and of universal history. Christianity is no exception. Its creed professes that Jesus, its founder, will come again to judge the living and the dead and that there will be the resurrection of the body and life everlasting.

Eschatology, the theological treatise investigating the Last Things, has had quite a checkered career. After a long period of benign neglect it made at the turn of this century a dramatic comeback onto the theological scene. Among Roman Catholic theologians, Karl Rahner (1904–84) played a key role in reenvisioning eschatology. Unfortunately there have been no monographic studies on his eschatology. The present work, which is an exposition and critique, is intended to fill this gap.

After locating eschatology within Rahner's overall theological achievement, the work proceeds to situate his eschatology in the context of contemporary eschatologies. The first part examines what Rahner calls transcendental eschatology. Since for Rahner eschatology is anthropology read in its mode of future fulfillment in christological terms, those aspects of his anthropology which have a direct bearing on eschatology are examined. These are grouped under three rubrics: the unity of humankind's final consummation, the conditions of possibility for eschatological fulfillment, and the anticipation of the Kingdom of God. This part concludes with an investigation of Rahner's most influential contributions to eschatology, namely, his principles for interpreting eschatological assertions.

The following two parts examine Rahner's categorical eschatology, that is, his understanding of the particular *eschata*. In the course of the exposition it will be apparent, I hope, how the previous reflections on his anthropology and hermeneutics will pay handsome dividends, as it becomes clear that without them Rahner's theology of the particular *eschata* would be well-nigh unintelligible.

Traditionally eschatology is divided into two parts, individual and collective. Regarding this division two questions, one material, the other methodological, need be addressed before we begin the task of expounding

Rahner's categorical eschatology. The first question concerns the contents of the two parts of eschatology and the relationship between them. Older neo-scholastic manuals tended to provide a considerable amount of detailed information on the other side of life, which they derived from the eschatological assertions of Scripture and tradition, taking these as advance reportorial descriptions of things to come.[1] In reaction to this tendency, some contemporary Catholic writers go to the other extreme of keeping an almost total silence on or at most giving only a cursory treatment of the fate of the individual and concentrate instead on the collective eschatology.[2]

Rahner has not written a systematic treatise on eschatology, and hence it is impossible to determine exactly how he would structure his own treatment of the subject. However, from his proposed scheme of dogmatic theology,[3] his hermeneutical considerations,[4] his *Foundations of Christian Faith*,[5] and his sundry articles on aspects of eschatology, it is apparent that Rahner intends to give a balanced treatment to both the individual and collective eschatologies without falling into the error either of treating eschatological assertions as reports on the afterlife or of reducing individual eschatology to collective eschatology and vice versa.

As regards the relationship between the two parts of eschatology, from his considerations of human beings as substantial unities of spirit and matter, of soul and body, and of their intrinsic sociality, it is clear that Rahner considers the two as constitutive parts of the one eschatology. For pedagogic reasons, they have to be treated separately since one cannot say everything at one time. But their indissoluble unity is unmistakably clear, even from the way Rahner entitles the two parts as "the *one* eschatology as individual eschatology" and "the *one* eschatology as collective eschatology." "In eschatology," asserts Rahner, "we always have to speak both collectively and individually, both spiritually and corporeally, just as we have to in anthropology. This duality cannot be subsumed and transcended, but neither can this duality be understood as indiscriminate statements about quite different realities."[6]

This brings us to the second methodological question, namely, which of the two eschatologies should be treated first. As I explain in chapter 1, traditional textbooks often treat individual eschatology first. A notable exception is Michael Schmaus's massive *Katholische Dogmatik*, vol. 4, pt. 2 and his later, more popular *Dogma 6: Justification and the Last Things*.[7] Rahner has not addressed himself expressly to the question. In his proposed scheme of dogmatic theology he had intended to treat death and the possibility of hell as private destiny under the heading of anthropology, and under the heading of eschatology he had planned to discuss the relation between individual eschatology and collective eschatology. However, in his distribution of the various elements of eschatology, he did not make any separation between individual and collective eschatology. In *Foundations of Christian Faith*, Rahner presents individual eschatology first without giving any justification for this order. One may think that Rahner merely follows the customary way of structuring the treatise on eschatology. Perhaps it is not implausible to suggest that this order mirrors Rahner's view of the development of individual human persons who become themselves in the "first otherness" in themselves and then in "the second otherness," namely, with other human beings and God. In my exposition of Rahner's eschatology I will adopt Rahner's order in *Foundations of Christian Faith*.

Under the rubric of individual eschatology, we will discuss Rahner's theology of death (chapter 4), of the intermediate state and "purgatory" (chapter 5), and of heaven and hell (chapter 6). Under collective eschatology, we will consider Rahner's theology of Christ's Resurrection and Parousia and of the resurrection of the body (chapter 7) and of the final consummation (chapter 8).

It is my greatest pleasure to record here my profound gratitude to Prof. Joseph Laishley and Prof. Anthony Baxter of the University of London and Prof. Brian Hebblethwaite of Cambridge University for expert advice and to Dr. Linda Stinson of the University of Texas at Arlington for her careful reading of the manuscript and critical comments. I also thank Dr. Thomas Carroll for his generosity of spirit and the typically Irish hospitality he gave me during my trips to the isle of saints and scholars and on many other occasions. My warm thanks are given as well to Dr. Dennis Slattery and Dr. and Mrs. A. Nicholas Fargnoli for their friendship and inspiration. I am also grateful to Mrs. Nancy O'Boyle for her encouragement and support. James and Monique Lynch and their family have always been magnanimous in their kindness and affection and to them my sincerest thanks. My gratitude also goes to Mrs. Jeri Guadagnoli who typed parts of the manuscript and Mrs. Alice Puro who was most helpful in obtaining research materials on interlibrary loan. My family, especially my parents, have constantly supported me, and to them I express here my eternal gratitude. Lastly, I owe particular thanks to Dr. David N. Wiley, director of Susquehanna University Press and his staff, in particular Ms. Lauren Lepow and Ms. Beth Gianfagna, for their generous and competent editorial services.

Of course for the shortcomings of this work I alone bear the responsibility. I hope that in spite of its deficiencies this book will not only help the reader obtain a grasp of Rahner's eschatology but also will serve as a useful introduction to contemporary eschatology in general.

Eternity in Time

Introduction: Eschatology and Rahner's Theology

> Der Traktat der Eschatologie ist noch sehr im Anfang seiner Geschichte; das Geschichtlichste hat in der Theologie des Christentums noch am wenigsten Geschichte gehabt. Es ist aber in einer Situation, die durch das moderne naturwissenschaftliche Bild einer Werdewelt, durch die Entfesselung des Willens zur vorausschauend-planenden und rationalisierten Änderung aller Verhältnisse des Menschen als des sich selbst und seine Umwelt schaffenden Wesens, durch die Möglichkeit einer Ausweitung des menschlichen Dasensraumes über die Erde hinaus, durch neuzeitliche politisch-militante Welthäresien eines innerweltlichen Utopismus usw. gekennzeichnet ist, nötig, dass die christliche Eschatologie sich, mehr als bisher sich selbst durchdenkend, selber finde. (*LThK*, 3:1095)

I. Eschatology in Christian Theology: A Brief Introduction to the Theme

Few treatises, if any, in Christian dogmatic theology have undergone such dramatic shifts of emphasis and mutation of contents as eschatology or the doctrine of the Last Things. Rooted in the articles of the creed professing Christ's future coming to judge the living and the dead and our expectation of the resurrection of the body and life everlasting, the Christian doctrine of the Last Things from the beginning was animated by a twofold conviction. On the one hand, it held fast to the reality of salvation already brought about by Jesus Christ in his life, death, and Resurrection. On the other hand, it resolutely directed the believers' eyes toward the imminent eschatological event, Christ's Parousia. The Lord, who was born, lived, died, and was raised and exalted to God's right hand for us and for our salvation, would return on clouds of glory to consummate the new age: the dead would be raised, the final judgment pronounced, the whole created order restored, and Christ would hand his kingdom over to the Father, so that God may be "all in all" (cf. 1 Cor 15:28). Meanwhile the Church, a pilgrim people on the march between the two poles of Christ's glorification and his final manifestation, by responding to God's gift of him-

self in the Spirit, advances in hope toward the Kingdom of God. Thus,
Christian eschatology is centered on Jesus Christ, the *Eschaton*. Its dimensions are essentially christological, ecclesial, and cosmic.

The expectation of the Kingdom of God[1] *as such* is of course not a peculiar trait of Christianity. Indeed, Jesus' message of the imminent coming of
the Kingdom of God can only be properly understood against the background of the expectation of that Kingdom by the people of ancient Israel
and late Judaism, even though the concept of Kingdom of God was given a
radically new interpretation by Jesus. Together with the master ideas of
covenant out of which it grew, messianism in the broader sense lies at the
heart of the Old Testament and intertestamental Judaism.[2] There was a
persistent expectation of an age of salvation at the end of time that would
culminate in the installation of the Kingdom of God. Messianism is, of
course, a very complex concept and one that has undergone several stages
of development.[3] Nevertheless, the flame of hope in a future deliverance,
in a Kingdom where universal justice and peace reign, whether to be
brought about by a descendant of David's dynasty or directly by Yahweh
himself, whether at the end of history or outside of it, was kept burning in
the spiritual hearth of the people of God by their prophets, their liturgy,
and their apocalyptic visionaries. Nor was this hope less fervent outside of
the canonical Hebrew Scriptures. If anything, it was intensified and expressed with the help of the most fantastic and extravagant imagery. It was
nourished by the expectation of a new world and a new age that would be
ushered in by the victory of God over the powers of evil. God's triumph in
this final cosmic struggle would bring about the collapse of the visible
world.[4]

The New Testament presents Jesus as the fulfillment of the expectation
and destiny of Israel. By giving Jesus the title Messiah-Christ, the early
Church identified his person with the object of Israel's millennial hope,
namely, the Kingdom of God. Thus, the Jesus who had preached the coming of the Kingdom of God became the Christ embodying the Kingdom in
the kerygma of the Church. This shift of the center of gravity was legiti-
mized by the Jesus of history himself. The Synoptic Gospels consistently
attest Jesus' consciousness of the unique character of his relation to the
Kingdom of God and its earthly manifestation (Mk 1:15; Mt 4:17; Lk
4:43). In his baptism he was declared by the heavenly voice to be the Ser-
vant of God and the Lord's Anointed (Mk 1:10–11; Mt 3:16–17; Lk
3:22). This messianic awareness is underscored in Matthew and Luke
through the reconstruction of the temptation scene in which Jesus rejects
some conceptions of the Kingdom of God current in contemporary Jewish
expectations (Mt 4:1–11; Lk 4:1–13). Jesus performs his miracles as a
declaration of war upon the 'Kingdom of Satan' (Mk 3:24) and as demon-
stration that in his own person (Lk 17:20) or through his mission (Lk

11:20; Mt 12:28) the Kingdom of God has become a present reality. The presence of the Kingdom here and now in Jesus is strongly emphasized above all by John with his themes of the judgment of Christ, the "Light of the world" (1:9; 8:12; 12:46) and the gift of the Paraclete (14:16, 26; 15:26; 16:7).

On the other hand, the New Testament also professes no less firmly that the Kingdom of God is a future, i. e., eschatological, reality. It is already inaugurated within history, in the death and Resurrection of Jesus, but it will reach its final and perfect form only in the ultimate future into which we are invited to enter (Mt 5:20; 7:21; 18:3; 19:23; 21:31; 22:12; 22:13; 25:10, 21, 23; Mk 9:47; Jn 3:5). This future dimension of the Kingdom becomes very clear in a variety of contexts: when we are urged to pray for its coming (Mt 6:10); when the eschatological meal is described (Mk 14:25; Lk 22:30); when the marriage feast and its guests are represented (Mt 8:11; 22:2–13; 25:1–12; Lk 14:16–24); when the Kingdom is identified with eternal bliss (Mt 5:3–10; 13:43; Lk 12:32, 37); when the Kingdom is said to dawn with the Parousia of Christ and his judgment separating the good from the wicked (Mk 9:11; Mt 16:28; 25:31–36).

In sum, as Rudolf Schnackenburg puts it, "Since the Kingdom of God with all its salvific power is present in Jesus and his ministry its complete and perfect revelation in the future is already assured. But this fulfillment is as yet an object of hope, and the working out of salvation in this present time is but a suggestion, a beginning or a sign and anticipation of what is to come."[5] The early Church, consequently, was always conscious that the Kingdom of God under Christ was still on the way, and the Church itself was a pilgrim people, strangers and sojourners in this world, constantly watching and yearning for the definitive inbreak of the Kingdom. And nowhere is the orientation of the Church toward the future coming of the Kingdom more explicitly revealed than in the Eucharist, which anticipates the eating and drinking at the Lord's table in the Kingdom (Lk 22:30).

It is common knowledge that the postapostolic Church kept the hope in the future coming of the Lord very much alive.[6] Furthermore, the close connection between the Easter events and the fate of the individual Christian as well as that of the world was firmly maintained.[7] This eschatological consciousness was eloquently expressed by martyrdom, exacerbated by heretical sects such as Montanism and millenarianism, and later nurtured by monasticism. In patristic theology, the essential connections between individual eschatology and collective eschatology were well preserved; the fate of the individual human being and the destiny of universal history and the cosmos were seen as indissolubly intertwined. Perhaps more than anyone else, Origen looked forward to an *apocatastasis*, the salvation and restoration of all beings in Christ.[8] In the West, Augustine became deeply interested in God's action in history, and in books 19 to 22 of the *City of*

God he explicitly discussed the end and punishment of the Earthly City and the eternal bliss of the City of God. At the same time, in this context Augustine also dealt with the Last Things of the individual, so that a happy balance between the individual and collective eschatologies was preserved.

This equilibrium was further maintained in the Middle Ages. Augustine's sense of history was preserved in Isidore of Seville and later in the twelfth century, particularly in Hugh of Saint-Victor. The eschatological awareness was also fomented by the various religious orders that sprang up in the course of time, by the heresies of Joachim of Fiore and the Fraticelli, by medieval biblical exegesis with its anagogical sense, by the first systematic treatment of the Last Things in Peter Lombard's *Book of Sentences* (bk. 4, distinctions 43 to 50) and by Thomas Aquinas's discussion of the end of man in *Summa Theologiae* (1ᵃ IIᵃᵉ, qq. 1–5) and of the life beyond in his commentary on the *Fourth Book of the Sentences* and in *Summa contra Gentiles* (bk. 4, qq. 79–96).

Unfortunately, the Reformation and the Counter-Reformation lost sight of the collective eschatology. Their attention was absorbed by the fate of the individual and their energy dissipated by controverted questions, such as the existence of purgatory, the nature of the beatific vision, and the nature of the fire of hell. Indeed, it can be said with justice that ever since Benedict XII defined that the direct vision of God—in the case of the just who are fully purified—and the punishment of hell for those dying in mortal sin begin even 'before' the general judgment,[9] the fundamental structure of the treatise on eschatology (*De Novissimis*) with its division into two parts, individual and collective eschatologies, became fixed, and the basic truths regarding the Last Things were universally and peacefully accepted. And, in the same process, eschatology unfortunately became a secondary and irrelevant appendix of dogmatic theology. Dealing with matters beyond the range of human experience, it quickly degenerated into empty speculation on irrelevancies.[10] As proof of this scarce theological interest, it is enough to note that the multivolume *Dictionnaire de théologie catholique* of 1913 devoted to eschatology only one column, and not a complete one at that, where it was said among other things that the term 'eschatology' had generally not yet acquired the right of citizenship in French theology. The state of affairs was not better in German theology: the *Lexikon für Theologie und Kirche* of 1931 devoted a mere forty-nine lines to the entry on 'eschatology'. Writing on the history of the treatise on eschatology, Rahner wryly remarked: "The history of the revelation of the Last Things down to and including the whole New Testament, is long and rich, but the history of eschatology is meagre in comparison with that of other sections of dogmatic theology, at least within the limits of ecclesiastical orthodoxy or in contact with this."[11]

II. Eschatology and Its Place in Rahner's Theology

It is against the barren, stultified neo-scholastic eschatology as expounded in seminary manuals that Rahner directed his scathing criticism in one of his earliest essays. Reviewing dogmatic treatises on eschatology published up to 1954, he remarked:

> We may consult any bibliography we like, and yet be horrified by the thinness or the entire lack of properly dogmatic investigation into the theology of death. Poets and philosophers reflect on it; but in our theology all we find is a few chilly remarks on death as a penal consequence of original sin. And that is pretty well all. What is said about it in Eschatology is at most a tenth of what we could learn from revealed sources, if we really read them with all our mind and heart. What thinness and lack of interest in Eschatology itself. Why can we find no work, at least no exact, thorough and patient work, on the rules of interpretation of eschatological utterances in the revealed sources? The eschatological reality itself and the mode of its manifestation inevitably act as co-determinants of the *genus literarium* of such utterances. And yet all we find on the question as to what is content and what form in such utterance is *ad hoc* improvisation. Who has ever written a theology of the concept of time and of our understanding of it? Until as late as the eighteenth century there was at least some speculation about Heaven and its local character. Today we say that Heaven is a place and that no one knows where it is. Simple, but a little too convenient. Surely there is more to be said than that. In the field of eschatology a great deal more could be done from the point of view of history of dogma alone.[12]

This long text not only gives a clear expression to Rahner's profound dissatisfaction with neo-scholastic eschatology but also exhibits his deep interest in the subject already at the early stage of his theological career. Moreover, it lists a number of themes (e. g., death, hermeneutics of eschatological assertions, theology of time, etc.) on which he will make significant and highly original contributions. As an appendix to the article from which the quotation is taken, Rahner proposes a scheme for a treatise of dogmatic theology that he had constructed many years earlier in collaboration with Hans Urs von Balthasar.[13] Of course, because it is nothing more than a sketch composed of cryptogrammic titles, it is not possible to form a clear idea of how Rahner himself would develop the themes indicated and how he would relate them to each other in the concrete. Nevertheless, the scheme on eschatology[14] is extremely interesting both because it indicates the way in which Rahner would structure his subject matter and because some of the themes he suggested were not usually treated in an average textbook on eschatology in the fifties. It is significant, for example, that in his projected treatise, Rahner did not follow the hallowed tradition of dividing into two parts, individual and collective eschatologies, and attempted to overcome such dichotomy by including a specific discussion on the relation between the two eschatologies. It is also of great interest that he placed the topic of death under the rubric of theological ✓ anthropology and not eschatology proper in order to avoid a too restricted treatment of it.[15] Moreover, it is noteworthy that he drew attention to the need for both a special hermeneutics of eschatological assertions and for an investigation of general concepts such as time, matter, and spirit for an intelligible discussion of Christian eschatology. Finally, it is highly significant that he emphasized the priority of collective eschatology over individual eschatology.[16]

In another article prepared for the second edition of the *Lexikon für Theologie und Kirche* some five years later,[17] Rahner expanded considerably his discussion of the nature of the dogmatic treatise on eschatology. First of all he pointed out that new factors urgently called for a renewal of eschatology: the evolutionary view of the world in modern sciences, the ability of human beings to manipulate themselves genetically and to plan their future, the possibility of extending the living space for humanity beyond the earth, and the militant activism of worldwide secular utopian ideologies.[18] He reiterated the need to elaborate a basic principle for determining the nature of eschatology and distinguishing it from false apocalyptic and to formulate a hermeneutics of eschatological statements.[19]

Not content, however, with repeating his past recommendation, Rahner moved on to suggest that the dogmatic treatise on eschatology should deal with both the universal propositions of eschatology and particular themes, the former as the context for making the latter intelligible. The universal propositions would constitute a transcendental eschatology or, as Rahner termed it in a later essay, an "eschatology of transcendental theology."[20] Such a transcendental eschatology, he suggested, would discuss, among other things, the intrinsic finitude and historical nature of time stretching from a genuine beginning to a genuine irreplaceable end; the 'once for all' character of each part of sacred history; death and the event of change effected by God as the necessary mode of genuine fulfillment of time; the fact that the end is already given in the Incarnation, death, and Resurrection of Jesus; the presence of this end as constituting the fact of the victorious mercy of God; the special character of time 'after' Christ; the permanent element of strife and conflict (the presence of the Antichrist) during this time that is intensified as the end approaches; the convergence of the natural and supernatural ends of the individual and the cosmos.[21]

Furthermore Rahner directed our attention to the following particular themes that neo-scholastic eschatology often ignored: the final abolition of the cosmic powers of law and death; the judgment as the consummation of the world; the abiding significance of Jesus' humanity for beatitude; the positive meaning of the inequality of the glory of heaven; the beatific vision as vision of the abiding mystery; the relation of the heaven of the redeemed to the rejected world of the devils; the positive meaning of the persistence of evil and the nature of the latter; the metaphysical nature of glorified corporeality; the one Kingdom of God composed of angels and human beings.[22]

As is clear from neo-scholastic manuals, one of the weak points of traditional eschatology is the gaping chasm separating individual eschatology from collective eschatology. This artificial division gives a flavor of mythology to the eschatological assertions and renders them unconvincing to modern hearers. To overcome this danger Rahner urged that attention should be paid to the necessary dialectic between the statements regarding individual *eschata* and those regarding universal *eschata*. Such a dialectic between these series of affirmations must be maintained; it should not be eliminated either by artificially dividing them and treating them separately (e. g., immortality of the 'soul' in individual eschatology and resurrection of the 'body' in collective eschatology) or by discarding one of the eschatologies in favor of the other.[23]

Finally, Rahner recommended that eschatology be integrated with other treatises of dogmatic theology, in particular, protology, the theology of history, theological anthropology, christology, soteriology, and ecclesiology, and that a confrontation of Christian eschatology be made with secular utopias and the eschatologies of other religions.[24]

In the meantime, from 1959 when his programmatic article on eschatology first appeared until his death on 3 March 1984 Rahner did not content himself with simply dispensing prescriptions on how to write on eschatology. Of course he never produced a complete treatise on eschatology as such nor a general synthesis—a sort of a *summa*—of his theology in which eschatology would find a place. His preferred genre always remained the essay.[25] Over the years, however, he wrote, besides a monograph on the theology of death, a sizable number of articles dealing with different aspects or themes of eschatology.[26]

Rahner's interest in eschatology remained constant. Not only did he write on eschatology, he also periodically assessed the theological writings on the subject. As he had done in 1954, he undertook some twelve years later a survey of eschatological literature. What he found did not fill him with enthusiasm:

> Finally we must include everything which can come under the heading of dogmatic eschatology. We lack a real hermeneutics of eschatological statements; there must be much more radical thought about the relationship between individual and collective eschatology if our pro-

clamation of the 'last things' is to be really worthy of belief today. The fundamental tenor of modern people's existence by no means exempts them from the danger of falling back into an Old Testament attitude toward the 'beyond'; the hope and postulate of an eternal life for the individual are not common assumptions forming a basis for discussion, as in the time of the rationalistic Enlightenment, but attitudes into which people of today and tomorrow must first be carefully 'initiated'. Christian eschatology has not yet been obliged to face up sufficiently to the secular and utopian 'eschatology' of the age beginning now, with its view of a single humanity, its 'hominisation' of environment, and our manipulation of ourselves—a period in which the person's *practice*, as opposed to what was previously his *theory*, appears in a totally new way as his highest and as his specific characteristic. A theology of hope has yet to be developed out of the dry attempts textbooks have made concerning the theological Virtue of Hope. We have as yet no theological ontology of hope, showing the human person as essentially one who exists *in hope*, and whose hope springs from an independent and original source that cannot be explained adequately simply in terms of a knowledge of the organic and evolutionary character of being and its possibilities. Only such a theology of hope as this could really come to grips competently with the Marxist conception of man.[27]

This lengthy quotation, in comparison with its counterpart cited above, is again extremely illuminating. Not only does it contain Rahner's basic critique of neo-scholastic eschatology of more recent vintage and the fundamental themes of his own eschatology, but it also clearly shows an enlargement and development, quite homogeneous to be sure, of his theological horizon.[28] There is now a more pronounced emphasis on the need for an ontological grounding of Christian hope and on the sociopolitical dimension of Christian eschatology.

Again one year later, in his article, "Theology and Anthropology," Rahner observed not without a touch a humor:

It seems to me that academic eschatology is still not far enough beyond the mentality of the professor of dogmatics who says he never maintained that the Archangel Michael's judgment-trumpet was a 'tuba materialis' but he would certainly defend the view that the sound of this trumpet was a 'tonus materialis'. Instead of really being theology, which always essentially involves criticism of images and models, academic eschatology is often a sort of puzzle in which one tries to unite into a single picture the images of Scripture, which cannot be so fitted together in a plastic form, neither do they claim as much.[29]

That eschatology occupies a central place in Rahner's theology is confirmed not only by his early interest in the subject, his repeated criticisms of the eschatology of the manuals, and his own voluminous explorations on the theme, but above all by his understanding of the Christian creed and the position of eschatology in it. Ever anxious to proclaim the Christian message in a credible manner to the men and women of our pluralist and militantly atheistic age, Rahner pointed out the necessity of a 'short formula' of the Christian faith. He was of course aware that because of our cultural and theological pluralism it is no longer possible to devise any one single and universally valid basic formula of the Christian faith applicable to the whole Church. Nevertheless it is urgently required that different basic formulas of the faith be composed. These, on the one hand, should contain only the essential (and, hence, christological) elements of the Christian faith, keeping in mind the "hierarchy of truths" as taught by Vatican II, and, on the other, in spite of their brevity, should be such as are readily intelligible to the hearers and brought home to them without recourse to lengthy commentaries.[30] Disclaiming any universality and binding force, Rahner proposed a three-part creed. The first formula is called "theological," the second "sociological" or "anthropological," and the third "futurologist." Of topical interest is of course the third formula, which reads: "Christianity is the religion which keeps open the question about the absolute future which wills to give itself in its own reality by self-communication, and which has established this will as eschatologically irreversible in Jesus Christ, and this future is called God."[31] This essentially eschatological character of Christianity is already explicity mentioned in the first formula. In it, it is said that "the eschatological climax of God's historical self-communication, in which this self-communication becomes manifest as irreversible and victorious, is called Jesus Christ."[32] This eschatological character is also *implicitly* affirmed in the second formula insofar as it is therein said that, because of the eschatological, victorious, and historical climax of God's self-communication in Jesus Christ, God is loved at least anonymously in the individual's love for the neighbor.[33] Thus, it is indisputably clear that for Rahner all Christian theology is in a very genuine sense eschatology, since for him Christian eschatology is nothing but Christian anthropology read in the future tense,[34] and Christian anthropology in turn is necessarily Christian theology.[35]

Lastly, the capital importance of eschatology in Rahner's theological system can readily be seen in the way in which he constructs his later 'searching christology' in an attempt to assist contemporary men and women to gain a clearer and more existential grasp of Christ. Of the three appeals of a "searching christology," two, the second and the third, are directly concerned with eschatology: the appeals to readiness for death and to hope in the future.[36] Furthermore there is a heavy eschatological emphasis in Rahner's ecclesiology, sacramentology, and theological anthropology.

III. Studies on Rahner's Eschatology

Rahner's theology, more than that of any other contemporary Catholic theologian, has been the object of numerous learned disquisitions. A cursory glance at existing Rahnerian studies[37] will show that most of these focus on Rahner's philosophical presuppositions,[38] his theological method,[39] his doctrine of God,[40] his christology,[41] his theological anthropology,[42] his theory of "anonymous Christianity."[43] and his theology of spiritual life.[44] These themes, without doubt, are essential in Rahner's theology and deserve careful and extensive investigation. It is, however, a regrettable lacuna that eschatology, despite its central importance for Rahner's theological system, has received scant attention. Secondary literature on the subject is composed mostly of articles, the majority of which are quite broad and are limited to the topic of death. Cornelius Ernst,[45] Lorenz Stampa,[46] Philip Lawler,[47] Enrique Laje,[48] Bernardo Mesa,[49] Florent Gaboriau,[50] Rosalie Ryan,[51] Juan Luis Ruiz de la Peña,[52] Nazareno Camilleri,[53] F. Szabo,[54] Josef Manser,[55] Hermann Wohlgschaft,[56] Herbert Vorgrimler,[57] Klaus P. Fischer,[58] Wolfhart Pannenberg,[59] Bartholomew J. Callopy,[60] William M. Thompson,[61] Norbert A. Luyten,[62] Leo J. O'Donovan,[63] Silvano Zucal,[64] and Robert J. Ochs[65] have discussed Rahner's theology of death in one way or another.

These authors, except the two last mentioned, because of the limitations imposed by the genre, could not deal with the theme in an exhaustive fashion. Ochs' book, *The Death in Every Now,* which grew out of his doctoral dissertation presented at the Institut Catholique in Paris, focuses only on Rahner's theology of death and not on his eschatology as such. Although the author has successfully orchestrated the various strands of Rahner's theology of death, freedom, and time, his study could have been improved by the inclusion of a discussion of Rahner's treatment of Christian life as a rehearsal for death and a development of the implication of Rahner's understanding of death for moral and spiritual theology. Zucal's study, on the other hand, is so far the most exhaustive and critical investigation of Rahner's theology of death. It not only offers a detailed exposition of Rahner's thanatology but also compares and contrasts it with Ladislaus Boros's hypothesis of a final decision in death. It could, however, be complemented by a more sophisticated analysis of Rahner's theology of freedom and his metaphysical presuppositions. In this way his theology of death may be more readily intelligible.

Other aspects of Rahner's eschatology have also been studied. Joachim McBriar has briefly explored the connection between Rahner's christology and his eschatology.[66] José Sánchez de Murillo discusses the relevance of his eschatology for Christian life.[67] Finally, Ferdinand Kerstiens touches upon the themes of hope and future in Rahner's theology.[68]

IV. Scope and Method of Treatment of the Present Study

With a view to complementing the existing studies on Rahner's eschatology, the work presented here is intended to offer an exposition and a
constructive evaluation of Rahner's eschatological doctrines. The work
is divided into three parts. After placing Rahner's eschatology in the context of the contemporary retrieval of eschatology both in Catholic and
Protestant theologies, the work will examine in Part 1 the anthropological
foundation and the hermeneutical principles of Rahner's eschatology.
There follows in Part 2 an exposition of Rahner's individual eschatology in
which the Last Things concerning the fate of each human being will be
considered: death, judgment, purgatory, heaven, and hell. In Part 3 I shall
examine Rahner's collective eschatology: the resurrection of the body, the
Parousia, and the communion of saints. In the concluding chapter the
question will be raised as to whether Rahner's eschatology has contributed
to a better understanding of Christian faith and existence and whether
there are in it any issues still open to further development.

The method will be both diachronic and synchronic. In each theme
Rahner's writings will be studied with an eye to their chronological order.
This is done in the first eight chapters and in particular in chapter 1 with the
intention to detect and identify lines of development in Rahner's eschatological thought. My thesis is that there was a homogeneous development from a somewhat individualistic, existential outlook to a more sociopolitical and historical perspective in Rahner's treatment of the Last Things.
Such a development is parallel to the one found in his theological
anthropology.[69] The last chapter will follow a predominantly synchronic
method, bringing together Rahner's various theological insights to determine his contribution to Christian eschatology.

1

Karl Rahner's Eschatology in Context

> If Jesus had not maintained his conviction of the victory of the
> kingdom of God through his death, if his faith as a belief in the
> coming of God had not remained victorious where everything is
> destroyed in death, if he had remained in death and not 'risen',
> his message would have no claim on us, would not exist for us.
> The outcome of his life, which is completed in his victorious
> death, is itself part of his message of the victory of the Kingdom
> of God. (*Our Christian Faith. Answers for the Future*, 96)

Von Balthasar's famous dictum that the eschatological office, which was
almost shut down in the nineteenth century according to Ernst Troeltsch,
has now been working overtime since the turn of the century, has become
the virtually classical description of the recent developments of eschatology
as a theological tract in our times.[1] There has been in the last eighty-odd
years a veritable rediscovery of eschatology in both Catholic and Protestant theology.

There are many causes for this renaissance of eschatology; but one of the
most influential contributors to it was, among Catholic theologians at least,
Karl Rahner. Rahner himself explicitly acknowledged the influence of diverse theological movements and thinkers upon his eschatology and occa-
sionally commented upon them. Consequently, for a proper understanding
of Rahnerian eschatology it is imperative to situate it in the context of
contemporary eschatologies.

I. Recent Eschatologies: The Diverse Modes of the Presence of the Kingdom of God

While a complete and exhaustive exposition of recent systematic eschatologies has still to be written, helpful overviews are readily available.[2] My
intention here is to sketch in rough outline the history of the rediscovery of
eschatology as the central theme of recent Christian theology so that

against this background an adequate understanding of Rahner's eschatology may be achieved.

Originating primarily as an exegetical problem within the biblical quest for the historical Jesus at the turn of the century, these eschatologies attempt to schematize the *eschaton* and to enter into dialogue with the historical consciousness characteristic of our modern times.

1. Consequent Eschatology

In stark opposition to nineteenth-century liberal theology, Johannes Weiss defended the thesis that the central purpose of Christ's mission was to proclaim the imminence of an otherworldly Kingdom of God to be established by a sudden intervention of God. Albert Schweitzer[3] further expounded a "consistent" or thoroughgoing eschatology, recently revived by Martin Werner,[4] according to which Christ shared with his contemporaries the expectation of an imminent end of the world and, when this proved a mistake, concluded that he himself must suffer in order to save his people from the tribulations preceding the last day.

2. Supratemporal Eschatology

In reaction to consequent eschatology, especially to its purely ethical interpretation of the Kingdom, the young Karl Barth insisted on the absolute transcendence of God and his Kingdom. Christianity is essentially eschatological, as Barth puts it forcefully in his commentary on the Romans: "A Christianity that is not rigorously and absolutely eschatological has rigorously and absolutely nothing to do with Christ."[5] Eschatology, however, is identified with God's transcendence, and eternity is opposed to time. To wait for the Parousia is not to expect an event to occur at some point in history but to lift one's eyes up towards God, the 'Wholly Other,' and to decide for him in faith.

3. Existential Eschatology

The atemporal presentist eschatology of dialectical or "crisis" theology was carried to its logical consequence by Rudolf Bultmann.[6] Going beyond purely exegetical research and relying on the philosophy of the early Martin Heidegger, Bultmann makes use of the distinction between *Historie* (the objective, neutral data of history to be critically examined in historical research) and *Geschichte* (history in terms of meaning and significance for the individual's present act of decision) to interpret the eschatological character of Christianity. The Kingdom of God that Christ proclaimed is indeed wholly future, but in the existential, not chronological sense. Fallen, sinful human beings, according to Bultmann, are oriented toward the past because the past is what is at hand, at our disposal. This existence is therefore inauthentic. Authentic existence, on the other contrary, tends toward the future that is made present by the individual's act of decision. Because human beings are possibility, they can reject the quest for security in their past (their *Historie*) and face the present moment in decision in authentic openness to the future as coming toward them (their *Geschichte*).

4. Realized Eschatology

In opposition to Schweitzer, Charles H. Dodd contended that the burden of Jesus' ministry was to proclaim the presence of God's Kingdom in himself. Eschatology is not future; it is already present in the life, death, and resurrection of Jesus. The dramatic urgency of Jesus' preaching did not result from any expectation of an imminent event but from the burning conviction that the Kingdom of God was already present in his own person. Eschatology is therefore nothing but a dimension of the present; it is a 'mythological' way of describing the present possibility of entering into contact with the salvation wrought by Jesus. Today the Church looks back at this decisive event enacted by Jesus; she celebrates it in the efficacious sign of the Eucharist, which Dodd calls "the sacrament of realized eschatology."[7]

5. Anticipated Eschatology

In radical opposition to Bultmann's existential interpretation, Oscar Cullmann proposed a theology of salvation history.[8] The Kingdom of God has its beginning at Creation, reaches its zenith or midpoint in Jesus Christ, and will be brought to completion at the Parousia. Eschatology, then, is indissolubly linked with definite historical facts. History itself is salvific; it moves with purpose and direction. In fact, Cullmann was opposed not only to Barth's atemporal and Bultmann's existentialist interpretations but also, more generally, to the intrusion of Greek metaphysics into an explication of the biblical understanding of time. The Greeks conceived of time as cyclical: history is a closed circle and salvation is a deliverance from the slavery to time into atemporal eternity. On the other hand, Cullmann suggested, the biblical conception of time is linear and chronological. Time is an ascending movement of past, present, and future; it is the field in which the divine plan of salvation unfolds with Christ as the midpoint.

6. Eschatology in Progress

So far the first five eschatologies have highlighted the two essential aspects of New Testament eschatology. On the one hand, the *eschaton* is other than human history, future and transcendent; on the other hand, it is active in history, present and immanent. The sixth model, eschatology in progress, promoted mainly by Joachim Jeremias,[9] attempts to maintain both aspects in unity by regarding eschatology as a process. The Kingdom is neither purely present nor purely future, for although it began with Jesus, it is not yet fully realized. Its total realization and manifestation will come only at the end of time. Meanwhile, the Kingdom of God is being progressively realized in human history.

7. Eschatology as Prolepsis

In dialogue with Ernst Bloch's philosophy of hope, new interpretations of eschatology have arisen, especially in German Protestant theology. One of these is eschatology as prolepsis, espoused by Wolfhart Pannenberg; the other is eschatology as hope, proposed by Jürgen Moltmann. In opposition both to Bultmann's existentialism, which dissolves history into an individual, subjective affair, and to Cullmann's theology of salvation history, which places salvation history on a different level from general, everyday history, Pannenberg[10] proposes that universal history is the most comprehensive horizon of Christian theology. Universal history, and not any privileged segment of it, according to him, is the sphere of God's self-revelation. Consequently, the eschatological fulfillment of revelation can only occur at the end of history. However, in the fate of Jesus Christ, whose fundamental message is eschatology, the character of the end of history has been made known to us, since in him God, who is the Absolute Future, is revealed. In Christ, therefore, the end is not only seen ahead of time but also is experienced by means of foretaste, anticipation. Pannenberg speaks of Jesus' Resurrection as *prolepsis* of eschatology.

Pannenbery further suggests that the dialectic between the future character and the actual presence of the Kingdom of God in history is to be resolved in the unity-in-distinction between the appearance and that which appears. That which appears is the coming of what is future. The future Kingdom of God is thus proleptically present in what appears in history. Pannenberg also identifies God with the future Kingdom since, he argues, in the Scripture, the being of God is identical with his power. God, then, is the future of the world.

8. Eschatology as Hope

Pannenberg's incipient usage of the future as a distinct theological category was transformed by Moltmann into the central and exclusive key to interpret eschatology and Christian theology as a whole. For him ". . . eschatology means the doctrine of the Christian hope, which embraces both the object hoped for and also the hope inspired by it. From first to last, and not merely in epilogue, Christianity is eschatology, is hope, forward-looking and forward-moving, and therefore also revolutionizing and transforming the present. . . . There is therefore only one real problem in Christian theology, which its own object forces upon it and which it in turn forces on humankind and on human thought: the problem of the future."[11]

With the future as a hermeneutic key Moltmann explores a new understanding of God and divine self-revelation. First of all, he clearly distinguishes between *futurum* and *adventus* ("Futur" and "Zukunft" in German). *Futurum* means simply what is ahead, that which is going to arise from the beginning, the temporal prolongation of being. *Adventus*, on the other hand, means the coming of something into the present; it is the equivalent of Parousia.

On the basis of this distinction Moltmann argues that God is to be conceived eschatologically as *Deus adventurus*, the Absolute *Zukunft* of the world whose being is *coming*, *adventus*, *Parousia*, *Zukunft*. Consequently, divine revelation is not "epiphany of the eternal present" but "apocalypse of the promised future of the truth."[12]

Since Christianity is future, there can be no 'eschatology,' that is, no *doctrine* of the Last Things, no collection of theses which can be understood on the basis of experiences that constantly recur and can be perceived by anyone. There can be no extrapolation of the *adventus Dei* from the factors and processes, past and present, in the way the *futurum* is predicted in futurology. The *adventus* can only be *anticipated* insofar as it has been promised (eschatology as *prolepsis*). The *eschaton* must be essentially open. However, Christian theology can give expression to the future as promised in the death and above all in the resurrection Jesus Christ.

The expectation of this *Deus adventurus* is not merely a theoretical interpretation of the future. God's *promissio* also means a *missio* for the Christians. Their task is to be 'co-workers' of the promised Kingdom of God and its universal peace and its righteousness. The Church must become 'the Church for the world': it has to grow into 'Christianity,' not in the sense of recovering the role of *cultus publicus* that it had during the Constantinian era, nor in the sense of maintaining the role of *cultus privatus* which bourgeois society has assigned to it, but in the sense of a social religious institution actively engaged in "the realization of the eschatological *hope of justice*, the *humanizing* of humanity, the *socializing* of humanity, *peace* for all creation."[13]

9. Secular and Political Eschatology

The above-mentioned eschatologies were of non-Catholic origin, but they exercised a profound influence on Catholic theologians in the sixties. The eschatology that we call secular and political certainly had deep roots in German Protestant soil. But it was developed extensively mainly by Catholic theologians, in particular by Johannes B. Metz, whose name is now officially linked with "secularization theology" and "political theology."

For Metz theology is essentially eschatological or, as he puts it, apocalyptic theology, with its recognition of the secularity of the world, its critique of privatization of faith and theology, its rejection of "bourgeois religion," its emphasis on the praxis of liberation, its understanding of the subject as essentially historical and social, its narrative of the dangerous memory of Jesus Christ, and its solidarity with the victims of oppression and injustice. In such a theology, hope is 'imminent expectation,' time is not a continuum in evolution but a process 'interrupted' by the dangerous memory of Christ's suffering, and the Kingdom of god is not a pure utopia achieved by means of human progress but the gift of God in response of our solidarity with the victims of society.[14]

The above brief sketch of the nine models of contemporary eschatology will serve as the context in which to approach Rahner's eschatology. Although Rahner has in the course of his writing referred one way or another to all the theologians discussed above, secularization and political eschatology are most significant since Metz's criticism, on Rahner's own avowal, is the only one he took seriously,[15] but also because Rahner enlarged the horizon of his eschatology precisely in response to such criticism.

II. Development of Rahner's Eschatology

Rahner's theological and literary career spans some fifty years. In half a century of unceasing, intense theological reflection and prodigious writing, there has inevitably been some evolution. Rahner himself explicitly acknowledged the existence of such growth. Asked by Andrew Tallon whether there has been a certain development in his concept of person, he replied: "I would answer: obviously and hopefully, because, I hope, I have not always repeated the same thing and certainly could not have said everything at one time, because, in my own history, hopefully, I have kept on learning something new."[16]

1. In Dialogue with Contemporary Eschatological Theologies

As part of the process of examining the development of Rahner's eschatology, it would be useful to look more closely at how Rahner reacted to
the various eschatologies we have discussed above. In all his writings
Rahner made only one explicit reference to Schweitzer, not however in the
context of the Kingdom of God and eschatology, but in that of the Christian's duty to work for peace.[17] Nevertheless, Rahner did discuss at length
the question of Christ's knowledge and the possibility of his being in error
regarding the imminent expectation of the Kingdom. These two themes are
of course quite apropos since they are implied in Schweitzer's thesis (and in
that of consequent eschatology) that Jesus was mistaken in his belief in the
imminent apocalyptic coming of the Kingdom of God.

First of all, for Rahner neither the perfection of Christ's human nature
nor his possession of *visio immediata* by virtue of the hypostatic union excludes the possibility of ignorance and of progressive growth in his human
knowledge. On the contrary, one of the conditions of possibility for the
exercise of human freedom is a certain degree of nescience in the human
subject. Indeed, unless there were some ignorance in his human knowledge, Christ could not really be a perfect man.[18]

Regarding Christ's eschatological consciousness, Rahner, basing himself
on Mk 13:12, simply notes that Jesus did not do all that he *could* have done
and indeed said *less* than he knew and could have said. Rahner further
adds that "the actual eschatological preaching of Jesus is quite understandable as a prediction about the completion of what Jesus proclaims about
himself and his mission in the present. For the content of Jesus' eschatology surpasses the eschatology of his times only in one point, which is however decisive and transforms all the rest: namely, that he himself in person
is salvation and judgment, at the present moment, in a way that can never
be surpassed."[19]

Rahner referred to Barth several times, in his discussions of trinitarian
theology,[20] of the sinful Church,[21] of secularization,[22] and above all of
justification and grace.[23] He did not, however, explicitly mention Barthian
eschatology, which we have described as supratemporal. Nevertheless it is
safe to say that Rahner's insistence on God as absolute and holy Mystery
would find an echo in Barth's thundering affirmation of God's transcendence. Furthermore, Rahner certainly shared Barth's rejection of the purely ethical interpretation of the Kingdom of God as championed by consequent eschatology. He would also agree with Barth's characterization of
Christianity as essentially eschatological. On the other hand, even though
Rahner's conception of eternity finds some resonance in Barth's, he would
repudiate the overly actualistic view of the presence of God's kingdom
implicit in Barth and in dialectical theology in general. In contrast to

Barth, Rahner laid a greater emphasis on the relevance of history and time
for the Kingdom of God.

If Rahner was opposed to the incipient form of ahistoric existentialism in
Barth, it is to be expected that he would be more adamantly so to its full-
fledged development in Bultmann. Of course Rahner would not deny the
similarities that existed between him and Bultmann; both were after all
indebted to a common philosophy, that of Heidegger. Rahner acknowledged the necessity of 'demythologization' for theology, especially in view
of preaching. For him, "The theology of the future must be a 'demytholo-
gizing' theology."[24] This applies especially to eschatological truths that,
more than others, run the serious risk of sounding mythological to modern
ears.

Nevertheless, Rahner firmly rejected Bultmann's devaluation of historical facts, in particular the Resurrection of Jesus. Although he adopted the
distinction between *Historie* and *Geschichte* already used by Bultmann,[25]
Rahner strongly upheld the factual reality of the Resurrection of Jesus over
against Bultmann's existential interpretation of it in terms of the cross.
Finally, in opposition to Bultmann, Rahner strongly emphasizes the future
coming of the Kingdom at the end of time.

Rahner referred to Dodd only once, in the context of the sacrament of
marriage, and quite indirectly.[26] Even though Rahner has never discussed
'realized eschatology' as such, he certainly would be very sympathetic to
Dodd's emphatic affirmation of the presence of God's kingdom in the person and ministry of Jesus or, to put it in Rahnerian terminology, of Jesus
as the Absolute Savior. Further, he would find the implications of Dodd's
'realized eschatology' for ecclesiology and sacramentology extremely con-
genial to his own theology of Church and sacraments. Nevertheless, he
would part company with the British exegete in retaining the futurist
dimension of eschatology.

Of all Protestant exegetes, it is Cullmann who was most acceptable to
Rahner as to most Catholic dogmatic theologians. Although Rahner made
only five references to Cullmann, and in a quite incidental way,[27] and
although no direct influence of the latter upon the former can be traced,
there is nevertheless a substantial agreement between the two in their
views of the Kingdom of God. This is no surprise since, as Stephen Travis
writes, ". . . of all the approaches to the coming of the kingdom and the
parousia . . . Cullmann's comes closest to the teaching of the New Testament and of Jesus himself."[28] Like Cullmann, Rahner most strongly
emphasized that Jesus constituted the *decisive* eschatological event and
that the tension between present and future, between the 'already' and the
'not-yet,' is fundamental to the understanding of the Church and to a theology of history. Rahner, however, has gone beyond Cullmann in overcoming one of the latter's most conspicuous weaknesses, namely, the lack of a

philosophical basis for a discussion of time, history, and eternity.

2. *From an Individualist-Existentialist to an Interpersonal to a Sociopolitical Perspective*

This mention of a philosophical framework will serve as a convenient springboard for a fuller discussion of the development of Rahner's eschatology as well as its parallels and similarities with the eschatologies of Pannenberg, Moltmann, and Metz.

A. FROM THE INDIVIDUALIST-EXISTENTIALIST TO THE INTERPERSONAL ESCHATOLOGY

It is common knowledge that Rahner's philosophical dissertation, *Spirit in the World*, intended to formulate a metaphysics of knowledge on the basis of Thomas's doctrine of the necessity of conversion to the phantasm as expounded in *ST* I, q. 84, a. 7. Rahner argues that the human spirit is essentially a dynamic desire for the absolute fullness of being, as is made clear in its act of reaching out (*Vorgriff*) for being in its totality. Because human beings are desire for the absolute being, they are spirit; but because the absolute being is present only as the horizon or condition of possibility for human knowledge, the human being is finite spirit. In terms of questioning, because human beings are *able* to question, they are spirit; but because they *must* question, they are finite spirit. In terms of intellect, as agent intellect human beings are spirit; but as possible intellect they are finite spirit. Further, because human beings as spirit exist in the world, the only objects they know and grasp as *objects* are the concrete, sensible things. Anything beyond the sensible world, e. g., God, human beings can only know *nonobjectively*, as the horizon against which they know the sensible objects. Rahner calls this nonobjective, unthematic knowledge of God who is coknown in every act of knowing the *Vorgriff*, that is, the act of the intellect's self-transcending anticipation of the absolute being. This *Vorgriff* Rahner identifies with the act of *excessus* of the agent intellect of which Thomas speaks.

My intention here is not to offer a detailed analysis of Rahner's metaphysics of knowledge but rather to explicate the perspective or horizon within which Rahner started his philosophical and, later, theological enterprise. It is clear that in *Spirit in the World* the object of analysis is epistemological, its method transcendental, and its purview the individual knower. There is no explicit mention of *person* in this work; its subtitle is *Towards a Metaphysics of Finite Knowledge according to Thomas Aquinas*. Its approach to humankind is therefore through the individual's mode of knowing rather than a metaphysics of freedom and relation; it is cognitional rather than dialogical or intersubjective.

On the other hand, as Tallon has convincingly shown,[29] there is already in *Spirit in the World* itself a solid foundation for a dynamic, intentional, and relational view of the person. Person is therein described implicitly as incarnate spirit. The human being's elements, spirit and matter, emerge as two irreducible constituents of the indissolubly and substantially one human being. This metaphysical affirmation is deduced from a transcendental analysis, not of the object known nor of the knower, but of the act of knowing. This act, which is an objective intuition, is shown to be an act of active self-transcendence of the subject. In the act of knowing, the individual becomes person through the process of self-enactment (*Selbstvollzug*), first by the act of incarnation of spirit in matter itself (the 'emanation' of matter from spirit) and secondly by the act of self-transcendence of the thus constituted unity of matter and spirit toward the Absolute Being, the absolute other. There is therefore in *Spirit in the World* an incipient form of and an ontological grounding for intersubjectivity.

This germinal intersubjectivity Rahner developed more explicitly in *Hearers of the Word*. Whereas *Spirit in the World* had intended to offer a metaphysics of human knowledge, *Hearers of the Word* proposed to show on the basis of the metaphysics developed in the earlier book the possibility of divine revelation or, alternatively, the human being as a hearer of a possible word from God. The term *person*, absent from *Spirit in the World*, occurs for the first time in this work. Human beings insofar as they are spirit are able to be self-conscious or self-present (*reditio in seipsum*) and are open toward the Absolute Being through their *Vorgriff*.

Despite the absolute self-luminosity of God and the openness of humanity, Rahner further points out, both God and the human individual are hidden because they are personal and free beings. This is the point where *Hearers of the Word* makes a decisive advance beyond *Spirit in the World*. Whereas the world of *Spirit of the World* is the *Umwelt (Dingwelt, Gegenstandwelt)*, that is, the world of things, that of *Hearers of the Word* is the world of persons, the *Mitwelt*.[30] Here Rahner speaks of God as the free unknown in his general ontology and of the human being as free listener in his metaphysical anthropology. Being free, God can choose to open himself to human beings or remain closed to them and they, also free, can choose to remain closed or open themselves to God. There is then a possibility of interpersonal relationship between God and the human being. "The human being as a spirit who knows the absolute Being, stands before the latter as before a *person* who freely disposes of himself."[31]

But should God will to reveal himself to humanity and should we decide to listen to God, where can this event occur? In history, Rahner answers, and again in this respect he has made significant advance over *Spirit in the World*: "The human being is spirit as an *historical* being. The place of his transcendence is always also an historical place. Thus the place of a possible revelation is always and necessarily the history of humanity."[32] Here we reach the heart of Rahner's philosophical anthropology as embodied in *Hearers of the Word*. Human persons, constituted historical not only by their materiality but above all by the freedom, must freely enact themselves, in space and time, within a community of persons. The interpersonal dimension, faintly echoed in *Spirit in the World* whose main concern is the cognitive act of the individual knower, is now repeatedly and eloquently affirmed in *Hearers of the Word*: "But there is history in the *human* sense only where, in a togetherness of free persons in their multiplicity, the activity of freedom expands in a world, i. e., in space and time, where the intelligible acts of freedom must, in order to become manifest, extend in space and time. . . . And precisely such a historicity is found in humans because they are essentially free, self-subsisting personalities, which must freely realize themselves through a multiplicity of such personalities as the total realization of the very essence of such a personality in space and time."[33]

In his later writings Rahner advanced from a dialectic of spirit and matter to that of nature and person, especially in his theological essays, where he elaborated a distinctly theological anthropology beyond his earlier philosophical one.[34] A shift is therefore made from the individualist-existentialist perspective centered on cognition to the intersubjective-interpersonal one centered on freedom, history, and love. Keeping this development in mind I submit that Rahner's early writings on eschatology, roughly from 1949 when his article on the theology of death first appeared to the first half of 1960 (that is, writings contained in *Schriften zur Theologie*, 1–7, including the essay "A Brief Theological Study on Indulgence" printed in vol. 8 but written in 1955), were composed, both in content and approach, under the perspective first of individual-existentialist and later of interpersonal viewpoints.

A glance at the titles of the essays and, above all, a close examination of their contents will, I hope, confirm my thesis. Of course, nothing in the nature of elaborate proof can and should be attempted here, since these writings will be studied in detail in due course. Suffice it for our present purpose to note that Rahner's first eschatological essays focused more on what in traditional textbooks of eschatology is regarded as the fate of the individual person. Despite statements in *Hearers of the Word* that can be interpreted as affirming the necessity of *interpersonal* love in community for persons to reach fulfillment, Rahner continued to speak mostly in terms of an *intrapersonal* becoming, i. e., of what goes on *within* the individual. That this intrapersonal and individualistic perspective is still heavily operative in the essays on death[35] and on freedom[36] is indisputable. The same is true of other eschatological essays, on concupiscence,[37] purgatory and indulgences,[38] the resurrection of the body,[39] beatific vision,[40] time,[41] and the life of the dead.[42] It is only with his essay on guilt that the interpersonal and social dimension of the human being began to emerge into clearer view.[43] It came to full bloom in his 1961 essay on love, where it is said that the development of love in the person is the gauge of the very becoming of that person.[44] It reached its peak in the 1965 essay on the unity of the love of neighbor and the love of God.[45]

B. FROM THE INTERPERSONAL TO THE SOCIOPOLITICAL ESCHATOLOGY

If his early essays on eschatology were written in the existentialist-interpersonal framework, Rahner made a noticeable move in the mid–1960s toward a more sociopolitical conception of human existence and hence of eschatology. So far the human person is conceived as a unity of spirit and matter, of intellect and will, related to other persons, human and divine, in knowledge and love, and through these interpersonal relationships growing toward full personhood. Now the human person is seen as a member of a political, legal, economic, social, cultural, and religious system and institution whose mode of organization and orientation, both on the national and international levels, can advance, retard, or thwart the human movement toward personhood. The fundamental duties of the human person, then, include not only assisting others in their individual needs but also removing oppressive structures and creating just economic and sociopolitical conditions for the exercise of the basic human rights, for the development and liberation of all victims of oppression and injustice.

A cursory glance at Rahner's eschatological writings after roughly 1965 will corroborate the claim of this change of perspective. In them collective eschatology came to the forefront, even though individual eschatology was not forgotten. Rahner now came to grips with secular, especially Marxist ideologies,[46] the problem of the future,[47] the question of hope,[48] the relation between Christianity and humanism,[49] the task of the Church in the contemporary world,[50] and the morality of revolution.[51] Of great interest, too, is Rahner's recent fascination with liberation theology and his editing and contribution of a two-page foreword to a book on Latin American liberation theology.[52]

Two factors seem to have provoked this new focus. First, the Second Vatican Council. As a *peritus* he made enormous contributions to the council. Nevertheless, it was not a one-way street; Rahner, too, benefited from the *aggiornamento* and the teachings of Vatican II. What Rahner learned from the council was not primarily particular teachings on a specific point of theology but rather a widening of perspective, an opening of new vistas, a dialogue with the world.

In this connection, mention should perhaps be made of the fact that in the postconciliar period, thanks to ecumenical dialogue, his growing inter-

national fame, and his worldwide travels, Rahner had many opportunities
for coming into personal contact with thinkers of different religious persua-
sions, not only theologians but also scientists in various fields. Among philosophers with whom Rahner dialogued in his attempt at understanding the
problem of hope and the future, the Jewish, atheistic, Marxist, revisionist
philosopher Bloch was the most significant. In his essays on Christian
humanism and on hope, he explicitly referred to Bloch's philosophy of
hope and its influence on political theology.[53]

The mention of political theology brings us to the second factor responsible for Rahner's shift from the "transcendental, personalistic and existential," as Metz puts it, to a more sociopolitical emphasis. Metz sees in
Rahner's anthropological theology the risk of producing a privatized,
bourgeois religion and to counteract that danger develops his own political theology.

Rahner himself welcomed such a development. Repeatedly since the
late 1960s he called for a 'political theology' as a form of the theology of the
future: "The theologian is aware that, since the necessary setting for the
individual's salvation is the Church as the unity of mankind and its history
theology must always be 'political theology.'"[54] In this context, Rahner
even claims that death, although a biological phenomenon, because it must
be freely enacted by the person, does possess "an intercommunicative or
'political' character."[55] Speaking of the future of the Church, he urges, in
language quite reminiscent of Metz, that one should arrive at a 'political
theology', "one which does not reduce Christianity from the outset to the
private and interior sphere."[56]

'Political theology', Rahner reminds us, should not be conceived as a
regional theology but as "a formal point of view inherent throughout in all
subjects for theological investigation."[57] It must seek to unfold the relevance of all theological statements for society. One of its tasks is "maintaining a constant critical reappraisal and calling in question of the social
system prevailing at any given time, seeing that there is a constant temptation to make an idol of this, and to establish it as absolute by unjust
oppression."[58] One is reminded here of Metz's "eschatological proviso"
and "creative, militant eschatology."

I hope to have shown that there exists in Rahner's theology as a whole
and in his eschatology in particular a homogeneous and gradual movement
from a transcendental, interpersonal, and existential consideration of
human and Christian existence to a more explicit emphasis on the sociopolitical dimension of such existence and the critical task of the Church.
Such development is intrinsic to the dynamism of Rahner's own theology,
but it was stimulated by such momentous events as the Second Vatican
Council, by his growing pastoral sensitivity to the needs of the Church and
the signs of the times, and by the challenge of diverse and often conflict-

ing eschatologies. In the next chapter we will see how this eschatology is grounded in his philosophical and theological anthropology.

Part I

Transcendental Eschatology

2

Anthropology as Eschatology

> Christian eschatology is nothing else but a repetition of every-
> thing we have said so far about man insofar as he is a free and
> created spirit who has been given God's self-communication in
> grace. Eschatology is not really an addition, but rather it gives
> expression once again to man as Christianity understands him: as
> a being who exists from out of his present "now" towards the
> future. . . . Because of man's very nature, therefore, Christian
> anthropology is Christian futurology and Christian eschatology.
> (*FCF*, 431)

In this first part we shall explore what Rahner calls transcendental eschatology. This chapter will focus on its anthropological presuppositions, both
philosophical and theological, and the next on its hermeneutics. An investigation of Rahner's anthropology is necessary since his anthropology is not
a mere background or context for his eschatology. Rahner's eschatology *is*
his anthropology conjugated in the future tense. I shall not present a complete survey of Rahnerian anthropology but shall limit myself to only those
aspects that are essential for an understanding of his eschatology.[1]

These aspects will be grouped under three rubrics of eschatology: the
unity of the final consummation (human beings as spirits in the world in-
teracting with each other in a community of persons); the conditions of
possibility for eschatological fulfillment (human beings as endowed with
freedom and living out eternity in time and history); and the anticipation of
the eschatological Kingdom (human beings as endowed with the supernatural existential and grace and yet at the same time weighed down by sin
and concupiscence).

I. The Unity of the Final Consummation: *The Human Person* as Spirit in the World and as a Social Being

Rahner points out that Christian eschatology cannot be correctly understood if one starts out with a rationalistic conception of the human being as

a mere aggregate of body and soul even if the latter is thought to be immortal. An authentically Christian, and hence unified, eschatology can only be maintained if the human being is conceived as a corporeal person with an indissoluble unity of matter and spirit and if human fulfillment is not understood as independent of the transformation of the world and of the resurrection of the flesh. It is this unity of body and soul in human beings and their sociality that provide the link between the individual and collective eschatologies.

1. The Human Being as Spirit in the World: The Unity-in-Distinction between Body and Soul

A. HUMAN BODILINESS AND SPIRITUALITY

Geist in Welt underscores Rahner's early and profound conviction about the metaphysical unity of the human being. Besides being the title of his first book, it is also an accurate caption for human existence. Within the framework of Thomistic epistemology Rahner expresses the unity of the human body and soul in terms of the unity of sense and intellect, abstraction and conversion to the phantasm, agent intellect (*Vorgriff*) and possible intellect (the cogitative sense), matter and spirit. In what follows, I will first briefly explain how in Rahner's analysis of the conditions of possibility for knowledge the human person emerges as matter and spirit, and then I will explicate in some detail Rahner's view of the unity of the human being.

Rahner suggests that Thomas's teaching on the necessity of the human intellect to return to the images in order to know (*ST* I, q. 84, a. 7) is an ontological affirmation of the materiality of human beings. The return to the images, however, presupposes sensation by which the images (*species sensibilis*) are formed in the knowing subject and in which the knower and the known achieve identity. In quasi-Hegelian language, Rahner asserts that knowledge as such is a being's presence to itself. A pure spirit's knowledge would be pure self-presence. An *incarnate* spirit's knowledge, however, is both self-presence and self-absence at the same time, corresponding to its dual nature. As intellect it is self-presence (*oppositio mundi*) and as sense it is self-absence (*praesentia mundi*). Thus human beings are spirits whose self-knowledge is necessarily mediated by the knowledge of another.[2]

Humans, however, are not merely matter; they have, or more accurately, *are* bodies. Whereas 'matter' is an intrinsic principle of itself indeterminate and in need of determination by a 'form,' by which a being is made spatiotemporal and subject to becoming, the body is constituted in its properly *human* species by soul and matter.

Although matter and body are the first things we encounter in our experience, what they are ontologically we can know only, says Rahner, by contrast to and derivation from our immediate knowledge of spirit: ". . . spirit is a reality that can only be understood by direct acquaintance, having its own proper identity derived from no other. It is only possible to say what matter actually is by contrast with spirit so known."[3] This is so because matter is conceivable only in relation to and for the sake of the spirit.

That human beings are spirit is clear from the fact that we can ask questions about being. In so doing we already transcend ourselves and are with being in its totality (*beim Sein im ganzen*).[4] In *Spirit in the World*, however, Rahner prefers to explicate human spirituality on the basis of the process of abstraction (the agent intellect) rather than on that of question. Two characteristics of the human spirit emerge. First, in abstraction human beings come back from the world in which they always are as sensibility and by means of objectification distance and distinguish themselves from the objects present in their sensation. As spirit, therefore, the human being is self-present or self-conscious (*reditio in* or *super* or *ad seipsum*). This ability to "return to oneself" Rahner also finds actualized in the intellect's act of judging (*concretio* and *complexio*).[5] This power for self-presence is identified with the agent intellect.[6]

The second characteristic is the spirit's openness or transcendence to being in general. In abstraction human beings form universal concepts from the experience of particular things. This means that the universal form represented in the concept is more than or is not exhausted by the sensible singulars that embody it. The individual objects are seen as limited, as not fulfilling all the possibilities of the essential form. But how can the intellect categorically or explicitly know that particular things are limited unless it also grasps unthematically or implicitly being in general as the background or horizon against which these things are known? Rahner detects therefore in the human intellect an inborn dynamic movement toward being in general as the condition of possibility for every act of knowledge. This act of unobjective tension toward being Rahner calls *Vorgriff*, an anticipatory reaching for the Absolute Being without grasping it as an object, and identifies it with Thomas's notion of *excessus* toward *esse*.[7]

Human beings, then, are spirits insofar as they can question being, return to themselves in the act of abstraction, and implicitly affirm the existence of God in the act of judgment. But, just as they are not simply matter but bodies, so also they are not merely spirits but souls. The soul, says Rahner in accord with the Thomistic tradition, is not a being but a principle of being. It is not an entity that exists for its own sake or has only fortuitously been united with matter. Rather it is ontologically ordered to matter and realizes itself only in matter. Together with the body it constitutes a consubstantial unity, the human being, so that every empirical characteristic we find in that being is an attribute of the whole person. The body is a specifically human body, the expression of the soul; and the soul acts in space and time and seeks the perfection of the whole person in the resurrection, and not simply in immortality.

B. THE HUMAN BEING AS UNITY-IN-DISTINCTION OF BODY AND SOUL

In emphasizing the distinct reality in human beings of matter and of spirit, Rahner is concerned to refute two pervasive errors, the spiritualizing Platonism that has always been the bane of Christian anthropology and the materialistic tendency of modern sciences. Nevertheless the central focus of Rahner's anthropology is not the distinction between matter and spirit, body and soul, but the ontological unity of these two principles in human beings. This theme of unity already figured preeminently in *Spirit in the World*. It is implicit in Rahner's treatment of the original unity of being and knowing, the unity of sense and intellect, the unity of the agent and possible intellects, the emanation of sensibility from the possible intellect, the conversion to the phantasm, and the cogitative sense.

Speaking more specifically of the unity of human body and soul from the epistemological viewpoint, Rahner argues from the sensible origin and hence the essentially receptive character of human knowledge that the soul is the form of the body.[8] Further Rahner adopts the Thomistic thesis that the soul is the *only* form of the body because, in his judgment, this thesis expresses more forcefully the human being's ontological unity.

From a theological perspective Rahner argues for the unity of spirit and matter at three levels, namely, their origin, their history, and their final end. First, both matter and spirit have one and the same origin, God. Secondly, spirit and matter have a unity in their history. The history of nature is included in that of the spirit and vice versa, just as the history of the spirit conditions and is conditioned by that of matter. The unity of the history of spirit and matter is exhibited most clearly in the process of evolution. In it the human spirit is the immanent product of the becoming of matter through active self-transcendence, so that we can see the history of nature and the history of the spirit as *one* history without having thereby to deny the essential gradation of being and of its development.[9] In this way, matter can be regarded as "a limited and in a sense 'frozen' spirit."[10] Matter is not something alien to the spirit, but a limited moment in the self-enactment of the spirit itself. Conversely, the spiritual soul, precisely as spiritual, is the form of the body, so that every reality in human beings, including every bodily reality, is the reality and expression of their spirit.

Thirdly, one in their origin and their history, matter and spirit are also united in their achievement and goal. For the Christian faith, matter is not a provisional element of history to be abolished at the end of time but a permanent factor of the final perfection itself.

Another way of approaching Rahner's understanding of the unity of matter and spirit and more specifically of body and soul is through his ontology of symbol.[11] 'Real symbols' (*Realsymbole*), in contrast to 'derivative symbols,' which are but 'symbolic representations' (*Vertretungssymbole*), 'signs' (*Zeichen*), 'signals' (*Signalen*), and 'codes' (*Chiffren*), are "the representation which allows the other 'to be there'."[12] Rahner's first basic thesis is that "all beings are by their nature symbolic, because they necessarily 'express' themselves in order to attain their own nature."[13] To understand this notion of symbol one must grasp Rahner's other related contention that any existent being is both one and plural: ". . . a being (i.e. each one) is multiple in itself and in this unity of the multiple, one [moment] in this multiplicity is or can be essentially an expression of another [moment] in this multiple unity."[14]

The plural moments of a being, therefore, are conceived as its 'self-expression' (*Selbstausdruck*), which is necessary for its 'self-enactment' (*Selbstvollzug*). In Rahner's view there is an 'agreement' between the original being and its derivative moments that is based upon the relationship of origin and is more profound than any agreement produced by an efficient cause. A being enacts itself by expressing itself in the 'other' and retaining the other as its own. This 'other' is precisely the 'symbol'. Or as Rahner puts it as his second thesis, "The symbol in the strict sense (symbolic reality) is the self-realization of a being in the other, which is constitutive of its essence."[15]

This ontology of symbol serves as a powerful framework for Rahner's explication of the unity between the human body and soul. If the soul is the *unica forma corporis*, then the body is the symbol of the soul in the strict sense. Rahner suggests that one should not ascribe to the body an actual being prior to the reality of the soul; otherwise the body cannot be a symbol of the soul but at best an expression of it. Rather the soul imparts itself to the *materia prima*, 'informing' it and giving it reality, so that anything that is act in this potentiality is precisely the soul. The body is "nothing else than the actuality of the soul in the 'other' of *materia prima*, the 'otherness' produced by the soul itself, and hence its expression and symbol. . . ."[16]

2. *The Individual as a Social Being in the Cosmos*

By the fact that they are spirits in the world humans are interpersonal beings living in solidarity with one another in a community and situated in a cosmos of space and time. For a correct understanding of Rahner's collective eschatology it is imperative that we consider these two further dimensions of human beings, their place in the society and in the cosmos.

Although its focus is the metaphysics of knowledge of the individual knower *Spirit in the World* contains an implicit ontology of the individual as an interpersonal being. As spirit, human beings enact themselves not only through the incarnation of the soul in the body through the *causalitas resultantiae* (the first 'otherness' of the spirit) but also through their unthematic self-transcendence towards the other. This second 'otherness' includes not only God but also other human beings. This is made clear in Rahner's ontology of the inner-worldly, efficient causality that he uses to explain the formation of the intelligible species.

What is of present significance in Rahner's explanation of the formation of the intelligible species is that human beings as sentient knowers in their acts of knowledge are both the agents and the patients. As agents we produce the intelligible species in which we know objects, but we cannot do so except as patients receiving it as an ontological determination of ourselves from without. As agents we are spirit; as patients we are spirit in the world, needing matter in order to enact ourselves precisely as spirit. What clearly emerges from this is that the individual needs another person for his or her becoming. He or she not only needs matter (first otherness) to become person (*intra*personal becoming, overcoming the first gap between matter and spirit) but also needs other persons (second otherness) for self-becoming (*inter*personal becoming, overcoming the second gap between the self as embodied spirit with other spirits, whether embodied or not).[17] Of course the immediate context of these reflections is epistemological. Later Rahner will identify the medium with 'person' and apply this interdependence of agent and patient to freedom, love, and ethics.

The social dimension of the human being, implicit in *Spirit in the World*, was explicitly developed by Rahner in his later writings. In *Hearers of the Word* Rahner describes human sociality in the context of our historicity, which is in turn based on our materiality.[18] Because his starting point is human materiality, the focus of Rahner's discussion is more on things than on persons. Despite this somewhat cosmo-centric emphasis, which Metz attempts to overcome in his second edition of the work by inserting five notes on the *personale Welt* or *Mitwelt*,[19] Rahner nevertheless categorically affirms the social dimension of the person. "An individual human person," says he, "can never exhaustively and at one time actualize that which belongs to him by way of possibilities as a material being. That is why referring to other beings of his kind, which every human being does as this particular individual, is not something unimportant; it is a referring to a multitude of human persons, to a humanity which, only as a whole, can really make manifest that which is essentially given to each individual human being deep down in his possibilities, but only as possibilities. Man is real only in a humanity."[20]

The unity of humankind is further emphasized by Rahner in his essay on monogenism. In fact he attempted a transcendental deduction of monogenism from what he called a "metaphysics of generation."[21] Even though he later abandoned monogenism as a theological theory,[22] Rahner continued strongly to insist on the unity of humankind as a biological species and as a community of persons. Because of their unity in origin humans are bound together in mutual solidarity in guilt as well as in salvation.

Human beings' mutual sharing in guilt occasioned another important essay in which our social nature is elaborated in detail. The relevant text is extremely rich and profound and deserves a thorough analysis; unfortunately it is quite lengthy and cannot be quoted here. The readers are referred to the text itself.[23] The central point Rahner is making here is that human beings can become who they should be only in relationship not only with God but also with the world of matter and the world of persons: "In short, the human being must constantly enact himself as a person in an 'intermediary reality' (*in einem Mittleren*), formed by the union of his animated corporeality and embodied spirituality together with their concrete, material and proportional objectifications, and by the external world of equally real persons and things as well as by the objectifications produced there by 'external' actions."[24]

Three other essays of Rahner's must be mentioned to complete our examination of his view of the human being's social nature. The burden of the first essay, "The 'Commandment' of Love in Relation to Other Commandments," is to show that love of God and of neighbor is the supreme act whereby humans become persons.[25]

It is, however, in the second essay, "Reflections on the Unity of the Love of Neighbor and the Love of God,"[26] that Rahner is most eloquent and forthright about the essential sociality of being human. Whatever Rahner had left implicit before 1965 about the necessity of other *persons* for self-fulfillment is now made the object of explicit and profound reflections. Here not only is it asserted that self-transcendence must necessarily be directed toward another human person in I-thou interpersonal love but also that love of neighbor *is* love of God.

The third and last essay, "Experience of Self and Experience of God,"[27] offers nothing essentially new on human sociality but summarizes and explicates in greater clarity and emphasis the primacy of the subject as *inter*subjective. The person is essentially relational, a member of a community. In Rahner's view, there is a strict unity of three experiences: the human being's experience of self, of another human person, and of God.

These experiences *mutually* condition each other; they all highlight the necessity of the other (*das* Andere of matter and *der* Andere of human persons and God) for the self-fulfillment of human beings.

B. THE INDIVIDUAL IN SOLIDARITY WITH THE COSMOS

That humans are matter already bespeaks their intrinsic unity with the cosmos. Since Rahner's view on the unity of matter and spirit has already been explicated, I will focus briefly on the place of humanity in the cosmos and its implication for eschatology. Becoming in the sense of active self-transcendence, that is, of becoming not only as becoming *other* but also as becoming *more*, is, for Rahner, self-transcendence into something substantially new, a leap to something *essentially* higher. Consistent with this notion of becoming, Rahner maintains that matter develops *out of its inner being* in the direction of the spirit, and more specifically that this is the case of the human being. In the human being the cosmos first becomes conscious of itself. If however human consciousness is self-presence and reference to the absolute totality and ultimate ground of reality, then the cosmos is referred to its ultimate ground not only as its origin behind it but also as its goal before it.

But if the history of the cosmos continues and is fulfilled in human history and if the history of human freedom is one of guilt and damnation, then the cosmos too stands under the judgment of God. Further, if, as the Christian faith professes, human history is enveloped by God's victorious grace, the history of the cosmos too as a whole will find its real consummation in and through the history of humanity. This consummation is called the immortality of the soul or, in Christian language, the resurrection of the flesh.

II. The Conditions of Possibility for the Eschatological Fulfillment

The Kingdom of God, which symbolizes the final consummation of the history of the cosmos and of the spirit, is God's deed and the fruit of his grace. Nevertheless, because it is the fulfillment of the human spirit, the question can and should be raised as to how human history as such can be brought to a definitive and eternally valid end. In other words, one should inquire into the conditions of possibility on the individual's part for the coming of God's Kingdom. For Rahner the conditions are human freedom and historicity.

1. Human Freedom as the Capacity for Definitive Self-Determination

Rahner first spoke of human freedom in *Spirit in the World* in the context of the *conversio ad phantasma*. The human spirit is free because in letting matter (sensibility) emanate from itself it is not lost in sensibility nor does it become sense but remains present to itself and preserves its *Vorgriff* toward the Absolute Being. Human freedom also asserts itself in the fact that the intellect in the act of abstraction apprehends the form of the object as limited and transcends it through its *Vorgriff* to *esse*. Thus the possibility of abstraction is grounded in the freedom of the spirit.[28]

In *Hearers of the Word* this narrow epistemological framework was expanded to include an explicit discussion of will, freedom, and history. In his later writings Rahner moved beyond philosophical considerations of freedom and discussed it theologically in connection with sin,[29] the Church and institution,[30] and sickness.[31] For our purpose I shall attempt to show that for Rahner freedom in the Christian and theological sense must be understood as the capacity (a) to determine or dispose of oneself, (b) in a definitive way. Such freedom by its very nature can be exercised only (c) with reference to God, that is, as received from and directed toward him, and (d) in a historical situation of sin and guilt. This theology is crucial to an understanding of the nature of human death and eternity.

A. TRANSCENDENTAL AND CATEGORICAL FREEDOM

As one of the human being's existentials, freedom, says Rahner, should not be conceived as a particular datum of human reality alongside others. On the contrary, freedom, i. e., transcendental freedom, is "the capacity to make oneself once and for all, the capacity which of its nature is directed towards the freely willed finality of the subject as such."[32] Transcendental freedom ultimately means the subject's responsibility in disposing of the self, not only in knowledge, and hence not only as self-consciousness, but also as self-actualization. Like subjectivity and personhood, freedom and responsibility are realities of transcendental experience. We become aware of them when we experience ourselves as subjects and as persons, as beings who are self-conscious and open to the Infinite Being. Of course, because we live and act in history, our transcendental freedom cannot exist separately but must always be embodied in particular, concrete choices and actions, just as the transcendental *Vorgriff* is always incarnated in particular acts of knowledge of individual, concrete objects. Hence, transcendental freedom is never exercised apart from categorical freedom; rather, it occurs within and through day-by-day categorical choices.

Another approach to transcendental and categorical freedom involves the use of Rahner's distinction between 'nature' and 'person'.[33] 'Nature' defines human beings insofar as they are at their own disposal. It is what we are born with. It includes such things as body, social and cultural environment, religious background, 'world', not as something separate from us but ourselves as the material given to ourselves for self-transformation in freedom. 'Person' defines human beings as they freely dispose of or determine themselves by their fundamental option in and through their particular choices, insofar as they possess themselves as their own definitive reality that they themselves produce. True human freedom, then, is the transcendent freedom that belongs to a human being as person.

B. FREEDOM AS THE CAPACITY FOR DEFINITIVENESS AND FINALITY

Freedom as freedom to *become oneself* and not just *to do something* is by its very nature the subject's capacity to determine himself or herself once and for all, definitively and finally. Through our decisions we become who we want to be forever. Our actions are not just transitory modifications of our identity for which we are rewarded or punished according to some arbitrary decision of a judge and that we are able to shed as if they were accouterment worn for special occasions. On the contrary they combine to shape our character and determine our eternal destiny. Through freedom we have the power to shape the *whole* of our existence, to decide for or against ourselves, to achieve or thwart our definitive self-fulfillment, to attain salvation or damnation, so that we *ourselves*, and not simply our acts, are good or evil.

C. FREEDOM AS THE *VORGRIFF* OF LOVE TOWARD GOD

Freedom as definitive self-determination of the person can be exercised only against the background of the infinite Good, which we may call God. In the act of freedom the subject must necessarily, although implicitly, affirm the absolute value as the horizon or goal against which a particular value is chosen. We know and desire individual objects as partial goods only in relation to the good itself. Our will, which is never satisfied by any particular good it possesses, drives beyond all particular goods and reaches our toward the infinite Good as its asymptotic goal.

Moreover, Rahner maintains that human freedom is not only related to God as its condition of possibility and sustaining ground but also that it is always and ultimately freedom vis-à-vis God. That is, human freedom must necessarily confront God as an 'object' that it chooses or rejects. This freedom implies, says Rahner, "the possibility of a 'yes' or 'no' towards its horizon and indeed it is only really constituted by this."[34] Of course in rejecting God human freedom rejects the condition of its own possibility and hence contradicts itself. This is a frightening possibility and a tragic paradox since in rejecting God freedom at the same time affirms him as the condition of possibility for its act of rejection.

D. FREEDOM AS RADICALLY THREATENED BY GUILT

Human freedom is a *created* freedom enacting itself in a situation of *guilt*. That it is a created freedom is shown by two facts. First, human freedom experiences itself as borne and empowered by its absolute horizon, which it does not create but which freely opens itself to it. Secondly, human freedom is always exercised in a context in which certain forces are antecedently operative and therefore cannot be planned or controlled. It is inevitably determined by these forces. Its task consists precisely in appropriating them as its own intrinsic and constitutive elements.

That the world of persons in which human freedom realizes itself is determined by guilt and that human freedom must be liberated is something not only known in everyday experience but also disclosed by Christian revelation. Christianity asserts that this codetermination of the salvation of every person by the guilt of others is something universal, permanent, and therefore also original. It can be called 'original sin', sin understood not in the univocal sense of an act of freedom (as in the *peccatum originale originans*), but in the analogous sense of *our own situation of guilt* determining our freedom (the *peccatum originale originatum*).[35]

2. *The Individual as a Historical Being: Between Time and Eternity*

Modern anthropology has consistently emphasized historicity as one of the fundamental existentials of human beings. It is to be expected that having been influenced by German philosophical thought, especially the historically oriented systems of Hegel and Heidegger, and above all steeped in the Judaeo-Christian tradition, Rahner would take history very seriously. Already in *Spirit in the World* Rahner attempted to ground human time and hence human historicity in motion. Human time, however, cannot be properly understood on the basis of motion, even if this motion is internal. In *Hearers of the Word*, although still retaining materiality and hence receptive knowledge in sensibility, as the ground for human historicity,[36] Rahner offers a fresh approach to human historicity on the basis of human spirituality and freedom. For our purpose we will examine Rahner's theology of time and eternity and his concept of Absolute Future.

A. TIME: GENUINE BEGINNING AND DEFINITIVE END

The starting point of Rahner's theology of time is the Christian teaching that the world is not 'eternal' but has been created in time and with time, and that it has a 'beginning'. To clarify how time is finite and hence has a beginning and an end, Rahner suggests that the finitude of time can best be grasped if we consider time not as something external to human beings, as a quantifying, measuring, continuous, and homogeneous field,[37] but as intrinsically connected with human freedom. Time is first seen as the condition of possibility for the exercise of human freedom, and freedom is what confers meaning to time and makes it not merely *Historie* but *Geschichte*.

This concept of time—'internal time'[38]—is 'extrapolated' in the second moment to the time of the world as a whole, the 'external time'. External time is not and cannot be abolished. Human freedom needs external time as the 'other' (symbol) in which its internal time is realized. However, external time can be understood only in the light of the internal time of human freedom.

Because time is an element of the history of freedom, it has a genuine beginning, a definitive end, and an irreversible course. By genuine beginning is meant not simply the chronologically first unit in a series of comparable units but that initiation of a whole which alone makes the history of the whole possible. A beginning is genuine only when it is the beginning of a personal being, where what is begun is a new whole and not merely a phase of another movement. The beginning remains open with respect to its end and only attains itself in its end. In this sense the end preserves, perfects, and reveals the beginning. The beginning contains a task that is imposed upon human freedom, which is fulfilled or frustrated by humanity's future free acts of choice. The past is revealed in the light of the future; the emergence of the future gradually reveals the origins.

Since freedom is the capacity for finality and definitiveness and since time is the concomitant of freedom, time has an end that is final and definitive. The end for the individual history of freedom is, of course, death. This end, however, is neither a negation of existence nor an arbitrary interruption of indefinitely continuing time, but the fulfillment of time. Time is taken up into the absolute validity of a freedom that has realized itself in time. The end is at once present because the individual has to take up an attitude with regard to it and at the same time outstanding because its outcome depends on the free choices still to be made.[39]

Because time has a genuine beginning and a definitive end, its course is irreversible. It has a 'once for all' character. Irreversibility of time does not merely mean that what has been done cannot be undone. It also means that what has been carried out in freedom cannot be lost. Rahner makes it clear that what passes away at the end of time is the process of becoming and not what we have become, both good and evil, which will acquire definitive validity before God:

> Hence you can say: your whole life remains always preserved for you; everything you have done and suffered is gathered together in your being. You may appear to have forgotten it, yet it is still there. It may appear to you as a pale dream even when you do remember what you

once were, did and thought. All this you still are. All this has perhaps been transformed (it is to be hoped) and incorporated into a better, more comprehensive framework, has been integrated more into a great love (indeed, the great love) and silent loyalty towards your God which was, remained and grew throughout everything life did with you; but everything has remained in this way, nothing has simply ceased, everything which happened—as long as we are pilgrims of maturing freedom—can still be retrieved and transformed into the one action of the heart in what you do today: the good of your past life, by taking up once more in its proper nature what remained and what through sin became the power of evil; the evil, by taking the good—without which the empty evil cannot exist—out of this obstructing evil . . . and by opening it up to the breadth of freedom which really belongs to every genuine reality such as was concealed even in your evil actions, by opening it up to the breadth of freedom which belongs to the pure goodness of God.[40]

B. ETERNITY: TIME FULFILLED AND MADE DEFINITIVE

As Rahner's understanding of time is intimately connected with his theology of freedom, so is his notion of eternity. As freedom is not the capacity of making an indefinite number of revisable choices and as time is not an infinite succession of states, so eternity should not be conceived as unlimited continuation of time after death, never-ending time running on into infinity on the other side of this world, with one moment coming after the other, as though "things go on" after death. This widespread misconception of eternity is, in Rahner's estimation, responsible for the present-day weakening of faith in life after death. Such misrepresentation of eternity, albeit unavoidable because of our spatiotemporal imagination, is not only incredible but also pernicious. For then one cannot see how 'heaven' can be bliss, since we are doomed to roam forever, in search of final destination without ever reaching it.

To form a more adequate concept of eternity, Rahner relates it to freedom, just as he has conceived time in terms of freedom. Freedom is not a ceaseless quest to achieve ever-fresh changes at will but the capacity for finality and definitiveness. Whenever something is achieved with finality and definitiveness in time, either by particular acts of freedom or by the act of freedom par excellence, namely death, there eternity comes to be. "In reality," says Rahner, "eternity comes to be in time as time's own mature fruit, an eternity which does not really continue on beyond experienced time. Rather eternity subsumes time by being liberated from the time which came to be temporarily so that freedom and something of final and definitive validity can be achieved. Eternity is not an infinitely long mode of pure time, but rather it is a mode of that spiritual freedom which has been exercised in time, and therefore it can be understood only from a correct understanding of spiritual freedom."[41] Thus for Rahner there is constituted an inseparable triad of time, freedom, and eternity. Eternity is not outside, above, after, beyond time; rather it is *in* and *from* time, time having acquired final and definitive validity before God through the exercise of freedom.

Rahner suggests three possible ways in which we can have an experience of eternity in time, of how time is made definitive by becoming eternity. First, there is the experience of change in which the changing phenomena replacing one another are manifestations of a permanent, persisting reality. This reality sustains these changing appearances, bringing them together into a whole, a unified history. Secondly, there is the mental experience that combines past, present, and future into a unity. Here, time is not simply there as something to which we are subjected; it is something we confront actively, gathering it up together into a unity of past, present, and future, something that is more than a succession of moments each destroying the other. Lastly, there is the experience of free decision that by its very nature does not permit what it has posited simply to disappear into the void of nothingness. In free decisions the subject bears an ultimate, inescapable responsibility for what he or she has done. In the act of absolute self-disposal, something irrevocable and irreversible is accomplished. Here, says Rahner, "time really creates eternity and eternity is experienced in time."[42]

There still remain two points to be discussed in Rahner's theology of eternity. First, can this anthropological approach to eternity, based on human freedom, be employed to form a notion of the eternity of God? And, secondly, does God's eternity have anything to do with time? First of all, Rahner finds the traditional understanding of God's eternity inadequate. It is based on the model of duration, in this case of course without cessation in either direction, without beginning and without end. Although such a model was popular in the past, Rahner suggests that it should not be adopted today. As time is best understood not on the model of physical motion (external time) but on that of freedom, so God's eternity can best be understood through the analogy of internal time, *per modum negationis et eminentiae*.[43]

Secondly, as to whether God's eternity has anything to do with time, Rahner maintains that Christian theology must hold firm to the 'immutability' and eternal 'timelessness' of God 'in themselves'. At the same time, however, because of the act of creation and above all because of the Incarnation of the Logos, it must be said that God not only has created time but has also freely assumed it as a specification of his own self. God, although 'immutable' and 'eternal' in himself, has *himself*, in the otherness of the world, undergone change, history, and time. The time of the world becomes God's own history.

To differentiate this becoming of God from our becoming, Rahner makes it clear that God does not become something else out of need (*Bedürftig-keit*). Rather his becoming is a sign of perfection: "Moreover, this possibility is not to be understood as a sign that he is in need of something, but rather as the height of his perfection. This perfection would be less perfect if he could not become less than he is and always remains."[44] Just as God creates the human reality by assuming it and assumes it by creating it in the Incarnation of the Logos, so one can say that God creates time by assuming it (*"assumendo tempus creat tempus"*). He thereby causes his own eternity to be the true content of time. He creates time in order to impart to it his own eternity.

C. ESCHATOLOGICAL FULFILLMENT OF TIME: THE ABSOLUTE FUTURE

In his later writings Rahner shifted his emphasis upon eternity as a present dimension of time, time made definitive and final through individual acts of freedom here and now, to eternity as the future reality to be brought about by the communal effort of humankind and by God as his free gift.[45] Increasingly the category of future was used both as a new paradigm for describing the transcendent nature of God and for delineating the mission and tasks of Christianity.

Rahner recognized that orientation to and preoccupation with the future has become a predominant feature of our time. There is even a new science called futurology whose task is to research into the future, shaping, planning, and interpreting it. Rahner begins his discussion of the relationship between futurology and Christian eschatology by drawing an important distinction between inner-worldly future and what he calls the absolute future. "The absolute future," says Rahner, "is God himself or the act of his absolute self-bestowal which has to be posited by him alone. . . . It is a specification of the world as a whole, comprehending the whole of reality and determining where its consummation is to be achieved. To this extent it has a transcendental character. Properly speaking, therefore, it cannot be planned or brought about by human either, because as the total consummation of reality as a whole it cannot *per definitionem* be brought about by any one particular element within this reality."[46]

The inner-worldly future, on the other hand, is that which human beings plan for, control, and calculate. It is something to be achieved within this world and within the dimensions of space and time and belongs to this world as one of its particular events or specific states. Human beings are discovering that they are 'operable'. Rahner distinguishes two kinds of intramundane future: (1) that which comes about because of a predetermined evolutionary pattern (e. g., reproductive fertility will issue forth in the future continuance of the race), and (2) that which results from human creativity and freedom, producing the genuinely and radically new. Only this second kind of future is properly speaking the *utopian future*. It contains a creative element that is underivable from previously existing factors by a process of evolution. In this future we do not simply extend further our own past or present, but in a real and radical sense surpass it in active self-transcendence. This utopian future, even though it is the object of human planning and manipulation, constitutes for Rahner "an open, and abidingly open question."[47]

Postponing to a later part of this work our considerations of Rahner's reflections on the tasks of Christianity in view of this new orientation toward the future, we will simply note here that this future utopia pursued by contemporary humanity, in Marxism for instance, should not be seen, in Rahner's estimation, as necessarily contradictory to the eschatological tendency of Christianity. Christianity can accept the contemporary utopian movement toward the future because it is "the religion of the future" and, furthermore, "the religion of the *absolute* future."[48] Christianity may appear to believers and unbelievers alike as something extremely complex. For Rahner, however, what is specific and proper to Christianity is ultimately something utterly simple. It is "the question, maintained in openness, of the absolute future which is God or—which is saying the same thing—the question of God who is the absolute future."[49]

III. Anticipation of the Eschatological Kingdom: The World of Grace

The Absolute Future is not only an eschatological reality still to come but also already anticipated in a mysterious yet real way in history. In traditional terms, the beatific vision, which constitutes the essence of eternal beatitude, is already anticipated in grace. Transcendental eschatology, which deals with the theological foundations for a categorical eschatology, must therefore attend to the reality of grace. In what follows we will consider grace and guilt insofar as these realities impinge upon the eschatological fulfillment of human beings.

1. The Supernatural Existential and Uncreated Grace

Commentators have often pointed out that the doctrine of grace forms the heart of Rahner's theology, and quite correctly so.[50] Of the many aspects of Rahnerian theology of grace, two items, his theory of supernatural existential and his understanding of grace as Uncreated Grace, are of topical interest.

A. THE SUPERNATURAL EXISTENTIAL

Rahner has sharply criticized the extrinsicist notion of grace espoused by average neo-scholastic textbooks according to which 'nature' and 'grace' are as it were two layers one placed on top of the other, and the *potentia obedientialis* of nature to grace is merely a nonrepugnance. He maintains that there exists in concrete human beings a 'supernatural existential' in virtue of which—antecedently to justification by grace, received sacramentally or extrasacramentally—they are already subject to the universal salvific will of God and *are* already redeemed and absolutely obliged to tend to their supernatural end.[51] This supernatural existential is a real, intrinsic modification of the human being that necessarily precedes our free actions and determines them. Because it is not owed to the person precisely as a creature and not simply as a sinner, it is called *supernatural*. In this way its absolute gratuitousness is made clear. Further, Rahner calls it *existential*, using Heidegger's terminology, because it is a fundamental structure of *Dasein*.

The point of these considerations is to show that for Rahner the eschatological fulfillment of human beings is not something accidental or artificially added to our nature. Rather it is the consummation of what is most intimate and essential to us; it is the fulfillment of ourselves. Conversely it also shows that failure to achieve this goal does not affect merely some secondary part of the person but his or her very self.

B. UNCREATED GRACE

Another aspect of Rahner's theology of grace that is of great import for his eschatology is his understanding of grace as primarily Uncreated Grace, that is, the indwelling of the divine persons in the justified. Because revelation and grace are God's communication of himself and not of something other than himself, the creature is healed, justified, and made eternally blessed by God's own being.[52]

In Rahner's view, the neo-scholastic textbook notion of grace as primarily created grace cannot provide an adequate understanding of God's self-communication in Christ. If grace is seen simply in terms of efficient causality by which God produces some accident in the human soul (an activity *ad extra* of God and hence to be attributed to God in common, or at most attributable to each divine person only by appropriation), it cannot be the ground of a presence of God in the human soul that would be essentially different from God's causal presence in the rest of the creation.

As a corrective to this understanding of grace, Rahner suggests that another kind of causality, namely, the formal and material causality, be employed in conceiving God's self-communication. In justification, as in

the beatific vision, the three divine persons communicate their own being
to the human soul as Uncreated Grace. Since this communication is the
communication of God's own self, it can only be understood in terms of
quasi-formal causality. Grace as such and as strictly supernatural is first
and foremost God himself communicating himself with his own nature:
Uncreated Grace. It is Uncreated Grace, and not the created grace, that is
primary. Created grace is not the efficient cause of Uncreated Grace;
rather, it is its material cause, the material disposition for the 'form', namely, Uncreated Grace. In communicating itself, Uncreated Grace actively
produces this disposition as its own condition so that the two realities,
created and Uncreated Grace, condition one another in reciprocal causality.[53] The profound implications of this understanding of grace for eschatology, especially for the question of the beatific vision, will be unfolded
in due course.

2. Guilt and Concupiscence

Because of his theory of the 'supernatural existential' with its numerous
corollaries on the possibility of salvation, Rahner has sometimes been accused of excessive optimism regarding the condition of human existence.
Of course as a Christian he is convinced that God has already triumphed
over evil, definitively and irreversibly, in the death and Resurrection of
Jesus. Nevertheless, Rahner's consciousness of the human bondage under
sin and guilt is no less acute than his sense of the universal presence of
God's grace. Grace for Rahner is not only *gratia elevans* but also *gratia
sanans*, not only sanctifying but also healing and forgiving.

What is of interest to us here is the effect of sin and guilt on the human
exercise of freedom, for, as has already been said, it is through our acts of
freedom that we shape our eternal destiny, definitively and irrevocably,
before God. This pernicious effect is traditionally called *concupiscence*.
Concupiscence in neo-scholastic theology, Rahner notes, is understood as
"the sensitive appetite (*Begehrungsvermögen*) and its act, insofar as this
strives after its sensitive object *in opposition to* the law of the moral order
independently of the higher, spiritual conative power, and thus resists the
free spiritual decision of man's will."[54]

Against this narrow and moralistic interpretation of concupiscence,
Rahner suggests that concupiscence should be understood as "man's
spontaneous desire, insofar as it precedes his free desire *and resists it*."[55]
Three characteristics of concupiscence as desire are implied: its spon-
taneity, its connection with human freedom, and its resistance to the
human act of self-determination. First of all, as an act of a mere natural
dynamism (*appetitus naturalis*) responding to a partial good (*actus indeliberatus*), concupiscence is the necessary condition preceding the human

being's free decision (*actus deliberatus* or *dictamen rationis*). This spontaneous, nonfree character of the act of the appetite makes it essentially premoral. Secondly, the human act of free decision is primarily an act of self-determination, of disposing oneself *as a whole* in reference to God as the absolute Good. Concupiscence is the necessary precondition for this act of self-determination. Thirdly, because concupiscence *resists* this act of self-determination, the individual's effort at complete self-disposal will never be fully successful.[56]

The nature of concupiscence could be better grasped if Rahner's distinction between 'nature' and 'person' alluded to above is kept in mind. Elevated by grace human beings attempt to bring 'nature' into the realm of the 'person' by their free acts so that their free decision should include and transform the spontaneous act, making it no longer purely natural but personal. Now, concupiscence, insofar as it is the spontaneous act of desire (*actus indeliberatus*) resisting the person's attempt at self-integration, is the act of 'nature' against the 'person'.

Rahner points out, however, that this resistance of concupiscence against the 'person' works both ways, not only when the person chooses to do good but also when he or she chooses to do evil. In contrast with pure spirits (angels), human beings, because of their materiality, temporality, and subjection to concupiscence, cannot engage themselves totally in any single act, whether good or evil. Thus, if there is a supernatural existential of grace in human beings, there is also a negative existential of concupiscence in them that at times prevents this supernatural existential from being fully realized and at other times, fortunately, also prevents it from being totally destroyed.

The purpose of these reflections on Rahner's theology of concupiscence is to show that concupiscence (and, as we will see, death too) is not just the manifestation of sin. In the order of salvation it is not just what is left over in the justified, something to be overcome eschatologically because it actively resists the ultimate fulfillment of humanity's goal; it is also the form in which Christians experience Christ's sufferings and suffers them themselves. Eschatology, therefore, is not simply something that will happen only at the end of the person's life, but also a reality present throughout his or her entire existence, in the form of *prolixitas mortis*.

IV. Eschatology as Anthropology in the Future Tense?

What we have expounded in this chapter is what Rahner tentatively calls "an eschatology of transcendental theology"[57] or, more simply, transcendental eschatology. Rahner is quite optimistic that "the dissatisfaction which is so generally felt with the existing state of traditional eschatology could be removed by an eschatology expressed in terms of transcendental theology, if this eschatology conceived of man as a being destined to an absolute future in a transcendental anthropology which included within its purview the self-communication of God to man."[58]

What emerges from this transcendental anthropology is a being endowed with several interconnected 'existentials' (*Existentialien*): The human being is a corporeal-material being, living in a biological community of life with its material surroundings; a spiritual-personal, cultural being with a diversity of personal communities; a unity of matter and spirit, of spiritualized matter and materialized spirit; a being gifted with freedom by which he or she can self-enact in an eternally valid way; a historical being with a genuine beginning, a definitive end, and an unknown, uncontrollable future; a being called by God to share in his Triune life and ontologically transformed in his or her very nature for this purpose; and yet at the same time a being laden with sin and guilt who must achieve his or her goal gradually and with difficulty by overcoming internal resistance.

One recurrent theme throughout these characterizations of the human being is that we are ineluctably oriented toward a future that is now already present but still outstanding. As matter, we are immersed in the process of an ongoing evolution whose transcendental goal is made clear, namely, the stage of perfect self-presence and consciousness, but whose categorical realizations are as unpredictable as history itself. As spirit, we are dynamically riveted upon the Absolute Being as our asymptotic horizon who recedes and eludes our grasp as the infinite and (as revelation tells us) gracious Mystery. As transcendentally free beings we can never quite catch up with our goal of total self-disposal that we necessarily aim at in our categorical acts of freedom and which remains a distant goal until our death. As temporal beings we are caught up in the movement of history from past through present to future, a future that is ultimately uncontrollable and unpredictable, despite our efforts of utopian planning and manipulation. As beings healed and elevated by God's self-communication, we are now living by the life of God, but this grace is only a beginning, a seed of the beatific vision yet to come.

This future, or more precisely, this absolute future is what transposes Rahner's anthropology into eschatology. Rahner has stated quite plainly: "Eschatology is not really an addition, but rather it gives expression once again to man as Christianity understands him: as a being who ex-ists from out of his present 'now' towards his future. . . . Because of man's very nature, therefore, Christian anthropology is Christian futurology and Christian eschatology."[59]

There is no doubt that this transposition of anthropology into eschatology in terms of futurity lends superb consistency, simplicity, and unity to Rahner's theological system. It conjoins the two poles of his method, transcendentality and historicity; it supplies an effective hermeneutical tool for interpreting traditional eschatology in Christian theology; it forges an indissoluble link among the various themes of theology that so far have been left disparate; it provides a solution to the vexing problem of the unity between individual and collective eschatologies.

But has Rahner bought this precious pearl at too high a price? Has his method been far more transcendental than historical? Leaving aside the question of whether his interpretation of Thomas's epistemology is historically faithful, is his doctrine of *Vorgriff* defensible? Is his ontology of *Realsymbol* sound? Does his anthropological approach to time and eternity by linking them to human freedom do justice both to eternity and time? Is eternity simply time made final and definitive or are there other ways of conceiving it? Is the concept of the Absolute Future as God-with-humanity-and-cosmos an effective paradigm for divine transcendence and for human historicity? What is the exact ontological status of the supernatural existential?

These are but some of the critical questions that must be addressed to Rahner's anthropology-transubstantiated-into-eschatology, and of course they cannot be answered until his categorical eschatology, both individual and collective, has been examined. For the moment let us attend to the hermeneutical principles Rahner employs in interpreting the eschatological assertions.

The Hermeneutics of Eschatological
Statements

> Thus I may be permitted to express my decided and radical mis-
> trust of any attempt to reduce theology in any adequate sense to
> the methodology employed in it, or to reformulate it in these
> terms. Theology always is, and always will be, even in the future,
> something more than its own hermeneutics. . . . Theology can-
> not be reduced merely to theological hermeneutics or a for-
> malized system of teaching on the subject of speaking about
> God. . . . In the long run theological methodology will only be
> convincing when it brings more into immediate contact with
> the subject-matter itself. . . . ("Reflections on Methodology in
> Theology," *TI*, 11:83–84)

The title of this chapter contains a much-discussed and perplexing word,
hermeneutics. It is common knowledge that hermeneutics as the science
and art of interpretation has recently been the object of extensive scholarly
debates. A glance at the issues under discussion will reveal both the range
and complexity of the issue: the hermeneutical themes in German idealism
and later in ontological existentialism; Anglo-Saxon philosophy of linguistic analysis; hermeneutical motifs in phenomenology, psychoanalysis,
sociology of knowledge, and critique of ideology; recent developments in
cultural anthropology, epistemology of the sciences, logic, semiotics and
semantics, and biblical literary and historical criticism. All these endeavors, just to mention a few at random, revolve around the plexus of
knowing, understanding, and interpreting the text or the reality communicated in the text.[1]

Rahner is clearly not a hermeneutical theorist in the way Friedrich
Schleiermacher, Wilhelm Dilthey, Martin Heidegger, Hans-Georg Gadamer, Emilio Betti, and Paul Ricoeur are. Nevertheless, his influence on
contemporary hermeneutics, especially in Catholic circles, is far from
negligible. He has written, besides the article on the hermeneutics of
eschatological assertions, many other essays on related topics, such as

the development of dogma, the relationship between biblical exegesis and systematic theology, the interpretation of magisterial documents, the ontology of symbol, and so on.

In this chapter we will first of all briefly consider Rahner's hermeneutical practice in relation to some contemporary theories of interpretation. Secondly, we will examine Rahner's specific prescriptions for the interpretation of eschatological assertions.

I. Rahner and Modern Hermeneutical Theories

Spirit in the World is ostensibly an interpretive study of Thomas Aquinas's *ST* I, q. 84, a. 7. However, Rahner's approach and method betray an understanding of hermeneutics far different from the then prevailing purely exegetical and philological analysis of texts. Of course the strictly historical investigation of the thirteenth-century Thomas is not neglected, as the abundance of quotations from his various works and the close textual analysis readily testify.

However, in terms that are reminiscent of Schleiermacher, Dilthey, and above all Heidegger, although none of these is cited in the book, Rahner maintains that in order to grasp the really philosophical in a philosopher, one has to join him in looking at the matter itself. It is only then that one can understand what he or she means. It is not enough to collect everything and anything Thomas has said; rather one must get back to the "original philosophical event" in Thomas.[2]

The act of abandoning oneself to the subject itself, of joining with the author of the text in looking at the matter itself, of getting back to the original event of thinking is not for Rahner primarily a psychological reconstruction of the mental processes of the author as Schleiermacher and Dilthey would have it. Rather it is a creative dialogue with the text in order to bring out into the open what is left unsaid or even could not be said by the original author. In this Rahner is more akin to Heidegger than to the other two hermeneutical theorists. In many ways the hermeneutics of *Spirit in the World* is similar to that of Heidegger's *Kant and the Problem of Metaphysics*. As Heidegger was not primarily interested in repeating what Kant had said about the limits of human knowledge but rather in what Kant had left unsaid about the possibility, not the destruction, of metaphysics on the basis of the transcendental imagination, so too Rahner was not concerned with "paraphrasing" Thomas Aquinas's theory of knowledge but with what can be said about the human being's metaphysical structure as spirit in the world on the basis of the intellect's *conversio ad phantasma* in light of the Kantian critique of knowledge.

Rahner followed the same procedure later when he interpreted biblical and magisterial teachings on diverse matters and, in particular, on eschatology. Just to cite a few examples, Rahner reinterpreted Chalcedonian christology in light of the evolutionary theory, death in light of Heidegger's existential analysis of *Dasein*, and purgatory in light of the widespread belief in reincarnation.

However, as he proceeded to investigate properly theological themes, Rahner echoed more strongly Schleiermacher's and Dilthey's emphasis on interior or lived experience as a necessary medium for understanding religious realities. Contrary to mainstream neo-scholastic theology of grace, Rahner constantly defended the possibility of consciousness of sanctifying grace and even of actual grace. His apologetical "mystagogy" consists in making possible for contemporary men and women the experience of the hidden Mystery transcendentally present in day-to-day, mundane categorical experiences: moving around, sitting, seeing, laughing, eating, sleeping, and working.[3]

Like Schleiermacher, Rahner in his hermeneutics, especially in his interpretation of the God-question, turns from the objective content of the experience to the subjective human consciousness. This center of consciousness is the locus of the divine self-manifestions; the luminosity (*Gelichtetheit*) of the Absolute Being is its constitutive idea and the condition of possibility. Rahner recasts Schleiermacher's "feeling of absolute dependence" in terms of the experience of "creatureliness." Creatureliness, for Rahner, is an experience of radical difference from and radical dependence on God and is available only in the transcendental experience.[4] Furthermore, not unlike Schleiermacher, Rahner conceived of theology as transcendental anthropology in which the a priori, unthematic anticipation of the Absolute Being, rather than the categorical, a posteriori knowledge of discrete objects 'out there,' provides the methodological perspective for evaluating and reformulating past doctrines.

Lastly, just as in Schleiermacher, religious experience as the means of validation of Christian doctrinal assertions assumes an increasingly preponderant role as Rahner attempts to provide them with a transcendental, indirect justification. In fact, it plays a key role in his indirect method to demonstrate the reasonableness of the Christian faith. With increasing frequency Rahner describes, at times in lyrical language, the "experiences of the Spirit," especially in the light of Ignatius's teaching on the "consolación sin causa."[5] He succeeds in revealing the presence of divine grace in most unexpected and yet common phenomena, and not only in extraordinary mystical experiences of the saints. As Harvey Egan has correctly remarked, Rahner's theology "begins and ends in a mystical moment: the *experience* of the lived, root unity of self-possessing knowledge and love penetrated by God's self-communication."[6]

Rahner shares Heidegger's understanding of hermeneutics as a process of disclosing what could not have been said by the text, as a creative dialogue between the text and the interpreter, a thinking along with the text that is not a manipulation of the ideas expressed in the text but a bringing to light of Being hidden in it. The later Heidegger shifted from hermeneutics as the understanding of *Dasein* to hermeneutics as the interpretation of language since Being occurs and is revealed in language. Similarly, Rahner emphasizes the importance of language, especially of what he calls the "primary words" (*Urworte*) in contrast to the "technical, utility words" in opening up the unfathomable depths of reality in general.[7]

Further both Heidegger and Rahner adopt the human question about being as the starting point not only for ontology but also for the interpretive act. For both the question implies a certain circular structure in interpretation insofar as the question already signifies a prereflexive knowledge of the subject matter to be interpreted. Both, too, emphasize the importance of prereflexive, unthematic knowledge of being as such for constructing a metaphysics of knowledge. Moreover, both are keenly aware of the 'ontological difference' between beings and Being. Further, both maintain the existence of an original unity between knowing and being, that is, being as being-present-to-oneself. Finally, both underline the historicity and temporality of human existence and hence of human understanding.[8]

In conclusion, Rahner's theological hermeneutics combines Schleiermacher's and Dilthey's emphasis on lived experience and its nonreflexive character as the key to understanding, with Heidegger's and Gadamer's dialectics of retrieval, of what is unsaid in the text. Like Heidegger and Gadamer, Rahner rejects a purely psychological approach to hermeneutics as a reconstruction of the mental processes of the author. Rather, the act of interpretation is understood as a dialectical interaction with the text, not a servile reenactment but a new creation, a new event in understanding. For Rahner as well as for his predecessors, there can be no 'presuppositionless' interpretation; one always approaches the text with a certain preunderstanding that is given by the tradition in which one stands. Tradition and authority are not obstacles to understanding; rather understanding occurs only if one takes this tradition and authority as the horizon of one's understanding and attempts to broaden this horizon by the encounter with the text and the reality revealed and concealed by the text. For Rahner there is in interpretation and understanding what Gadamer calls the "fusion of horizons," of different points of view (*Horizontverschmelzung*).

II. The Hermeneutics of Eschatological Assertions

We now come to the hermeneutical principles Rahner explicitly conceived for eschatological assertions. He formulates them in seven theses, some of which are divided into several subtheses.[9] His basic approach is dogmatic and not biblical. However, he is confident that his dogmatic hermeneutics will be confirmed by or at least not contradictory to a hermeneutics derived directly from biblical data.

Rahner is convinced of the usefulness of the critico-historical method and insists that it should be applied in the interpretation of biblical eschatology:

> . . . We should ask what are the principles of hermeneutics suggested by Scripture itself, where it makes eschatological assertions. We should listen carefully to these assertions; we should compare the various sets of concepts, disparate at certain levels, which lie behind the assertions; we should inquire precisely into their real origin, their *Sitz im Leben* or social setting, which in this case would really be the absolutely primordial experience of revelation, compared with which all other eschatological assertions are derivative and explanatory—and are meant to be so—; we should meditate on and compare the various eschatologies which are to be found in Scripture itself; we should apply the principle of the *analogia fidei* to biblical eschatology; we should investigate historically various eschatological notions, images, motifs, etc.; and then it would be quite possible to take the guiding line of the biblical assertions on eschatology and deduce certain principles, which will be those by which Scripture itself demands to be interpreted in these passages.[10]

These hermeneutical recommendations, laconically formulated here, are of great significance for several reasons. First, they demonstrate Rahner's vivid awareness of the almost unmanageable complexity of the task of determining and systematizing the contents of biblical eschatology. Secondly, they underline Rahner's conviction that one should abandon the naïve proof-text approach to biblical eschatology adopted by the average neo-scholastic treatise, *De Novissimis* and his genuine sympathy for the hermeneutical procedures of modern biblical exegesis. Thirdly, they evidence Rahner's position that the hermeneutical principles for eschatological assertions must not be imported from outside or conceived a priori but must be formulated on the basis of biblical eschatology itself. And finally, in line with what has been said in the previous section, hermeneutics is regarded not as a merely philological analysis of biblical texts, even though a careful investigation of eschatological notions, images, and categories is demanded, but as a properly theological task to be carried out on the basis of the *analogia fidei*.

In what follows we will expound Rahner's hermeneutical principles of eschatology, explicating them not just serially but grouping them together according to their intentions. In this way some kind of organic unity and intrinsic connections among them will be made evident.

1. Eschatology and the Hidden Future

Rahner's first four theses deal with the genuinely future character of Christian eschatological realities. These are known by God and can be revealed to humanity, but as essentially hidden and uncontrollable since their outcome depends on the freedom of God and of human beings.

a. *First Thesis*: "The Christian understanding of the faith and its expression must contain an eschatology which really bears on the *future*, that which is still to come, in a very ordinary, empirical sense of the word time."[11] Like Cullmann, Rahner takes eschatology in its chronological sense of future. He therefore rejects Bultmann's existential demythologization of eschatology as a purely present decision for or against the kerygma. For Rahner as well as for Pannenberg and Moltmann, eschatology deals with realities still to come, realities that belong not only to the ultramundane future but also to the Absolute Future. In interpreting eschatological assertions we must keep this futurity in mind and cannot dismiss them as mere symbolizations of presently occurring realities.

b. *Second Thesis*: "The Christian understanding of the nature, life and personal being of God takes his 'omniscience' not merely as a metaphysical axiom, but as a strict truth of faith, and makes it include God's knowledge of future events. Insofar as this knowledge embraces the realities of the world and mankind, there can be no denying or doubting, in metaphysics or theology, the fundamental 'abstract' possibility of the communication of such future events; they are known by God and they are human, and hence do not of themselves in principle go beyond the capacity of human understanding."[12] Two points are made in this second thesis: first, God's knowledge of future events of human history and secondly, the human capacity of understanding them should God choose to reveal them to us. Hence, eschatological assertions are not the result of philosophical speculation but are made known by God in a concrete history of revelation and salvation.

Further, even though human beings cannot impose a priori any limits on God's power to reveal futher events, nevertheless it is possible and necessary to define the framework within which God's communication about future events can be understood. This framework is to be constructed a posteriori on the basis of God's actual revelation and serves to delimit the manner in which human beings can receive such communication from God and hence the way in which these divine utterances must be interpreted. This is what the following thesis intends to do in two complementary statements.

c. *Third Thesis* (First part): "It is certain from Scripture that God has *not* revealed to humanity the day of the end."[13] This thesis does not merely assert that we happen to be ignorant of the exact moment when the end will come. It also affirms that the eschatological events have an essentially hidden character so that they are revealed *as* hidden, as unexpected, as mystery. Any hermeneutics of eschatological assertions that regards them as prediction or anticipated report of future events must therefore be false.

(Second part): "If human beings are beings involved in history. . . , they cannot understand themselves in any given present moment without an aetiological retrospect toward a genuinely temporal past, an 'anamnesis', and without prospect of a genuinely temporal future. Their self-understanding embraces the beginning and the end of their temporal history, both in the life of the individual person and of humanity."[14] Hermeneutics of the end of humankind must include within itself a consideration of human beginning. Eschatology includes protology, just as prognosis includes anamnesis and vice versa. The knowledge of the future is an inner dimension of the self-understanding of persons in their present moment of existence and grows out of it. This point is elaborated in the next thesis.

d. *Fourth Thesis*: "Knowledge of the future will be knowledge of the futurity of the present: eschatological knowledge is knowledge of the eschatological present. An eschatological assertion is not an additional, supplementary statement appended to an assertion about the present and the past of the human person but an inner moment of this person's self-understanding."[15]

Whereas the third thesis connects humanity's hidden future to our past, this fourth thesis relates our future to our present. Because man ex-sists into the future, the future in its hiddenness must be a real moment of the present self-understanding of the person. Indeed it can be known and understood *only out of the present*; it is the futurity of the present. Therefore the hermeneutics of eschatological assertions is ultimately the interpretation of the individual's present self-understanding in terms of his or her future fulfillment; it is, in other words, anthropology conjugated in the future tense. In Christian terms, this would mean that eschatology is the future fulfillment of the salvation already wrought by Jesus Christ and granted by God to human beings.

2. The Nature of Eschatology and Its Difference from Apocalyptic

On the basis of what has been said, especially in the third and fourth theses, Rahner attempts to define more exactly the nature and scope of genuine eschatological assertions and distinguishes them from false ones, which he calls "apocalyptic." Hence:

e. *Fifth Thesis*: ". . . We may say that biblical eschatology must always be read as an assertion based on the revealed present and pointing toward the genuine future, but not as an assertion pointing back from an anticipated future into the present. To read from the present out into the future (*Aussage*) is eschatology, to read from the future back into the present (*Einsage*) is apocalyptic. The eschatological assertion is part of human nature and when it is concerned with the present as revealed by God's word, it is Christian eschatology. The apocalyptic suggestion is either phantasy or gnosticism; it does not merely suppose, as Christians also must, that the future only exists in the inaccessible mystery of God as such, . . . it also unwittingly supposes that the future already leads of itself a supratemporal existence, of which history is only the projection on the screen of worthless time, and that time is not the real ground from which the eternal validity of the human person emerges, but a nothingness which is unmasked and really eliminated in this gnostic contact with the true reality, called apocalypsis."[16]

This thesis no doubt constitutes the heart of Rahner's hermeneutics of eschatology. First of all, the source of Christian eschatology for Rahner is the *present* situation of salvation, which consists in God's Trinitarian self-disclosure to humans in the grace of the crucified and risen Christ. "The Sitz im Leben," says Rahner, "the setting of eschatological assertions is therefore the experience of God's salvific action *on ourselves* in Christ."[17]

Secondly, it follows that the hermeneutics of eschatological assertions is an etiology. As protology is an etiological account from the present situation of sin and salvation back into the origins (Creation, humanity's elevation and Fall) and not a historical report of what transpired at the beginning, so too eschatology is an etiological account from the present situation of grace forward into its future stage of fulfillment and not an anticipatory description of what will happen at the end of time and beyond. Thus protology and eschatology mutually condition each other, in terms of both content and methodology.

Thirdly, if eschatology is the present situation of salvation transposed into the future mode of fulfillment, then the hermeneutics of Christian eschatology cannot treat it as an *additional* and quite different revelation about the future. Rather, it should be seen as christology and anthropology transposed into the future mode. Whatever the Christians know about their future fulfillment, they know it from the fulfillment that has already occurred in Christ.

Fourthly, two erroneous interpretations of eschatology must be rejected. The first consists in reading the eschatological texts of the Bible as anticipatory reports of what will happen at the end of time and transferring this information back into the present in order to discern therein clues of impending eschatological events. This hermeneutics Rahner terms "apocalyptic." The second hermeneutical error is a historical demythologization that so insists on the present, existential dimension of eschatology as to deny its real, still-to-come future. Both forms of hermeneutics are unacceptable. The former distorts the real nature of Christian eschatology, which does not consist in reading from the future back into the present but in transposing the present anthropology into its future fulfillment in terms of christology. The latter wrongly dismisses the real futurity of humankind.

3. Implications and Corollaries for the Hermeneutics of Eschatology

The *sixth thesis* unfolds some of the implications and corollaries of the fifth thesis for the hermeneutics of eschatological assertions.

a. ". . . The eschatology of salvation and of loss are not on the same plane. . . . True hermeneutical discourse must exclude the presumptuous knowledge of a universal apocatastasis and of the certainty of the salvation of the individual *before* his death as well as certain knowledge of a damnation which has actually ensued."[18] If eschatology is a transposition of the present existential situation of human beings into its mode of fulfillment and if this situation is one of salvation and sin, then one should speak of the open, real possibilities of salvation *and* loss for each human being. Hence, the exclusion of universal *apocatastasis* as a statement of fact[19] and of the certainty of the salvation of the individual before his death.

This does not mean that the Church cannot declare that certain individuals who have died in Christ (e.g., martyrs and holy men and women) have attained salvation, since its mission is to proclaim the triumph of Christ's grace. But it is not allowed to make a parallel declaration regarding the actual damnation of any individual. Hermeneutically, therefore, says Rahner, "on principle only *one* predestination will be spoken of in a Christian eschatology. And it contains only *one* theme which is there on its behalf: the victory of grace in redemption consummated. Possible damnation can only be spoken of, but must be spoken of, insofar as, and only insofar as it is forbidden to us to make the sure triumph of grace in the world as providing us with already fixed and acquired points in our estimation of an existence which is still to be lived out in the boldness of freedom."[20]

b. "All eschatological assertions have the *one* totality of the human person in mind, which cannot be neatly *divided* into two parts, body and soul."[21] Because a human being is a unity of body and soul, the statements regarding his or her final fulfillment must be understood as referring to the one *whole*. Of course there will necessarily be two sets of eschatological statements about the human being, since the distinction and difference between soul and body cannot be eliminated and therefore one cannot dismiss either set as mythological or physical and retain only one. Nevertheless these two sets of eschatological assertions must be read as statements not about two different and separate things but about the one human being. This principle will have profound implications for our understanding of the intermediate state and purgatory.

Further, since the person is both an individual and a member of society, there will be two eschatologies, individual and collective, neither of which can be eliminated or reduced to the other. Again these two eschatologies should not be seen as opposed affirmations about two entirely different realities. Human beings are individuals insofar as they are members of the society, and society cannot exist except as a community of individuals.

c. "There is no point, on our principle, in creating a fundamental, absolute opposition and antagonism between an imminent and a distant expectation of the *parousia*."[22] Thus Rahner offers a transcendental solution to the hermeneutical problem that vexed biblical scholars at the beginning of our century concerning the mode of presence of the Kingdom of God. If eschatology is the assertion about present salvation insofar as it tends toward its future, hidden fulfillment, the expectation of the Parousia is both imminent and distant. If it is not imminent, eschatology becomes a mere piece of curiosity, irrelevant for the present life of faith; on the other hand, if it is not distant, humanity's real futurity is denied its force.

d. "*Christ* himself is the hermeneutical principle of all eschatological assertions. Anything that cannot be read and understood as a christological assertion is not a genuine eschatological assertion."[23] Christology is therefore the criterion of the hermeneutics of eschatology. Rahner's eschatology, like Barth's, is decidedly christocentric. Further, one can see here the unity and compactness of Rahner's anthropology, theology, christology, and eschatology, with christology holding the center. To speak about humanity is to speak about God and vice versa. But one cannot speak about humanity and God except in the true God-man, Jesus. And when this Christ-talk is conjugated in the future sense, eschatology emerges.

e. From the experience of Christ as the formal principle, the contents of eschatology can be determined: "That time will have an end; that towards the end the antagonism between Christ and the world grows fiercer; that history as a whole ends with the final victory of God in his grace; that this consummation of the world, insofar as it is the incalculable act of God's freedom, is called God's judgment; insofar as it is the fulfillment of the salvation already real, victorious and definitive in Christ, it is called the return and the judgment of Christ. Insofar as it is the fulfillment of the individual, who cannot be wholly absorbed and lost in his function as moment of the world, it is called the particular judgment. Insofar as it is the fulfillment of the resurrection of Christ, it is called the resurrection of the flesh and the transfiguration of the world."[24]

4. The Remythologization of Eschatological Assertions

Seventh Thesis: "Our basic principle provides a fundamental criterion to distinguish betwen form and content in the eschatological assertions of Scripture and tradition. This does not mean that such a distinction could make a perfectly adequate and definite distinction between 'thing' and 'image'. This is impossible, if for no other reason than that no assertion about the thing is possible without some sort of image, and in this sense a 'myth' can only be replaced by another, but not by language utterly devoid of images."[25]

Thinking without images is impossible, as Rahner has demonstrated on the basis of Thomas's doctrine of *conversio ad phantasma*. Of course it is difficult to distinguish form from content, imagery from thought, in concrete eschatological assertions, since the line of demarcation between them is fluid. Nevertheless, the reformulation of eschatological assertions, which is one of the tasks of hermeneutics, is not a demythologization but remythologization or transmythologization, a clothing of the content in a more intelligible and contemporary set of images. The more modern reformulations must always remain connected with the ancient assertions. "Every eschatology," says Rahner, "no matter how modern, always remains a retrospective interpretation of the old, not a new and better assertion which replaces the old."[26]

In sum, the hermeneutical method of the dogmatic theologian in interpreting the eschatological assertions consists in the following four steps. First, interpreters must submit their sources and methods to a strict, critical examination. This they do often by relying on the researches of their biblical colleagues who employ the appropriate tools of literary and historical criticism to discover the meanings intended by the historical texts. Secondly, they then raise the question of what assertions are binding in eschatology by distinguishing the intended meanings from their amalgams. Thirdly, they must see if and how they can reduce these assertions to a small number of basic assertions from which their eschatology can be derived. Lastly, they must ask whether these basic assertions are elements of christology and anthropology transposed into their mode of fulfillment, distinguishing thus between authentic eschatology and false apocalyptic.[27]

III. Summary and Critical Questions

I have shown, I hope, that for Rahner the hermeneutical act is a multi-dimensional one. It consists not only in historical and philological analysis of what the text has said but also in retrieving what the text has not and could not have said. It requires not only a critical reading of the text but also abandoning oneself to the subject matter itself and thinking the thought of the author and along with him or her. Further, it is not merely a psychological reconstruction of the mental processes of the author or a purely intellectual, thematic explication of the hidden meaning of the text but requires a lived experience of the reality spoken of by the text as the key to understanding and validating doctrinal affirmations concerning that reality.

In his general hermeneutics Rahner stands in the tradition of the great German hermeneutical theorists, Schleiermacher, Dilthey, Heidegger, and Gadamer. As a Catholic hermeneutical theologian, Rahner maintains the intrinsic unity of Scripture and tradition and the properly theological character of the hermeneutical enterprise. Finally, as a dogmatic theologian, Rahner formulates hermeneutical principles for eschatological assertions that respect the hiddenness, the genuine futurity, and the present, existential import of the *eschata*.

Most importantly he defines eschatology as the transposition of anthropology into its mode of future fulfillment in christological terms, and hence as a reading from the present into the future rather than a reading from the future into the present as in apocalyptic. Such understanding of eschatology has profound implications for the interpretation of heaven and hell, of the unitary character of human fulfillment, of the presence of the Kingdom of God, and for the christological reduction of the contents of eschatology. Lastly, the interpretation and reformulation of eschatological assertions is not a stripping away of their images but a reclothing in more intelligible, more culturally appropriate images.

Once again one cannot help but marvel at the spectacular unity of Rahner's theology, the all-embracing comprehensiveness of his system, the tight connections among the various structures of his theological edifice. But once again one may wonder whether there are not tiny cracks here and there or perhaps, more seriously, foundation problems that will send the whole building tumbling down. One may ask, for example, whether Rahner's hermeneutics of "retrieval," which he appropriates from Heidegger, satisfies the "criteria of appropriateness" (to use Shubert Ogden's and David Tracy's terminology), that is, whether it can correctly discern the historical meaning intended by the text. It must be remembered that both Heidegger and Rahner have been accused of having distorted the sources they interpreted, the former the early Greek philosophers and the latter

Thomas Aquinas. Cornelio Fabro regards Rahner as a "deformator thomisticus radicalis," claiming that Rahner has hopelessly distorted Thomas Aquinas on all levels: texts, contexts, and principles.[28] Is Rahner so concerned with meaningfulness (the criteria of adequacy) that he has missed the meaning of the text and the past teachings of the Church? Is his "christological reduction" a sufficient guarantee for correctness of interpretation? Should we direct to Rahner Emilio Betti's objections to Gadamer's hermeneutics, that it confuses *Auslegung* with *Sinngebung*, consequently jeopardizes the legitimacy of referring to the objective status of objects of interpretation, and thus renders questionable the objectivity of the interpretation itself?[29]

Further, does Rahner's appeal to religious experience as a validation of doctrinal teachings resuscitate the ghost of Modernism, as George Vass suggests?[30] Does his insistence on the unthematic dimension in religious experience (*fides qua*) run counter to the role that the Church defines for the *fides quae*?[31]

Most importantly, is his anthropological reduction of eschatology tenable? In this case, can eschatology surprise us with something not only future but genuinely *new*? By considering eschatology as the transposition of the present situation into its mode fulfillment, has not Rahner already provided us with too much information on this fulfillment despite his firm and repeated insistence on its hiddenness? Further, is Rahner's characterization of apocalyptic sufficiently based on a thorough knowledge of apocalyptic literature? Apart from whether 'apocalyptic' is a mot juste to describe the kind of theological genre Rahner has in mind, has Rahner sufficiently appreciated the positive impact of such literature on the struggle for liberation from an unjust social situation or persecution?

These are but a few of the questions that we will have to keep in mind as we attempt to evaluate Rahner's eschatology. Meanwhile, as the exergue of this chapter has made clear, method and hermeneutics, although a necessary part of any theological enterprise, are not the whole of theology. In the next two parts of this work we will examine the contents of Rahner's eschatology itself, first individual, and then collective.

Part II

The One Categorical Eschatology as Individual Eschatology

Christian Death

> The death of Christ is not simply an event of the past. On the
> contrary it is, as all Christendom believes, an event which, even
> though in the external and superficial sense it belongs to the past,
> still has an eternal validity in God's sight. . . . But the Christian
> has to think of this death of Christ in such a way that he reverent-
> ly and solemnly accepts its enduring validity. . . . And in order
> to do this, and in order really to understand what the message of
> this death is meant to convey to him he must strive to gain an
> understanding of the nature of death in general. Of course he
> can learn something of the meaning of death in general precisely
> *from* this message of the death of Christ. ("On Christian Dying,"
> *TI* 7:285)

Of all aspects of Rahner's eschatology, death is the one most often and
most extensively studied. This is so partly because Rahner's earliest and
major writing on eschatology deals with death[1] and partly because it is to
this topic that he made original, important, and controversial contributions, a topic to which he returned repeatedly in his theological career. It is
also the study wherein, as the quotation above makes clear, the transcendental method with its twin poles of transcendentality and historicity is
consistently applied. According to Rahner, in their attempt to understand
death, the Christians must begin with the death of Christ as it occurred in
history. But in order to understand this historical event one must investigate the nature of death in general and its conditions of possibility as a
basis for understanding the death of Christ. On the other hand, the nature
of death and its conditions of possibility are clarified by the historical event
of Jesus' death itself. There is therefore a mutual conditioning between
transcendental reflections and historical considerations on death.

It is common knowledge that death, although often banished as a taboo
from the public consciousness of our industrial and technological society
and quarantined in antiseptic hospital rooms, has recently been the object
of extensive and profound reflections in existentialist philosophy,
psychoanalysis, and Marxism. The huge bibliography compiled by Albert

J. Miller and Michael J. Acri on the subject is an eloquent witness to this fact.[2] Whether death is seen with Heidegger as a permanent determination of human existence ("Sein-zum-Tode") and a radical "ontological possibility" for *Dasein*'s authentic or inauthentic existence, or with Freud as a fundamental drive that comes into conflict with Eros and without which life would be like a Platonic romance or a game played without stakes, or with Marx as an expression of the alienation to which the individual is subjected in a capitalistic society, there is no doubt that death is not considered as a merely biological phenomenon but has acquired a distinctly human face. It is in this anthropological perspective that Rahner's theology of death can properly be understood and evaluated.

In the past, theology focused its attention not so much on death, whose nature, after all, was supposed to be obvious from the daily experience of death, as on what comes *after* death. Death was regarded as the person's indifferent transition from one state to another, a transition without any anthropological significance and hence not a worthy object for investigation in systematic theology. At best it received pious considerations in moral and ascetical theologies where the primary intention is to prepare the faithful for a holy death (the *artes moriendi*). And yet, as Rahner points out, there are at least three reasons why death itself, and not only what comes after it, should be studied in its own right by systematic theology. First, it contains in itself all the mysteries of human existence; secondly, according to the Christian faith, the death of one man, Jesus, is the fundamental event of salvation and world history; and thirdly, it is the event in which humans achieve their definitive destiny.[3]

In what follows we will first examine Rahner's view of death as a universal event affecting the whole human being. We will then proceed to consider his understanding of death as a 'natural' and 'personal' act. In this connection we will enquire whether his view of death as a personal act is identical with the hypothesis of a final decision (*Endentscheidungshypothese*). Next we will expound his notion of death as a consequence of sin and will conclude with a discussion of how Rahner understands death as a dying with Christ.[4]

I. Death as a Universal Event Affecting the Whole Human Being

In formulating his theology of death, Rahner is faithful to his own hermeneutical principles. He is not content with simply deducing a theology of death from the statements of Scripture and tradition but carries out a theological work "which only begins when the doctrine of the Church has been clearly determined, and compares the single propositions of this doctrine with each other, confronts them with other types of knowledge and goes on to elaborate more fully the concepts they involve, in order to secure a more precise understanding of what has been directly heard in faith."[5] From this multileveled hermeneutical labor, two basic statements regarding death emerge: death is a universal phenomenon, and death is the event affecting the whole person.

1. The Universality of Death

That all human beings are subject to the law of death and will in fact die is, in Rahner's judgment, a teaching of the Christian faith. This statement regarding the universality of death seems at first sight to be a banal platitude based on an empirical observation of repeated occurrences of death. However, Rahner insists that it is not a biological or medical affirmation but a theological one. Even though there is no contradiction between the former and the latter, the purely biological aspects of death, with which medicine is concerned, are only one element of a more comprehensive reality. Humans are not merely a biological phenomenon but persons endowed with spiritual freedom and responsibility and hence capable of eternal validity. It is about this free, spiritual reality as a whole that the Christian affirmation of the universality of death is made. It is different from the biological statement at least in two respects.

First, it does not merely assert that the person in general ("*das Man*") will die, but that *I* have to die. My death and dying is a truth that I must accept and opt for as an act of my own freedom. I must really understand that ". . . I have to die, that I myself am already on the way to this death, that all my life through I am advancing inexorably and undeviatingly towards this moment of my death."[6]

Secondly, the Christian affirmation of the universality of death intends to be of absolute, and not merely provisional, validity. Biological or medical statements about the universality of death may be taken to mean that human beings die unless and until medical progress becomes able to prolong life indefinitely (as the statement, "Many die of pestilence," was formerly true but is no longer so). On the contrary the Christian assertion of the universality of death, in Rahner's judgment, intends to affirm that *all* human beings will *necessarily* die. This is so because it is not based on physiological considerations but on two theological factors.

First, as we will see later, death, besides being a biological phenomenon, is also a consequence and a manifestation of sin, both original and personal. And since all human beings are sinners, in virtue of both the original sin and their own personal sins, they all must die.

Secondly, Rahner's understanding of human freedom as the person's capacity for definitiveness and final validity enables him to explain why death is necessary. Death is the only way in which a free and historical being can pass from the continuous flux of time to the definitive state of eternity. "The deepest and most ultimate reason for the connection with and orientation to death which is most intimately inherent in man, which makes him mortal and in virtue of this fact renders all humans now and forever subject to death in the truest sense, is the freedom of the spirit. It is this, ultimately speaking, that makes man mortal, and mortality in the biological sense is only the manifestation and the realization in the concrete of this mortality, which has its origin and basis in the freedom with which man is endowed as spiritual."[7] If freedom is not the capacity of making forever revisable choices but of definitive self-determination and if death is for spatiotemporal beings the only way in which they can break the mere prolongation of temporal existence and bring about finality and definitiveness, human beings should be willing to embrace the enduring fulfillment of who they are and what they have accomplished in time through death.

On account of both human sinfulness and human freedom death then is ineluctable. Rahner is convinced that humans will never be able to abolish death since it is not merely the accidental or natural result of purely biological processes that perhaps the sciences will someday be able to understand and control but is demanded by human nature itself. Rahner reminds scientists who may be inebriated by the technological advances of our times that "this intoxicating experience of infinity will always end up in cruel disillusionment—at the latest in death."[8] Scientific attempts at prolonging life at any cost, Rahner warns us, may produce not happiness but boredom and damnation, because this interminable existence would prevent humans from reaching their fulfillment: "We are able to prolong human life and in fact have already done so. But what a laughable alteration would it really be if we were all to become 120 or 180 years old? Who has ever claimed or prophesied that he could do more? And who—even if he were to give but a little thought to such a utopian idea—could even merely hope or wish to live forever in the kind of human existence which is the only one given to us? The *inner* finiteness of human existence would turn the *external* endlessness of life into utter madness—into the existence of the eternally wandering Jew—and into damnation, since what is unique in a finite sense is impressive and sweet only if, and because, it is not always available; a time which I could really have to infinity whenever I liked condemns the content of each moment to absolute indifference, since it is absolutely repeatable."[9] Death, therefore, and the readiness to die is what keeps life 'alive' in our spatiotemporal existence. And the responsible acceptance of death, not in general and in the abstract, but as *my* death and my readiness to die *my own* death, is what makes my existence authentic and genuinely human.

2. Death as the Event Affecting the Whole Person

Rahner prefaces his theology of death with a basic principle that faithfully reflects his understanding of the substantial unity of the human being: "Death is an event which strikes the person in his totality."[10] With this statement Rahner distances himself from the Platonizing tradition of Christian theology and at the same time reveals his sympathy for the concern of modern anthropology to maintain the fundamental unity of the person. "Man in the Old Testament writing," asserts Rahner, "is very un-dualistically and unplatonically a unity in his being and history, and the world is seen from the very beginning as an environment intended for man. Man comes quite unashamedly from the earth and is therefore seen even in Scripture . . . as the product of the material cosmos, without Scripture thereby allowing this one man in the paradoxical duality of his origin to break up into two quite independent realities called spirit and matter. Consequently, for the Old Testament writings in particular, the *whole man is made to suffer by death*."[11] Death, therefore, affects human beings not only in their bodies but in their souls as well, not only "at the level of the material and the biological, but on the plane of self-awareness, personhood, freedom, responsibility, love and faithfulness; man whose mode of existence is such that it is charged with the responsibility of his self-awareness and his freedom."[12]

Because death is the event of the whole human being Rahner is critical of the Stoic attitude that so separates the body from the soul that death is regarded as affecting only the body and therefore can be borne with equanimity and even indifference.[13]

As we have seen in chapter 2, the human being is a unity of nature and person; we are, that is, beings who are endowed with, prior to our personal free decision, a certain mode of being with its definite laws of development and, on the other hand, with the capacity and task of determining ourselves through our freedom. Death as the event that affects the whole person possesses therefore both personal and natural aspects. In the traditional language of Christian doctrine, the natural aspect of death is expressed by the statement that death is the separation of soul and body and its personal aspect by the statement that it means the definitive end of our state of pilgrimage. We will now examine these two aspects of death successively.

II. The "Natural" Aspect of Death:
Death as the Separation of Body and Soul

The doctrine of death as the separation of body and soul, even though neither explicitly contained in nor denied by the Scripture, is so widely used by the tradition from the earliest Fathers down to the catechism of

Cardinal Gasparri that from the theological point of view, in Rahner's judgment, it can be considered as the classical description of death. Despite its long-standing popularity and its not insignificant merits, Rahner finds such description inadequate in several respects and attempts to complement it with his thesis of the 'pancosmic' relation of the soul after death.

1. A Critique of the Traditional Description

Rahner recognizes that the description of death as the separation of body and soul does express an important truth about the relationship between the body and soul after death: "It refers, first of all, to an indisputable truth, that the spiritual life-principle of man, the soul, assumes in death, to put the matter vaguely but cautiously, a new and different relation to what we usually call the body. The soul no longer holds the structure of the body together as a distinct reality, governed by its own immanent, vital laws and delimited from the rest of the universe. The body lives no more, and in this sense we can and must say that the soul separates from the body."[14] Another Christian truth that is also contained in this description is the doctrine of the immortality of the soul, which asserts that the spiritual soul does not perish when the structure of the body is dissolved but maintains its personal, spiritual life, although in some wholly different manner of existence. The fact that this traditional formula embodies these two fundamental truths may justify its continued use.

Nevertheless, the inadequacies of this description of death are quite serious. Rahner points out three of them. First, it does not specify the distinctively *human* character of death: "It is absolutely silent . . . about the characteristic feature of death, that it is an event for man as a whole and as a spiritual person."[15] It does not make clear that death, as has been shown above, affects the *whole* person, body and soul. Further, it does not distinguish between the death of a plant or an animal and that of humans. A plant and an animal 'perish'; their 'death' is a merely biological process of corruption. Human beings, on the contrary, 'die' as spiritual and free persons. A beast dies less of a death than a human being does.

Secondly, the traditional description does not make clear whether the soul separates itself from the body of its own volition or whether it is separated from the body against its will. Is death something that the person must resist at all costs or is human existence itself a being-towards-death, so that death is "the result of the soul's own deeper dynamism toward its own fulfillment,"[16] the act in which humans achieve themselves freely and definitively? Rahner will consider this question when he discusses the personal aspect of death.

Thirdly, the description is inadequate because its concept of 'separation' is obscure and capable of different interpretations. First of all, since the soul is at one with the body and since the body is part of a material whole, the soul must have some relation to that whole, the totality that constitutes the unity of the material universe. This whole, both metaphysically and cosmologically, Rahner notes, is not to be conceived as a merely conceptual sum of individual things nor as the mere unity of an external interaction of individual things on one another. However the nature of this whole is to be determined more exactly, there is no doubt that the soul, by being united to its body as its *unica forma corporis*, is also related to this whole of which the body is a part. Now Rahner raises the question of whether in being 'separated' from the body the soul is also separated from this material whole so that it becomes totally acosmic or whether, no longer limited to an individual bodily structure in death, the soul can enter into a much closer, more intimate relationship with that material whole, that center or core of the material universe, so as to become pancosmic ("allkosmisch").

Such a question may at first sound preposterous, especially in the context of that prevalent Christian philosophical and theological anthropology heavily influenced by Neoplatonism. It is simply assumed as a matter of course that the soul's return to God is equivalent to its abandonment of the world. In such a view, relation to matter and nearness to God increase in inverse proportion. But if one overcomes for a moment this unchristian assumption and is willing at least to entertain the possibility of the soul's relation to the center of the material universe, then, perhaps, the hypothesis of the pancosmic relation of the soul after death may not appear as theologically untenable. That is what Rahner attempts to show.

2. The Hypothesis of the Pancosmic Relation of the Soul

Rahner states his hypothesis as follows: "Death does not simply withdraw a person from the world and make him acosmic; rather it transposes him into a new and more comprehensive relationship to the world, freed from the limitation to a single point in space and time characteristic of his earthly existence."[17]

What are the grounds for such hypothesis? Rahner offers both philosophical and theological justification for it. On the philosophical level, he alludes to the older Thomistic metaphysics of the soul, the more modern doctrine of 'life-entelechies', and the phenomena of parapsychology.

First, Rahner recalls that in the older doctrine of the relationship between the body and the soul, the informing of the body by the soul is not an act distinct from the soul itself, something accidental to it, but is "the substantial 'act' of the soul, the very reality of the soul itself, to the extent that soul's own substantial being is, so to speak, built into the material reality, as an act which is not really distinct from the soul."[18] Consequently, the soul, which 'survives' the body in death, cannot be what it is (*forma corporis*) unless in some way it continues to be the 'act' informing the body. Hence, it must be said that the soul after death, in virtue of its informing the body, has a transcendental relationship to matter and that such a relationship is required by its very essence.

Secondly, Rahner finds some basis for his hypothesis in the recent doctrine of 'life-entelechies' and their relation to matter. This vitalistic philosophy conceives the entelechies as forces actively guiding and sustaining the activities not only of human beings but also of subhuman beings, rendering them capable of genuinely teleological action. Further, these entelechies have an aspatial and supraindividual character; they not only direct and sustain individual organisms but also are related to the meta-empirical ground of material reality. This idea, according to Rahner, makes it impossible to think of death in the subhuman realm as the simple cessation of an entelechy, as scholastic cosmology used to hold. Rather, says Rahner, "death even in the sub-human realm appears as the surrender of the entelechical relation at a certain space-time point in the world, while the entelechical powers persist as constituents of the universe."[19] If it is true of subhuman entelechies that after the death of the organisms they continue to be related to the material world, a fortiori or at least analogously, so Rahner argues, it should be affirmed of the human soul that after the death of the human being whose entelechy it is it does not become acosmic but 'pancosmic'.

Thirdly, with this hypothesis of the 'pancosmicity' of the soul, Rahner contends, certain parapsychological phenomena might be more easily explained. Rahner does not mention any specific examples, but one can think of spiritualist phenomena and alleged communications with the dead through mediums during seances. These phenomena seem to indicate that the dead are not entirely cut off from the world.[20]

Before proceeding to provide theological grounding for this hypothesis, Rahner cautions the reader against two possible misunderstandings. First, the pancosmicity of the soul does not mean that at death the entire world becomes the 'body' of this particular soul in the way in which its own body was its own: "The pancosmic relation does not imply a substantial informing of the world in its space-time structure by the soul, in the way in which for scholastic metaphysics the soul informs the body."[21] Secondly, the hypothesis does not mean that the soul is omnipresent to the whole cosmos, precisely because in death the soul gives up its determinate spatio-temporal location within the world and within the mutual interrelations of individual beings.[22]

To prove the pancosmicity of the soul Rahner draws our attention to two facts. First, the animated body, even in its lifetime, is an open system in relation to the world; the body does not end with its skin. Secondly, the spiritual soul through its embodiment is in principle open to and remains in communication with the whole world; it is never a closed monad. If one keeps these two facts in mind, one might not object to the possibility that "the soul, by surrendering its limited bodily structure in death, becomes open towards the universe and, in some way, a co-determining factor of the universe precisely in the latter's character as the ground of the personal life of other spiritual corporeal beings."[23]

As for the theological justification of his hypothesis, Rahner offers three indications: the nature of angels, purgatory, and the resurrection of the body. First of all, one may think on biblical, theological, and metaphysical grounds that angels, prior to their actual individual spiritual decision and self-determination, and previous to any particular influence through efficient causality on individual things in the world, possess a permanent and continous relation to the world as a whole, not in spite of, but precisely because of their incorporeality. If this is true of the so-called pure spirits, then one cannot rule out the possibility that the human soul possesses some such relationship to the world and that this relationship is not abolished in death but is rather, for the first time, perfected since it is no longer mediated by the individual body.

Secondly, the Catholic teaching on purgatory may be invoked to support the hypothesis of the pancosmicity of the soul. The doctrine that human beings continue to mature after death, in accord with their final decision during life, may be made more understandable if it is held that "the soul, freed from the body, is not removed entirely from the world, but that the soul, after surrendering its bodily structure and through that surrender, experiences in its morally free self-determination more clearly and acutely its own harmony or disharmony with the objectively right order of the world, and conversely, itself contributes to determining the latter."[24] Further, if purgatory is the penal consequence of venial sins and if venial sins are possible only in material beings, since only material beings are capable of acts that do not involve a total disposition of themselves, then for the soul to undergo a self-purification after death as the result of venial sins would imply the soul's relationship to matter.

Finally, the resurrection of the body seems to confirm the pancosmicity of the soul. If death as such brings about a total release of the soul from the body and its complete break with the world, it would be difficult, Rahner argues, to understand how the resurrection of the body could be a positive component of human perfection desired by the soul itself. On the contrary, if after death the soul does not lose its relation to the world, it would be possible to secure a better understanding of the possibility of the resurrection and the qualities of the glorified body. As Paul describes it (cf. 1 Cor 15), the risen body is perfectly pliant to the spirit of the human being now divinized by grace. Further, despite its corporeality, it is not confined to a particular place to the exclusion of another but enters into free and unhampered relations with everything. "In this way," says Rahner, "the glorified body seems to become the perfect expression of the enduring relation of the glorified person to the cosmos as a whole."[25]

With these philosophical and theological considerations Rahner is able to overcome the limitations of the traditional description of death as separation of body and soul, while acknowledging its substantial merits. As a 'natural' event, death is a biological act, and in this respect the death of a person is similar to that of a beast. But because death is also a *human* act, it possesses certain peculiar characteristics that are not explicitly taken into account by the traditional definition. To remedy this deficiency Rahner gives detailed consideration to these elements in his theology of death. Moreover, in line with his view of the substantial unity of the human being Rahner attempts to overcome the Neoplatonic dualism implicit in the traditional formula with his hypothesis of the pancosmicity of the soul. Whether such a proposal is fully adequate will be examined at a later stage. In our critique of this hypothesis we will do well to bear in mind, as I will mention at the end of this chapter, that Rahner appears not to have attached too much importance to *how* the soul's relationship to the world after death is explained. What is of supreme importance for him is that the soul is not conceived as totally cut off from the world after death.

III. The "Personal" Aspect of Death: Death as the End of the Human Pilgrimage

We have seen that for Rahner death is both a natural and a personal act and that it is the latter aspect which distinguishes the death of a person from that of a beast. This personal aspect, Rahner claims, is implicit in another traditional description of death, namely, that death marks the end of the human being's earthly pilgrimage and the beginning of an unchangeable, eternal destiny.[26] Rahner develops this teaching further by means of his theology of freedom, time, and eternity.

1. Death as the Definitive and Final Act of Freedom

As we have seen, human freedom for Rahner consists in the capacity for self-determination in a definitive and final way vis-à-vis God. Further, time is not merely a succession of moments in which the present moment devours the preceding one only to be devoured in its turn by the next. Rather, time as internal and personal time is an irreversible movement endowed with a genuine beginning and a definitive end and is indissolubly connected with human freedom. Eternity is not a never-ending continuation of time but the definitive and permanent outcome of time. The substance of Rahner's theology of freedom, time, and eternity is well expressed in following compact statement:

> Humans are not a thing that is simply pushed through the space-time dimension as though they were only in possession of the transient moment which is called the present. Humans are subjects. They possesses themselves. They are at all stages capable of taking themselves as a whole. And for this reason, in spite of the continuous process of change and the alternation of action and passion in the time to which they are subject, they have before them their time *as a whole.* As their life advances they *retain* the past and go forward into a future *that they have already worked out beforehand.* By the exercise of their freedom they make the time allotted to them present to themselves as a whole, past and future together. Now, because of this, the totality of human existence is saved and redeemed in its complete and consummated state; in other words, the eternity toward which the human person is advancing in his time, does not constitute a further period appended to, and following upon his life in any true sense, as a further projection of it which could be conceived of in linear time as extending into an unending future. Rather this eternity is the enduring validity of human existence before God as lived in freedom. It is the abiding faith, the sheer definitive consummation of the person's time and of the person's time as a whole. . . . The human person gathers up the totality of his life as freely lived, he achieves himself *in the fullness of his subjectivity and freedom as determined by the content of his life,* just as at every moment of his temporal life he has already obtained a degree of self-possession such that it embraces *the totality of his own life-span* considered formally as *an empty space to be filled out with content.* . . . He does not bring his temporal mode of existence to an end by quitting it, but by compressing it, so to say, and bringing it with him in its totality into his eternity which is his time as summed up and completed.[27]

In this context it is easy to understand how death as the last act and last moment in human temporal existence is neither merely our end nor our mere transition from one mode of existence to another, both having something essentially in common, namely, indefinite temporal sequence. Rather, says Rahner, "death ends time by being its consummate validity and therefore eternity."[28] This view of death as the act that brings human temporal existence and our history of freedom to a definitive end implies that death is not only a biological act that we have to undergo passively but also an act that we must perform actively in our freedom. How death can be an act of human freedom is something we will have to examine shortly.

At any rate, it is to be noted here how this view of death takes this earthly life with radical seriousness: "It (i. e. this life) is truly historical, that is, unique, unrepeatable, of inalienable and irrevocable significance."[29] And it is *this* life that is made eternal, and not something that follows *after* this life is ended. Writing in 1949, Rahner rejected on the basis of the definitive character of death any possibility of reincarnation or metempsychosis: "There is no eternal return of all things; there is only a history, happening once and for all. There is no migration of souls for which every life is only a provisional attempt open to complete revision at a later date, which in turn, for better or for worse, may be repeated."[30]

In an article written some thirty years later, however, Rahner, although maintaining substantially the same position, is somewhat more open to the possibility of reincarnation.[31] Of this we will speak at greater length in the next chapter. In any case, the teaching that death constitutes the irrevocable end of the human earthly pilgrimage does not totally exclude the further development of the person after death nor does it imply a static concept of the human being's eternal life with God. On the contrary, it is impossible to conceive of eternal life otherwise than as "a never-ending movement of the finite spirit into the life of God."[32]

Since humankind stands in solidarity with the world and since the world can have a history only within the human history, just as the cosmic and external time can be understood only in analogy to the human, internal time, the death of humankind, which brings their history to a close, also brings the history of the world to a definitive end. Hence, in Rahner's judgment, the world cannot go on forever. Of its own intrinsic dynamism it tends toward its own immanent consummation, which is, however, also the result of an unforeseeable intervention from without: "The total, created reality of the world grows in and through incarnate spiritual persons. Their death slowly brings the universe to its own final stage. This immanent maturing of the world toward its consummation, like that of the individual human being, is, at the same time, in a mysterious dialectical unity, a rupture, an ending from without, through an unpredictable intervention of God through his coming in judgment."[33]

2. Death and Particular Judgment

Traditional eschatology often speaks of a particular judgment of the individual person by God at the moment of death, in contrast to the general judgment at the end of history.[34] While a few theologians have denied that there is a particular judgment,[35] Rahner believes that the reality of the particular judgment, however its precise nature is to be determined, must be maintained. The ground for this is the dual nature of the human being who is both matter and spirit, an individual and a member of the society. What is at stake here, therefore, is the relationship between the general and the individual eschatologies. In Rahner's view, neither Bultmann's attempt to demythologize the general eschatology by reducing it to the individual eschatology nor the opposite move of some Protestant theologians to cancel the individual eschatology in favor of the general eschatology does justice to the complexity of human nature. Both introduce a dichotomy between the two elements of the one consummation of the person. This one fulfillment, however, because of the duality of the human being, must be expressed in two dialectically united series of affirmations of individual and general eschatologies.

But how is this particular judgment to be understood, and how is it related to death? Is this judgment, which makes the person's history of freedom definitive and irrevocable, an essential, intrinsic constituent of death itself, or is it something that comes after death or is linked with it merely by God's decree? As Rahner puts it: "Does God turn death into judgment because humans themselves in and through their death determine their own final condition, or does judgment follow death, because God has so ordained that it is this judgment, different in itself from death, and the final happiness or unhappiness bestowed by God in this judgment, which brings about the finality of the personal attitude which death by itself could not produce?"[36]

Rahner is aware that this is an open question in Catholic theology since the magisterium has not pronounced in favor of either alternative. However, relying on the authority of John Damascene and Thomas Aquinas, Rahner holds that "the finality of the personal life-decision is an intrinsic constituent of death itself as a spiritual and personal act of the human person."[37] The reason why Rahner opts for this solution is neither that he wants to make a concession to the modern tendency to "downgrade" God's role as judge and "upgrade" the human being's, nor simply to remove the scandal of God's presumably vindictive justice in condemning to eternal suffering those who have rebelled against him. Rather, his position in this matter is consistent with his view of human freedom as the capacity for definitive self-determination vis-à-vis God and of death as a natural and personal act. One could say that for Rahner death is the act by which humans bring their history of freedom to a definitive end, and, in this act of dying as a freely accepted act, they express their position vis-à-vis God, a position that they have taken throughout their history of freedom but which is now recapitulated and made definitive in this last personal act of death. In this way humans "judge" themselves and God ratifies their self-judgment as his own.

3. Death as Passion and Action

A. THE TWOFOLD MEANING OF DEATH

Traditional theology of death commonly regards it almost exclusively as an event that happens to humans, something they have to undergo passive-

ly. This idea is further strengthened by the pains, agony, or unconscious-
ness that often accompany dying, suggesting that humans are purely passive in death. Rahner does not deny this aspect of death; indeed, as we will
see, when speaking of death as the consequence of sin, he describes the
reality of pain and darkness inherent in death in starkest terms. However,
he is concerned to preserve the unity of the human being as spirit and
matter, freedom and necessity, person and nature in his attempt to understand death. Because humans are all of these at the same time, Rahner
maintains that there is a dialectical unity of passion and action, of 'suffering' and 'doing' in death, a dialectics that he has already discovered in the
act of knowing.

> If death is the end for the whole person, that is, if through death the
> whole person arrives at the end of that temporal existence which is
> characteristic of human life and which finds its termination precisely in
> death, then this end must have its impact upon the whole person, the
> soul included. Not, obviously, in the sense that the soul ceases to exist,
> but in the sense . . . that in death the soul achieves the consummation
> of its own personal self-affirmation, not merely by passively suffering
> something which supervenes biologically, but through its own person-
> al act. Death, therefore, as the end of the human being as a spiritual
> person, must be an active consummation from within brought about
> by the person himself, a maturing self-realization which embodies the
> result of what the person has made of himself during life, the achieve-
> ment of total self-possession, a real effectuation of self, the fullness of
> freely produced personal reality. At the same time, death as the end of
> the biological life is simultaneously and in a way which affects the
> whole person, an irruption from without, a destruction, the interven-
> tion of the Fates, an external event what turns up unexpectedly, so
> that a person's own death, from within, through the act of the person,
> is at the same time an event of the most radical spoliation of the per-
> son, activity and passivity at once.[38]

This is one of the most celebrated passages of Rahner's writings on
death; it attempts to hold in dialectical unity the two aspects of death corresponding to the duality of the human being: action and passion (*Tat* and
Leiden), fulfillment and end (*Vollendung* and *Ende*), self-possession and
destruction (*Sich-in-Besitz* and *Zerstörung*). While it may be obvious that
death is passion, end, and destruction, what does Rahner mean when he
affirms that death is also action, fulfillment, and self-possession?

To understand Rahner's thesis one must briefly recall to mind his understanding of human existence, of time, and of death. Humans are both 'nature' (that which is preestablished for free personal control and serves as
the norm of this decision) and 'person' (what this being in freedom makes
of itself and what it understands itself to be). Because of this duality they

can experience something coming from without as imposed upon them, e.g., pain, suffering, anxiety, fear, etc. But because humans are also 'person', they can accept or reject freely and actively this experience as a contradiction to their nature. Rahner calls this external opposition to human nature *insofar as it is received or rejected by him in freedom* "passion." There can be a "passion" only where there is a person.[39] But "passion" ultimately means death, which affects, as we have seen, the whole human being, as nature and person: "Every Passion is a moment in the person's subjection to death . . . every Passion is an existentially exercised process by which the person is brought face to face with his basic questionableness which he himself alone cannot solve but one with which he is presented by death."[40]

In response to this threat of death, the individual can adopt either of the following two attitudes. In describing these Rahner follows Heidegger almost to the letter. On the one hand, "the person can . . . try to run away from the 'ontological structure of his being' ['*Eigentlichkeit seines Wesens*'], from this 'being made for death' which concerns the whole individual. He can try to cover up this his death-situation by talk, by keeping himself busy, by immersing himself in the daily routine, by taking flight into the anonymity of 'everyone'; he can therefore also take the sting out of every Passion—by trying as much as possible to avoid it, by taking flight into amusements, into harmlessness, into bourgeois optimism, by the soporific of a hope for improvement (of an individual or social kind)—and he can cover up its character of the relentless approach of death and of a '*prolixitas mortis*'."[41] In other words, one can fall into an 'inauthentic existence'.

On the other hand, one can assume death with courage as the comprehensive horizon of one's historical and finite being, accept it as one's own unique possibility, as the light that illumines everything of one's existence, transform one's own "project." Hence, one accepts death not as a merely biological act but as a personal event to be enacted in freedom. As Rahner puts it, "When the individual makes a personal, existential decision with regard to this death-reality of his human existence, then this decision can only consist in a 'yes' to this reality. For only by saying yes to it, can a free person turn a necessary fate externally imposed on him into a free act of the person itself. A 'no' would preserve the free power of the person over itself only if by this 'no' he were to succeed in excluding the imposed fate from himself as a person; in other words, only if by this 'no' he could turn death into a purely biological event which takes place within the a-personal nature without affecting the person himself precisely as a person. Total, free self-determination (and that means a person) and an imposed total fate (and that means the death of the finite, suffering nature of a person) can become one only by the person's turning its total fate into a personal deed by freely saying yes to it."[42]

Humans not only can and should freely accept death as their personal
act, but, because their freedom is enacted in time and because time is
orientated toward its goal, they should also voluntarily anticipate it in their
daily life, not obviously as a form of death wish or suicide, but as a form of
asceticism and renunciation: "Thus, the person practices asceticism in the
proper sense whenever he looks his death-situation 'straight in the eye' by
saying yes to it, whenever he personally says yes (for whatever reason) to
this subjection to death and realizes this yes existentially—by voluntarily
anticipating this dying which is realized bit by bit in the whole life."[43] Because their freedom intrinsically desires its own fulfillment, which can
come about only in death, and because their historicity is not only *anamnesis* but also *prognosis*, humans must not simply assent freely to the necessity of death and anticipate it but love it as well. As Rahner puts it in a
striking sentence: "Wherever there is real liberty, there is love for death
and courage for death."[44]

It is only in this perspective of death as a free, personal act that, Rahner
argues, one can understand two important elements of Christianity which
in turn shed light on the meaning of death as action, fulfillment, and self-
possession, namely, the possibility of salvation for all human beings and
martyrdom.

B. DEATH AND ANONYMOUS CHRISTIANITY

I have already in several places referred to Rahner's theory of anonymous Christianity. It is not my intention here to discuss this theory,[45] controversial in itself, but only to examine the role Rahner assigns to death in
it. Because death as an act of nature is suffering and destruction of the
whole self, it cannot but appear as a dark and meaningless event against
which the person instinctively rebels. But if a person affirms and accepts
through an act of free self-disposal the meaningfulness of his or her life, he
or she can do so only by the grace of God bestowed in Christ. Rahner
concludes therefore that "the act performed in virtue of the grace of
Christ, whereby man positively accepts the comprehensive sense of his human existence in face of the sinister appearance of meaningless death, can
and must necessarily be called an act of faith: the surrender of the whole
man in the incalculability and impenetrability of human existence to the
incomprehensible God. . . . There a man is not dying the death of Adam,
the death of the sinner in his love of what is nothing provided it is at his
own disposal. Whether he knows it or not, a man is dying the death of
Christ, for only Christ's death gained this grace for us and only his death
freed our death into the life of God himself."[46]

One may object that such a death cannot be thought of as Christian since
there is the possibility that it is merely an *actus honestus* of natural moral-

ity. A person could die, accepting death as God's will in a morally right surrender of the self, that is, he or she could die a nonsinful death, and yet because that person lacked faith, perhaps inculpably, his or her death could not be an act of faith and hence could not be termed Christian.

To this objection Rahner gives a series of replies. First, cases of such nature are extremely rare. In the normal situation people are confronted by either faith or unbelief; hence, when they die they either die the death of faith or the death of unbelief, that is, the Christian or the unchristian death.

Secondly, and more fundamentally, Rahner rejects the actual existence, although not the abstract possibility, of morally significant but supernaturally neutral acts. Following Juan Martinez de Ripalda, Rahner maintains that the possibility of merely natural, good moral acts is never actually realized in the concrete, historical economy of salvation. On the basis of the transcendentality of the human spirit both in cognition and volition, God's universal salvific will, and the distinction between unthematic and thematic knowledge, Rahner suggests that the grace of faith in the mode of offer (the 'supernatural existential') is not an intermittent intervention of God's part but a permanent existential of humans as creatures endowed with spiritual faculties and of the world in general. Moreover, since grace produces a new formal object, humans are conscious, although not thematically, of this offer of grace.

Because of this transcendental offer of grace that transforms the intrinsic nature as well as the consciousness of the human being, Rahner maintains that there are no purely natural moral acts in concreto. It follows that whenever humans are obliged to make a moral decision, they are always deciding between their salvation and perdition, so that in the concrete they are always making moral decisions within the supernatural order as such: "Whenever the person arrives at a free decision about himself, he is always capable of a *fides virtualis*, that is, capable of an interior attitude toward God which is morally of the same kind as faith proper, and which can thus become, when elevated by an interior grace, a saving act and (if the grace is not freely rejected) exist as such."[47]

On this presupposition, death, which is the supreme and last act of free self-disposal, cannot be a moral act of the merely natural order without consequence for salvation or perdition. Rather it must be the comprehensive act of either faith or unbelief. As a personal act death is therefore the event in which the dying person is offered the last opportunity of becoming at least an anonymous Christian. With this explanation of the nature of death Rahner is convinced he has offered a credible account of how there can be and actually are people who are justified and attain supernatural salvation and yet do not visibly belong to the Church as its official members during their earthly lives. This reality of anonymous Christianity does not prevent Rahner from upholding the necessity of faith in Christ for justification and salvation, and hence the necessity of missionary work of proclaiming Christ.[48] Nevertheless, he interprets that universal salvific will of God, which has been realized in Christ, as an objective and permanent existential intrinsically transforming human beings and enabling them to perform an act of at least implicit faith in Christ, above all at the moment of death. For Rahner, therefore, "Christian death is the freely exercised liberty of faith, which in reality and truth disposes of the whole of life, by accepting the incalculability of this mortal existence as a meaningful and loving disposition of God."[49]

C. DEATH AND MARTYRDOM

If death as action, fulfillment, and self-possession can clarify the meaning of anonymous Christianity, it also helps us grasp an essential element of explicit Christianity, namely, martyrdom. Here, the ambiguity of death as despair and unbelief disappears. The death of the Christian martyr is a "beautiful testimony of faith" (*marturein ten kalen homologian*: 1 Tim 6:13). Because it is a death caused by external violence that could be avoided by the victim, the fact that he or she willingly accepts it is a clear and incontrovertible evidence that it is a free death. "All the violence which causes it is only the secret device of God who provides the opportunity for this highest act of liberty. . . . In a violent death which could have been avoided and which is, nevertheless, accepted in freedom, the freedom of a whole life is gathered into the one burning moment of death. Then the death of life (in its totality and freedom) enters into the death of death, in an act of complete freedom affecting the totality of life and so life's eternal finality. The death of martyrdom is a death of genuine liberty."[50]

One might object here that the voluntary aspect of martyrdom does not of itself assure that the death of the martyr is a death of faith. After all, does not every moral decision remain ultimately enigmatic, for oneself and certainly for others? Further, an act that is good in itself is not necessarily good in execution. And finally, how can we tell the death of a genuine martyr from that of a simple hero or of a fanatic who also dies voluntarily and courageously? What makes martyrdom a death-in-faith and vice versa?

Rahner's answers to these questions, orchestrated in various steps, give us a deeper insight into death as a personal act. First of all, Rahner recalls that the Church is holy, not only by virtue of its 'objective' sanctity, that is, in its doctrine and its means of grace, but also of its 'subjective' sanctity, that is, the sanctity of its members. This objective and subjective holiness is both an essential characteristic of the Church and a motive of faith for the Church. Now, as a motive of faith, this holiness must be empirically perceptible. But where can it be apparent if not in the death of the martyr, in which what appears, that is, death with Christ for God, must really be present? On this basis one can understand why Christian tradition from earliest times attributed to martyrdom the same power of justification as baptism. Indeed, Rahner suggests that martyrdom, although it is not a sacrament in the strict sense, operates ex opere operato, as it were, since what is signified in baptism, namely, dying and being baptized into the death of Christ, is made present in martyrdom. In a certain sense martyrdom is more than a sacrament, since the latter may be validly celebrated and yet not efficaciously received due to the recipient's lack of proper disposition, whereas in the former such a discrepancy is ruled out from the start. What guarantees the efficacy of martyrdom and the complete coherence between the objective goodness of the martyr's death and the subjective goodness of the martyr is the nature of the Church, which is the visible manifestation of God's eschatologically victorious grace in the world and history. Hence, martyrdom is not only a fact in the life of the Church but also a motive for faith in the Church.

All these considerations, however, have not yet given an answer to the question of how one can distinguish between a genuine martyrdom and the death of a fanatic or a heretic. As part of the answer, Rahner suggests that "an essential characteristic of Christian martyrdom is the voluntary and believing acceptance of death itself and not merely the acceptance of the consequence of a struggle, as in the case of a brave soldier who seeks victory, not death."[51] Nevertheless, Rahner is aware that not every self-imposed death is necessarily a morally good one; suicide, for instance, is objectively wrong. Nor is every death inflicted by others without provocation and voluntarily accepted by the victim morally good either, since the death of a heretic or a fanatic is not regarded as martyrdom. Rahner is compelled, therefore, to uphold the decisive importance of the objective content or reason for which a person voluntarily accepts death as the criterion for judging the moral goodness of a death.

However, Rahner is quick to point out that this is only part of the story: "Voluntary death cannot be regarded as a morally neutral matter, which derives it significance solely externally from a particular motive divorced from the death as such."[52] Voluntary death must be a moral good in itself; otherwise one cannot explain why there is universal respect for persons who voluntarily accept an avoidable death, even though one may have reservations about why they choose to die.

The reasons, for Rahner, are twofold. First, whenever someone dies freely the whole of his or her life and history of freedom is present, and this presence of the whole life in the one act commands awe and respect. Secondly, a death that is refused, the ineluctable death of the unbeliever and the despairing, is not, even in its formal constitution, the same as the freely accepted death in faith and hope. They are not simply the same death directed toward two different objects. The difference in such opposed individuals' attitudes toward death implies a difference in the contents or objects of their deaths. The moral goodness of the subjective act flows from the moral goodness of the object, just as a moral evil of the object implies the moral evil of the subjective act. Rahner postulates that "there must be in some way a divinely ordained pre-established harmony between the subjective uprightness of the act and its intentional content; the materially good act cannot in the last resort be subjectively a perverse one, and vice versa."[53]

In practice, the difference between a good death and a bad death, a difference that is rooted in their different objects and their contents, is manifested and recognizable in the person's free attitude toward death. Liberty for the good, according to Rahner, is the stronger liberty, a freedom in which human beings are involved in their totality, a liberated freedom that reaches its fullness. On the other hand, "evil liberty fails, wills too little, shrinks from pure and unconditional giving; it is anxious, it counts and calculates; it is full of suspicion and is afraid of purifying suffering. Evil freedom, in comparison with true freedom, always displays outward symptoms of inferior objective and personal power."[54] If this is true of important moral choices, it is a fortiori true of the supreme act of freedom, namely, death, especially death freely accepted. In Rahner's judgment, therefore, a person's attitude toward death is a reliable index of the moral quality of his or her death: ". . . Good and bad deaths are differentiated from each other, not only by their respective motivations (when a voluntary death is in question), but also by the manner in which the death is accomplished. . . . When a person dies patiently and humbly, when death itself is seen and accepted, when it not merely 'happens' in the course of striving for something else and when perhaps death is not really envisaged through blind eagerness for something (flight from shame, something obstinately sought, etc.), when death is loved for its own sake, and explicitly, it cannot but be a good death. Whenever it is faced in a spirit of pure and free submission to the absolute decree, it is a good death. And this quality can be sufficiently verified by observation."[55]

Because a person's attitude toward death is rooted in the objective content of his or her belief, Rahner affirms that the Christian martyr's attitude of patience, peace, calm, and deliberate gravity and detachment must correspond to the Christian teaching on death. He even suggests that since this teaching is unique to Christianity and not found in other religions, martyrdom—at least on such a large scale—is a uniquely Christian phenomenon.

Rahner's emphasis on death as a personal act of freedom raises the question of whether his view is identical with the hypothesis of a final decision (*Endentscheidungshypothese*) expounded in particular by Boros.

IV. Death as a Personal Act and the Hypothesis of a Final Decision

There is no question here of a full exposition of the *Endentscheidungshypothese*. The hypothesis has been proposed by several contemporary theologians and has deep roots in the tradition.[56] I shall limit myself to a concise explanation of this hypothesis as proposed by Boros since his exposition is the clearest and the most systematic.[57] I will then examine whether Rahner's view is identical with this hypothesis.

1. The Hypothesis of a Final Decision in Death

Boros states his hypothesis of a final decision concisely as follows: "Death gives man the opportunity of posing his first completely personal act; death is, therefore, by reason of its very being, the moment above all others for the awakening of consciousness, for freedom, for the encounter with God, for the final decision about his eternal destiny."[58] To avoid equivocation, Boros emphasizes that by death he does not mean clinical death or relative death, but absolute death, that is, death understood in the metaphysical sense of "separation of the soul from the body."[59] It is at this moment that humans are released from their condition of temporality and attain their definitive and irreversible state of being. It is only at this moment, that is, *in* death, and not before or after death, that the final decision is made.

Further, Boros points out, this "moment of death" is not one moment in a temporal succession but "a mere line of demarcation between two moments without any temporal extension of its own . . . . Therefore, the moment of death, the transition itself, is—when looked at from the subsequent condition—the last moment of the preceding condition, and—when viewed from the preceding condition—the first moment of the succeeding condition."[60] Thus the transition in death is a nontemporal process, even though the person who performs the transition is in time and space.

It may be objected that if the moment of death is nontemporal, then the final decision, which implies several separate acts, cannot be performed since the mind requires some length of time, however short, to be able to posit these several acts. Boros responds by distinguishing three levels of time corresponding to three successive stages of being. The first stage is called "the sub-personal time-level." At this level, time is a regular, uniform succession of moments, each of which devours its predecessor only to be devoured in its turn by its successor. The second stage in the movement of being is that of the inner, personal sense of time. At this level, the successive moments no longer pass uniformly. Our personal duration takes on different and individually characteristic forms: impetuous speed, gradual advance, indolent dawdling. Humans can experience this level of time, even though they are never able to free themselves completely from the subpersonal time. Finally, there is the third level of time, namely, the moment of the soul's separation from the body, in which the soul becomes fully awake to its own spirituality: "In death the spiritual movement of being is liberated from the alien element of non-personal temporality. The spirit's succession now becomes entirely interior, that is, determined solely by the succession inherent in its exercise of its own being. This occurs in a total awareness and presence of being, and not in mere flashes that reach us only fragmentarily. Thus the spirit is no longer swept along by an alien succession. It is able to realized fully the whole continuity of its being, all at once, in one and the same act."[61]

After clarifying his basic notions of death, the moment of death, and the relation of the final decision to temporality, Boros goes on, with the help of the transcendental method, to gather support for his hypothesis, first in philosophy and then in theology. In philosophy, he finds confirmation for his hypothesis of a final decision in death in Maurice Blondel's analysis of volition, in Joseph Maréchal's analysis of knowing, in Henri Bergson's analysis of perception and remembrance, in Gabriel Marcel's analysis of love, in the dialectic of the two opposing curves in the human person, namely, physical birth, growth, development, decline, and decease (the "outer man"), and spiritual growth (the "inner man"), in the poetic experience of essential proximity to and essential remoteness from the world, and in the kenotic actualization of our existence by which we come to being through nonbeing. These human acts and processes show that person is a being-towards-death and by anticipation realizes death in them as a fully personal act.

These reflections bring Boros to a reevaluation of the traditional definition of death as the separation of the soul from the body. Like Rahner, Boros judges it unsatisfactory because it obscures the substantial unity of human beings. The separation of the soul from the body cannot be conceived simply as a sundering of two complete beings. Since the soul is essentially the act of the body, the latter being its external self-expression, it cannot be completely separated from the body without being exposed to destruction. Boros fully subscribes to Rahner's hypothesis of the pancosmicity of the soul as a necessary corrective to the Neoplatonic influence on the Christian understanding of death.[62]

On the theological level, as confirmation of his *Endentscheidungshypothese*, Boros appeals to the doctrines that death is the end of our state of pilgrimage; that salvation is a personal fellowship with Jesus Christ; that God wills all humans to be saved; that death is not only punishment and manifestation of sin but also the sign of God's mercy and kindness; that not only the debt of temporal punishment (*reatus poenae*) but also the imputability of unforgiven venial guilt (*reatus culpae*) must be removed before beatific vision is granted; and that Jesus chose to save us by his death rather than in any other way. Each of these six theological doctrines will become, according to Boros, understandable and acquire greater depth if the hypothesis of a final decision is accepted.[63]

In Christian language, the *Endentscheidungshypothese* sees death as a sacramental situation. If death is an encounter with Christ that a person achieves both in his complete presence to the material world and in total self-presence, then death should be viewed not as one of the seven sacraments but "rather as the 'basic sacrament' mysteriously present in the other sacraments and inwardly supporting them at the same time as it transcends them."[64]

2. Rahner and the Endentscheidungshypothese

It is abundantly clear that there are not only parallels between Rahner and Boros in their theologies of death (e. g., the consistent application of the transcendental method and the use of some specific theological arguments) but also a direct and extensive influence of the former upon the latter. Indeed, the Hungarian theologian has explicitly acknowledged his debt to the German theologian. In particular, he appropriates Rahner's hypothesis of the pancosmicity of the soul, his interpretation of Christ's descent into hell, his theory of "hominization," his notion that angels are intrinsically related to the world, his theory of the supernatural existential, his distinction between nature and person, and his notion of concupiscence. Not only has Boros taken over many of Rahner's key ideas, but he has also developed them in a systematic fashion and provided them with an explicit philosophical and theological underpinning that in Rahner is often relegated to the background.

But is Rahner's idea of death as a personal act identical with the *Endentscheidungshypothese*? This question is important not simply because it requires a comparison between two influential theologies of death but also because the emerging differences, if any, will define Rahner's theology of death in much sharper relief.

Because of the numerous and profound similarities between Rahner and Boros, not a few commentators have regarded Rahner as a forerunner of the hypothesis of a final decision in death. These include Piet Schoonenberg, Joseph Pieper, Eberhard Jüngel, Amilcare Giudici, Giampiero Bof, Alois Winklhofer, Alois Spindeler, Georg Scheltens, Gisbert Greshake, and Edmund Fortman.[65]

And yet, quite often Rahner has explicity denied his paternity of the *Endentscheidungshypothese* and openly criticized Boros's proposal. He commended Boros, his former student, for having shown the relationship between sin and death.[66] But he sharply distinguished his position concerning the person's capacity for self-disposal before God from Boros's theory of a final decision in death. "This notion," says Rahner, "should not be understood in the sense of a hypothetical decision as Ladislaus Boros proposes in *Mysterium Mortis*. The author has never supported this hypothesis and his conception is much broader. Nothing is stated here about the historical moment in which a man actually takes this decision."[67] Again, speaking of the state of sickness as a radical challenge to human freedom to decide finally for God, Rahner noted that he did not share the "hypothesis of a final decision" supported by Boros.[68] He wanted to emphasize the fact that dying is an event occurring throughout a person's entire life, of course with varying degrees of intensity, whenever by a free act of choice a person accepts or protests against death present in his or her life. Because of the *prolixitas mortis*, Rahner warned us not to regard death simply as an event coming at the *end* of life and not to ascribe to it peculiarities that are denied in principle to other moments of time within the life of a human being. Rahner believed that Boros made that mistake: "But in principle to ascribe to the moment of medical decease a theological significance that cannot belong to any moment in the rest of life, to assert that in the moment of clinical death and only at that point there occurs man's real and comprehensive act of freedom in the total disposal of his existence for or against God, since this passing along offers an adequate situation and opportunity for it: this is an assertion which is not probable in the light of empirical psychology and biology, can be supported only with the aid of ideas savouring of mythology, and which theologically is neither probable nor necessary."[69]

While Boros seems to identify the moment of death as the only time when the definitive act of self-disposal occurs, Rahner concedes that he does not exclude the possibility in certain cases of a more or less exact coincidence in time of the final basic option for God and clinical death. However, he also maintains that such a basic option can occur within the course of life either explicity or implicitly, given the presence of death in life itself.

These important differences between Rahner and Boros did not escape the notice of some Rahnerian scholars. Vorgrimler, Ruiz de la Peña, Fischer, and Zucal have in one way or another pointed out the radical differences between Rahner's understanding of death as a personal act and the *Endentscheidungshypothese*.[70]

To be fair to Boros, however, it must be pointed out that he does not entirely neglect the fact that death is a continually present reality in life. He expressly appropriates Heidegger's analysis of death as "*a fundamental modality of living*, concrete existence"[71] and quotes Augustine's sayings to the effect that humans begin to die from the moment they are born.[72] Further, he explicitly warns that "the hypothesis of a final decision rightly understood does not in any way at all represent *a devaluation of the decisions made during life*. . . . The final decision is in part determined by the preparatory decisions taken during the course of a life-time . . . . It grows out of them to exactly the same degree as it stands above them by giving its final, conclusive judgment on them."[73]

It is true, however, that this aspect is secondary in Boros's *Mysterium mortis* where the hypothesis is systematically proposed. Moreover, Boros has nowhere said that such a definitive decision can in principle be made during a person's life. Indeed, for him, "death gives man the opportunity of posing his *first* completely personal act."[74] Here, Rahner parts company with him and therefore cannot be regarded as the father of the *Endentscheidungshypothese*, at least in the form proposed by the Hungarian theologian.

V. Death as the Consequence of Sin

Rahner's reflections on death as a personal act should not obscure the fact that death—with its attendant elements of destruction and darkness— is also for him a consequence and manifestation of sins both original and personal. So far Rahner has analyzed the three traditional teachings regarding death: its universality, its nature as the separation of the soul from the body, and its effect as the termination of the human pilgrimage. Now he considers death as the death of Adam and of the sinner. There exists a causal connection between death and sin, especially the sin of Adam, the head and progenitor of the human race. To clarify the meaning of death as the consequence of sin, Rahner first of all examines whether death can be regarded as a 'natural' event and, if so, what constitutes this natural element. He next discusses the penal character of death, that is, death as the consequence and manifestation of original sin. Finally, he shows how death can also be a personal mortal sin.

1. Death as a Natural Act and as Expression of Guilt

A. THE NATURAL ESSENCE OF DEATH

Traditional theology often refers to the paradisal state as one in which humankind was endowed not only with supernatural grace but also with preternatural gifts: the gifts of immortality, integrity, knowledge, and impassibility. The question is raised then as to whether Adam, had he not sinned, would have had to die. Rahner answers affirmatively but notes that in this case death would have been the perfect consummation of life rather than its destruction. It would have been an end, an active consummation of the whole being from within, a 'death without death', that is, without the violent separation of the soul from the body imposed from without.

This question regarding the necessary death of the paradisal man is not at all an idle speculation. It has important implications for the theology of death, for it shows that not every aspect of death can be regarded as a punishment for sin. In other words, death is not purely and simply a consequence and manifestation of guilt. In certain respects it can be considered as a natural event. Rahner reminds us of the Church's teaching against Michel Baius that death is an immediate consequence of the human constitution as body and spirit.[75] Further, were death only a punishment for sin and not also a natural event, Rahner argues, one would not be able to see how there can be a dying with Christ, that is, a participation in and appropriation of his redemptive death. "There must be in death, as it is an actual event for each individual, some common element, neutral, so to speak, which permits us to say that, in a true sense, all humans die the same death (although death as it afflicts each individual actually is indeed salvation or damnation, and although 'same' as used in context cannot refer to death taken in its comprehensive meaning)."[76]

But what precisely is this common natural element of death? The answer to this question will clear the ground for the identification of the penal character of death. One may think that the natural essence of death consists in the end of the biological life and the dissolution of the bodily constitution. Rahner concedes that this answer is correct, but it is not fully adequate. It does not say clearly that death is a natural event, a goal inwardly striven for, in the sense that "it is part of the nature of a creaturely history of freedom to reach a definitive consummation in a unity of restraint and freedom, a consummation which might as such also be called 'death' and which is prior to the distinction between guilt and innocence."[77] To say that death is a natural event in this sense does not, however, imply that the actual death of each human person in the concrete, historical order is something neutral, irrelevant to his or her spiritual destiny. For, in fact, each death is always either a manifestation of sin or an act of faith. It is never a *merely* natural process, although it must also be a natural process, for it is the way in which the history of human freedom can be brought to a definitive end, either in salvation or in damnation.

Now if the appointed ending of the human being's history of freedom *as such* is the natural element of death, that element cannot be the consequence and manifestation of sin. In what then does the penal character of death consist?

B. DEATH AS A CONSEQUENCE AND MANIFESTATION OF ORIGINAL SIN: THE HIDDENNESS
OF DEATH

Rahner finds the traditional distinction between death as *poena* for the
sinner and death as mere *poenalitas* for the justified unsatisfactory. For it
does not make clear how the one reality, which is a necessity for both
justified and sinners alike, can be a punishment at one time and a mere
poenalitas at another. After all, death as the termination of biological life
can be a mere *poenalitas* even for the sinner. Further, the understanding of
death as *poenalitas* for the justified does not bring out the positive importance of death for salvation.[78] Methodologically, Rahner suggests that the
penal character of death must be located in something which is present in
death but ought not to be there. This element is what Rahner calls "the
hiddenness of death, insofar as this is or can be experienced as something
that ought not to be, relative to the person's supernatural elevation, at
least as a retarding factor that must be overcome in the development of
human life under the influence of grace."[79]

To understand what Rahner means by the hiddenness of death (*die
Verhülltheit des Todes*) and why it is something that ought not to be, one
must recall to mind his distinctions between nature and person; between
death as passion and as action, as the 'natural' and 'personal' act; between
end as termination and as fulfillment; and also his theory of concupiscence.
Death, as we have seen, is a unity of two dialectically opposed elements:

> The end of the human being as a spiritual person is an active fulfill-
> ment from within, an act of self-completion, a life-synthesizing self-
> affirmation, a person's total taking possession of himself, the final act
> of self-formation, the plenitude of personal reality. At the same time,
> inseparably and in a way which affects the whole human being, the
> individual's death as the end of a material biological being is a destruc-
> tion, a rupture, an accident which strikes the person from without,
> unforeseeable, with no assurance that it will strike him at the moment
> in which interiorly he has completed his life. Death is a blow of fate,
> a thief in the night, an emptying and reducing of the person to
> powerlessness, in fact, the end. This simultaneity of fulfillment and
> emptiness, of actively achieved and passively suffered end, of full self-
> possession and of being completely dispossessed of self, may, for the
> moment, be taken as a correct interpretation of the phenomenon we
> call death . . . . At this point we encounter that irreducible dialectical
> unity of death which we want to call its obscure, hidden character.
> Death appears both as act and fate, as end and fulfillment, as willed
> and as suffered, as plenitude and emptiness. It seems to involve an
> empty, unsubstantial uncanny character, a kind of de-personalization,
> loss of self, destruction, and at the same time the plenitude of a per-
> son's attainment of total self-possession, the independence and pure

immanence that characterize personality. Yet both these sets of aspects belong to the phenomenon of death.[80]

Along with the long quotation given a few pages back (documented in n. 38), the substance of which is repeated here, this passage is the locus classicus of Rahner's theology of death. Here he gives the essential reasons why death is an ambiguous and hence hidden event. The ambiguity of death results from the ontological structure of the human being as body and spirit, and *to this extent* it can be said to belong to the 'natural' essence of death. However, it is something that ought not to be present in death under the influence of grace. For it is not inconceivable, Rahner points out, that a subject of freedom, transformed by grace, in a history of freedom, and above all in the supreme act of definitive self-disposal in death, should experience the complete success of this process of integration and hence should be able to undergo death without fear and without doubt regarding an eternal destiny. And yet, given the permanence of concupiscence, no one possesses that certainty in death: "It is not possible to say whether the full term of life reached in death is not in fact the emptiness and futility which till then was concealed, or conversely, whether the emptiness apparent in death is only the outward aspect of a true plenitude, deceptive only to us who are not dead."[81]

By reason of this hiddenness, death for us is a punishment for original sin. Whereas Adam's death, had he not sinned, would have been a transparent and certain fulfillment of his life, our death, even though it is an act of freedom, is undergone in emptiness, obscurity, and suffering, and hence is the penalty of sin. Even though the freedom from darkness in death is an unmerited and supernatural gift and hence cannot be exacted, nevertheless it must be experienced by humans as some kind of 'need' or 'requirement', as a natural consequence of supernatural grace. Even in the postlapsarian condition, human beings still preserve that tendency toward the supernatural order in which their death would have been a pure and transparent maturation from within. That is why when experiencing death in its obscurity and hiddenness, they realize that it is something which ought not to be and therefore a punishment of sin.

It may be asked whether death, as the penalty for original sin, is something God imposes as it were from without, as a retribution meted out by his justice, but not intrinsically related to sin, or whether death is the expression of that sin, flowing immediately from its very essence. Following the teaching of Thomas on the divinizing grace of the first parents to whom immortality belongs as a connatural consequence, Rahner opts for the second alternative: "Death is primarily an expression and manifestation of the essence of sin in the bodily constitution of man, and as such, as a consequence, a punishment for sin . . . . Death is guilt made visible."[82]

2. Death as a Personal Mortal Sin

Not only is death in its hiddenness a penalty and a manifestion of original sin, but it is also a consequence of grave, personal (and unforgiven) sins, a fact to which traditional theology has not sufficiently adverted. As in the case of original sin, death is not merely an external retribution for sins but is an intrinsic, essential expression and visible manifestation of these personal sins in the entire reality of the person, body and soul. The reason why death can be a personal mortal sin lies in its hiddenness. Death, as Rahner repeatedly reminds us, is a dialectic of action and passion, of internal freedom and external constraint. The dying person is neither wholly self-directing nor wholly subject to control by another but halfway between these two. In death, a person must decide his or her own fate totally and irrevocably, and yet at the same time every power, every possibility, of autonomously controlling his or her own destiny is taken away. Hence death is "the act in which a man either *willingly accepts* or *definitively rebels against* his own utter impotence, in which he is utterly subject to the control of a mystery which cannot be expressed—that mystery which we call God. . . . Thus the exercise of his freedom taken as a whole is summed up at this point in one single decision: whether he yields everything up or whether everything is taken from him by force, whether he responds to this radical deprivation of all power by uttering his assent in faith and hope to the nameless mystery which we call God, or whether even at this point he seeks to cling on to his autonomy, protests against this fall into helplessness, and, because of his disbelief, supposes that he is falling into the abyss of nothingness when in reality he is falling into the unfathomable depths of God."[83]

Rahner has offered a penetrating analysis of the various forms in which this sinful denial of death can disguise itself. On the one hand, one can deny the ambiguity of death. This can be done in two ways: either one regards death as absolutely obscure and therefore utterly absurd and hence refuses in despair to accept any illumination or assistance from outside of oneself; or one can regard death as not obscure at all, as totally transparent, and hence interpret it positively and independently. On the other hand, one can look upon death as an act affecting the body and the soul. Once again, this can be done in two ways. The first, the spiritualist aberration, regards death as the liberation of the soul from the confines of matter and bodily existence, the soul being transferred into another mode of individual existence or absorbed into a universal spirit or transformed into a subject freed from the illusion of spatiotemporal individuality. The second, the materialist interpretation, conceives of death as a merely biological, natural process having no spiritual significance; death is simply a return to the world of matter.[84]

Because death can be a mortal sin, it is rightly dreaded. This horror of death is caused not simply by the purely biological instinct of self-preservation but by that orientation to divine life which still remains in the sinner and which, had it been able to find pure expression at the beginning of human history, would have eliminated death at the outset. Humans rightly dread death because of its ambiguity and hiddenness. We should not, Rahner warns, conceal this dread by explaining it away as a fact of life or by taking refuge in superficiality, despair, or tragic heroism. We would then make death into something truly terrifying: the advent of eternal death.

VI. Dying with Christ

So far Rahner has described the natural and, as it were, neutral element of death so that it is clear how death can be an event of either salvation or damnation. The focus of his interest, however, is not death as a consequence of original sin and as an act of mortal sin, but death as transformed by Christ, as "the revelation of our dying with Christ, the culmination of our appropriation of his redemptive death."[85] To elucidate this point, Rahner first considers the death of Christ; secondly, the death of the Christian who dies in the state of grace; and thirdly, the union between the death of Christ and that of the Christian, a union made visible in the sacraments.

1. The Death of Christ

Because of the reality of the Incarnation by which he is made like us in all things except sin, Christ died our death, the death proper to fallen humanity with all its manifold characteristics. Hence, says Rahner, his death cannot be similar to ours merely in externals, that is, as a merely biological act, but must contain all the essential elements of human death, as they have been analyzed so far, except its sinful aspect. This means that Jesus' death must exhibit the same complexity of action and passion, person and nature, fulfillment and end. Therefore, when Christian tradition refers to Christ's death as redemptive, we must understand redemption not on the basis of one single aspect of his death but on the basis of his death as a whole composed of several diverse elements.

It is here that Rahner finds the traditional theory of satisfaction less than satisfactory. It rightly maintains that Christ's redemption is brought about in his obedience, his love, and his free acceptance of death, yet because it holds that any other moral act of Christ would have an infinite value due to the dignity of his divine nature, it must assume that on principle God could have accepted any act of Christ other than his death as fully redemptive. Hence, were Jesus' death to have a saving efficacy, it would have it simply in virtue of a juridical decree of God to accept it.[86]

This satisfaction theory, according to Rahner, is inadequate on at least three counts. First, it does not make it intrinsically clear why it was through Christ's death that we were redeemed and not through any other act of his which would also have had an infinite value. To appeal to God's free decree is premature. Further, the Scripture seems to teach that Christ's death is redemptive precisely because of the characteristics which are proper to death alone (as a blood sacrifice) and not to any other moral act.

Secondly, the theory assumes that death as such is merely an event passively suffered, and not also an act freely performed. On this questionable assumption, the redemptive act of Christ would consist only in his patient acceptance of and obedient submission to the sufferings that caused his death and not in the death as such. Now, Rahner points out, if Christ was truly human, he must have experienced death in its hiddenness and ambiguity, as the manifestation and consequence of sin, even though he was not in the state of unbelief. Consequently, he had to enact his death actively and in freedom. Of course, unlike us, he could do this in absolute freedom, in virtue of a grace that necessarily belonged to him as a divine being, secure from the weakness of concupiscence. Nevertheless, it is true that, Rahner argues, "it is precisely in its darkness that the death of Christ becomes the expression and embodiment of his loving obedience, the free transference of his entire created existence of God. What was the manifestation of sin thus becomes, without its darkness being lifted, the contradiction of sin, the manifestation of a 'yes' to the will of the Father."[87] Further, the view that Jesus saved us precisely in his death makes it understandable how Christ saved us also in his life, since death is axiologically present in all the acts of freedom throughout life.

Thirdly, the satisfaction theory does not make clear how the death of Christ can be redemption for others because it does not show how in death Christ was related to other human beings and to the world. Making use of his theory of the pancosmicity of the soul after death, Rahner attempts to reinterpret the biblical teaching of Christ's descent into hell (cf. Rom 10:7; Eph 4:9; Mt 12:40). It may be recalled that for Rahner the soul after death is not cut off from matter; rather, no longer limited to an individual body, it enters into a much closer, more comprehensive relationship to that ground of the unity of the universe. Through death, humans in some way introduce the result of their life into the ground of the unity of the world as their personal contribution to the history of the world. Transferring this notion to Christ, Rahner suggests that through his death "Christ's spiritual reality, which he possessed from the beginning, enacted in his life, and brought to consummation in his death, becomes open to the whole world and is inserted into this whole world as its ground as a permanent determination of a real ontological kind."[88]

Hence, in death itself, Christ not only did not cease to be related to the world but became an intrinsic principle of it, so that the world, in which human actions are performed and death takes place, has been transformed and would have been different had Christ not died. With evocative images Rahner describes Christ's becoming the principle of the material world: "When the vessel of his body was shattered in death, Christ was poured out over all the cosmos; he became actually, in his very humanity, what he had always been by his dignity, the heart of the universe, the innermost center of creation."[89] In virtue of his becoming the center of the cosmos, Christ brought redemption and release to those who had died before him and who, even though at their deaths they were just and in principle saved, had to wait for the salvation brought to them by Christ when he descended into the realm of the dead. Further, those who die after Christ have the real possibility of descending into hell with him and being redeemed by entering into contact with that innermost center of the universe.

2. *The Death of the Christian as a Dying with Christ*

Death in its hiddenness can be a personal mortal sin. But because Christ has died this death in its hiddenness in obedience to his Father's will, in love and trust, this death can also be an act of faith: "It can be made into an enduring act of faith in the fact that our lives and destinies are being directed and controlled by another and that this direction is right; the willing acceptance of our destiny, the ultimate act of self-commitment to that destiny, a renunciation which we make in anticipation of our final end because in the end we must renounce all things; also because we believe that it is only by this poverty entailed in freely accepting our own destiny that we can free ourselves for the hand of God in his unfathomable power and grace to dispose of us as he wills."[90]

There is therefore beneath their apparent similarities a radical difference between the death of a sinner and that of a justified person. This difference does not simply consist, as traditional theology too superficially thought, in the fact that death is a *poena* for the sinner and for the justified only a *poenalitas*, that is, a mere consequence of sin and not a punishment. This purely juridical distinction is inadequate on several grounds. It obscures the fundamental difference between a sinful death and a holy one; it considers death exclusively as the consequence of original sin and neglects the possibility of death as a personal mortal sin; and it focuses on death as something to be suffered passively and not also as an act to be performed in freedom.

The New Testament, Rahner notes, speaks of the Christian's death as "dying in the Lord" (Apoc 14:13; 1 Thes 4:16; 1 Cor 15:18), a death that is no death at all because it is a dying with Christ which is life-giving (2 Tim

2:11; Rom 6:8). Thus, "the death itself of a person in the state of grace is a saving event. . . . We may even say that death is the culmination both of the reception and of the effecting of salvation."[91] This death, which is occuring every day, culminates in the last moment of life. Rahner is fond of quoting a saying of Eutyches, a sixth-century monk, to the effect that there occurs 'pragmatically' in death what has occurred 'mystically' in the sacraments, especially in baptism and in the Eucharist, namely, our assimilation to the death of Jesus.

How does one die with Christ, "die in the Lord," in the concrete? In answer to this question Rahner recalls that what distinguishes the death of Christ is that death, as the manifestation of sin, became in him the expression of grace. "The real miracle of Christ's death resides precisely in this: death which in itself can only be experienced as the advent of emptiness, as the impasse of sin, as the darkness of eternal night. . . and which 'in self' could be suffered, even by Christ himself, only as such a state of abandonment by God, now, through being embraced by the obedient 'yes' of the Son, and while losing nothing of the horror of the divine abandonment that belongs to it, is transformed into something completely different, into the advent of God in the midst of that empty loneliness, and the manifestation of a complete, obedient surrender of the whole person to the holy God at the very moment when the individual seems lost and far removed from him."[92]

If such was the death of Christ, an experience of emptiness and abandonment by God ("My God, my God, why have you forsaken me?") and a radical acceptance of and loving obedience to God in the midst of such emptiness and powerlessness ("Father, into your hands I commend my spirit"), then to die with Christ is to undergo that same dialectical experience of remoteness from and nearness to God, of doubt and faith, despair and hope, rebellion and love. "The trinity of faith, hope and love," says Rahner, "makes death itself the highest act of believing, hoping, loving, the very death which seems to be absolute darkness, despair, coldness itself. . . . Faith in darkness, hope against hope, love of God who appears only as Lord and as inexorable justice."[93]

Of course such a way of dying does not happen automatically. As preparation for it, Rahner mentions "Christian vigilance, remembrance of the Last Things, waiting for the Lord, joy at his nearness, the groaning of the creation for redemption, for the glorification of the body as it perhaps begins even in this life, through a slow approach to the ideal of Paradise, of freedom from concupiscence by means of an ascetical life."[94] But these are not the only means whereby the Christian can appropriate Christ's death. Rahner also highlights the sacraments as the efficacious signs in which Christ's death and the death of the Christian are visibly and publicly united.

3. The Visible Union Between the Death of Christ and the Death of the Christian in the Sacraments

The personal encounter between the Christian and Christ is not limited, of course, to the sacraments; it takes place whenever and wherever the person freely accepts God's grace. Nevertheless, Rahner notes, it is only natural that there should be and is an official, social, visible expression of this personal encounter in the efficacious signs of grace of the Church, namely, the sacraments. The sacraments constitute the basic acts by which the Christian appropriates Christ's redemption.

Now, since Christ's death is the redemptive event par excellence, it is also visibly and officially appropriated in the sacraments. In fact, there are, in Rahner's judgment, three sacraments in particular that, by their immediately perceptible form, by the meaning they express, and according to the teaching of the Scriptures, make us partakers of Christ's death and, consequently, make our own death a participation in his: baptism, the Eucharist, and the anointing of the sick.

Basing himself mainly on Paul (Rom 6:3–4; Phil 3:10), Rahner holds that there is "a real, intrinsic relationship between the mystical death in baptism and the actual death of the Christian, and not merely between baptism and the dying-to-sin during life."[95] Dying-to-sin, therefore, is not merely a metaphor for death; rather, it means our participation in Christ's death through our own real death, which is enacted constantly throughout our lives and consummated in our actual deaths. This real death, present throughout life, begins at baptism: "Baptism is the beginning of Christian death, because it is the imitation of the life of grace, by virtue of which alone death can be Christian. . . . Through baptism we are crucified with Christ and the crucifixion of our Christian life is consummated in the act we call our death. Baptism is the beginning of Christian dying."[96]

In the Eucharist there is a repeated and visible revelation and deepening of the Christian's companionship with Christ in suffering and death. It is "the continuously renewed celebration of the death of the Lord, making that death present here and now in our lives. . . . What is done in this mystery is the sacramental enactment of Christ's death, and what we receive in this mystery is the grace which became ours, in his death."[97] In order that Christ's death, which we announce in the Eucharist until he comes again, be effective in our own death, we must, Rahner forcefully reminds us, do as Scripture bids us: suffer with him (Rom 8:17), be conformed to his death (Phil 3:10), glorify him in our bodies (Phil 1:20), and be delivered into the power of death (2 Cor 4:10).[98]

Lastly, the sacrament of the anointing of the sick manifests the Christian's relationship to Christ's death by the situation in which it is administered, the sickness of the body. Just as death is not simply a biological act, so sickness is not merely a biological process. "As a way to death and a danger of death," says Rahner, "it is the visible manifestation of the power of sin and of the devil as well as of that weakness of the human person which, ethically and corporeally, is an expression of sin and of the danger of sin. Sickness is, therefore, eminently a situation of decision between salvation and damnation, and this just at the moment when the person, precisely because he is sick, is in danger of not meeting this situation properly."[99] Because of the substantial unity body and soul, sickness, either physical or mental, always affects the human being as a whole, as a single entity. Our concrete experience of sickness is never such that we are in a position unequivocally to distinguish between the spirit and the body as two completely separate compartments and clearly to assign a certain factor to what we have to suffer as coming from outside and another factor to what we have brought about freely from inside.

Hence, says Rahner, "in sickness humans are brought face to face with themselves in a particularly uncompromising way. They achieve a state of isolation with themselves. And yet they do not know exactly what this state is into which they have fallen, whether they are to regard themselves as the controller or the controlled. . . . Sickness sharpens a person's awareness of both factors in his life, both that he is in control and that at the time he is subject to control from without."[100] In other words, in sickness human beings experience themselves as mystery, as a question to which they have no answer.

It is only natural that in such a moment of trial, the Church strengthens the sick and the dying with another sacrament. The effect of this sacrament is salvation in both of its forms: restoration of bodily health or acceptance and endurance of death in a Christian manner. ". . . This sacrament assumes the character of a consecration to death, and becomes the visible manifestation of the fact that the Christian, confirmed by the anointment of the Lord, and in virtue of his grace, endures the last trial of his life, performs his last act, his own death, in companionship with the Lord."[101]

VII. Critical Questions

At the conclusion of this rather straightforward exposition of Rahner's theology of death and looking back at that theology as a whole, one cannot but be struck by its internal coherence, its consistency with other parts of Rahner's theology, in particular his anthropology, its fidelity to the tradition, and at the same time its openness to contemporary thought.

For one thing, one can see the effectiveness of Rahner's theological method. Applying its two poles, historicity and transcendentality, as the two blades of a pair of scissors, Rahner cut through to the reality of death from the point of view of both Jesus' historical death and transcendental reflections on the conditions of possibility for human dying. The result is a brilliant and original theology of death in which the historical event of Jesus' death and transcendental reflections on death mutually illuminate and enrich each other. In this way, the universality of death is shown to be rooted, not in the unavoidable biological corruption, but in the dynamism of human freedom. Again, armed with his anthropological reflections on the unity of matter and spirit, body and soul, Rahner is able to critique the Neoplatonic dualism inherent in the traditional understanding of death as separation of the soul from the body and overcome it with his hypothesis of the pancosmicity of the soul. As I have already mentioned, Rahner, in his later systematic writings on death, quietly dropped this theory or at least no longer espoused it with his initial enthusiasm.[102] Even so, his basic ideas concerning the relationship of the soul to matter after death remain unchanged.

Again, Rahner's distinction between nature and person allows him to retrieve a forgotten dimension of death, namely, its character as act and free decision. This perspective enables him to gather support for his theory of anonymous Christianity and to enfold the rich meaning of Christian martyrdom. Nevertheless, his repeated insistence on the *prolixitas mortis* throughout a person's life, both in his or her acts of free decision and in the sacramental celebrations, spares him from the unrealistic speculations of Boros's *Endentscheidungshypothese*. Finally, his reflections on the natural essence of death and on its hiddenness as the manifestation and consequence of original sin furnish him with an effective conceptual framework to explain how death can be either a personal mortal sin or an event of salvation and to develop a rich theology of the death of Christ.

A further assessment of Rahner's theology of death will have to be relegated to the last chapter of this work; meanwhile, a few critical questions can be raised here. First, methodologically, has Rahner preserved a necessary balance between the historical pole and the transcendental one? Specifically, in the analysis of human death, has he paid sufficient attention to the phenomenon of death as it really occurs or has he superimposed upon it a previous anthropology developed independently of and without regard for the fact of death? Again, in his interpretation of Jesus' death, has he taken into account all the data of the New Testament or has he forced upon it his anthropology of death?

Secondly, in his attempt to overcome the Neoplatonic dualism inherent in the traditional understanding of death, has Rahner done justice to the notion of death as the separation of the soul from the body? Has he not perhaps missed the positive point made by this notion, namely, that death is a real destruction of the substantial unity of the human being?

Thirdly, with regard to his hypothesis of the pancosmicity of the soul with which he hopes to overcome Neoplatonic dualism, are Rahner's arguments both philosophical and theological truly persuasive? What is the exact ontological status of the soul with regard to the 'heart of the cosmos'? Are there not less contrived solutions to this problem of the relationship of the soul to matter after death? It has already been pointed out that Rahner later abandoned this hypothesis. An investigation into the reasons why he did so would be extremely informative.

Fourthly, with reference to his conception of death as a personal act (*geistig-personale Tat*), is Rahner naïvely optimistic in minimizing the absurdity of death? Is not his attempt to find meaning in death totally futile or even misguided? Should he not be consistent with Heidegger's analysis of human freedom and maintain that it leads, not to fulfillment, but to nothingness?

Finally, has Rahner done justice to the satisfaction theory of redemption? Did Christ's redemptive work consist, as Rahner claims, in his accepting death *as such*, in its hiddenness and emptiness? Did it not rather consist in the death *on the cross*, for the sins of humankind, in obedience to his Father's will? In this connection, it may be asked whether Rahner's interpretation of Christ's *descensus ad inferos* is exegetically sound. Is Sheol indeed the "heart of the universe," a resplendent center of unity and meaning, or is it a dark dungeon of separation and absurdity? Once again, the obvious question looms large: Is not Rahner's theology too transcendental, and hence does it not prove to be too tight a casket, even for a theology of death?

5

The Intermediate State

> My intention here is not to deny the doctrine of the intermediate
> state. I should only like to point out that it is not a dogma, and
> can therefore remain open to the free discussion of theologians.
> ("'The Intermediate State'," *TI* 17:114)

The doctrine of what is often known as "the intermediate state" has been an untroubling possession of the Catholic Church at least since the promulgation of Pope Benedict XII's constitution, *Benedictus Deus* (1336). By the intermediate state is meant the intervening 'temporal' period between the death of a human person, if it takes place before the general resurrection, and the final consummation of human history and the universe, a period in which the soul continues its existence apart from the body (the doctrine of the *anima separata*). It is well known that Benedict's predecessor, John XXII, in a series of sermons preached in Paris in 1331, had suggested that after death the blessed enjoy only the vision of Christ's glorified humanity, the access to the vision of the Triune God being available only after the general resurrection; there is likewise, he went on to affirm a year later, a progressive retribution in the condition of the damned. His opinions aroused a fierce controversy that was finally settled by Benedict XII. The pope declared that the souls of the blessed—that is, those who had died before Christ or died after Christ and needed no purification, and those who died in need of purification and have completed their purification—all of these, immediately (*mox*) after death or immediately after their purification, enjoy the beatific vision, whereas the souls of those who die in actual mortal sin go down to hell immediately (*mox*) after death.[1] The doctrine of the intermediate state between death and resurrection, which is conceived as that of bodiless souls, was presupposed by the constitution and is taken for granted by most Roman Catholic textbooks on eschatology.

In recent years, however, there has been a growing challenge to this doctrine, not only on the part of Protestants, but Roman Catholics as well.

Connected with the doctrine of the intermediate state is the problem of the immortality of the soul, which we will treat in chapter 7. The attacks against the doctrine of the existence of a disembodied soul in an intervening period between death and the general resurrection are mounted from different vantage grounds: contemporary philosophical reflections on the unity of body and soul, researches on the biblical belief in the afterlife and the resurrection, and historical studies on the intended meanings and limits of magisterial pronouncements on the intermediate state.[2]

Rahner himself took part in the discussion on the intermediate state and related doctrines. In what follows I will first examine his thesis regarding the nature of the intermediate state, then his understanding of purgatory, and finally his reflections on the possibility of reincarnation.

I. Is There an Intermediate State?

1. The Intermediate State: Defined Dogma or Cultural Amalgam?

Rahner's own thesis regarding the possibility of an intermediate state is in itself minimal. Contrary to most Protestant theologians, he did not deny the existence of the intermediate state. For him it is simply a cultural amalgam: "It is by no means certain that the doctrine about the intermediate state is *anything more* than an intellectual framework, or way of thinking. So whatever it has to tell us (apart from statements about the commencement through death of the final form of man's history of freedom, and about the inclusion of the body in this final form) does not necessarily have to be part of Christian eschatology itself."[3]

For Rahner, Benedict XII's constitution, *Benedictus Deus*, did indeed assume that there is such a thing as an intermediate state between a person's death and his or her bodily glorification. But it was *only* an assumption, not the direct object of teaching of the constitution. What is being taught as Christian truths is the perfecting or condemnation of the soul immediately after death and the glorification of the body. Hence, if there is a way of maintaining these truths in their fullness without thereby postulating the doctrine of the intermediate state as defined above, then clearly this doctrine is nothing more than an amalgam; in other words, it is something said but not meant.[4]

To find support for his thesis, Rahner appeals to the data of the Scripture. There are, he points out, two series of statements, one of which affirms the future resurrection of the flesh, i.e., the one and total person, and the other the immediate vision of God after death (cf. Lk 23:43; Jn 5:24). On the one hand, the belief in the future resurrection of the righteous (later extended to all human beings) was based on the conviction that God wills the salvation of his covenanted people and that this salvation is demonstrated in the resurrection of the dead. But the resurrection concerns not only the body or only the soul, but the one and total person. Consequently, one cannot appeal to the Old Testament concept of Sheol as the equivalent of the concept of the intermediate state, since there is in the Old Testament no concept of the separate existence of the soul from the body after death. On the other hand, when it is affirmed in the New Testament that at the moment of death the person is already "in paradise" or "with Christ," one cannot assume that this means that his or her 'soul' is immediately enjoying eternal blessedness, while the 'body' is still waiting for the resurrection. Rather, for Rahner, this statement only means that "death, too, belongs to the powers and forces which ultimately cannot harm the man or woman who lives through his or her faith in Jesus Christ."[5]

Whether these two series of statements regarding the future resurrection and the immediate vision of God can be harmonized must remain, in Rahner's judgment, an open question. Certainly, the Scripture does not attempt to homologize them. Later theological tradition achieved their concordance by means of their twin notions of the intermediate state and the *anima separata*. It is, however, precisely these two concepts that have come under attack. Rahner noted first of all that in interpreting Christ's liberation from Sheol of those who had died before him, the majority of the Fathers understood it in light of the Jewish teaching as a *physical* resurrection and not as the freeing of their souls for the contemplation of God. Further, even Benedict XII's constitution does not rule out the possibility that the soul may enjoy *greater* blessedness *after* the resurrection of the body.[6]

From these considerations Rahner concludes that "the genesis of the idea of an intermediate state in the Middle Ages was a stage in the history of theology, but no more than that. It is the attempt to reconcile the collective and the individual view of eschatological perfection."[7] One may not object to this view by urging that to conceive of the unity of the individual and collective eschatologies without postulating the intermediate state would imply the dismissal of the collective or cosmic eschatology. This would not be the case, Rahner replies, because it is still possible to conceive of the individual eschatology as an intrinsic element of a progressive transformation of world history and of the cosmos in general.

2. Objections and Answers

The concept of the intermediate state, were we to regard it as more than a cultural amalgam implicitly assumed but not explicitly taught as a truth of faith, would run up against two formidable objections. First, how is it possible to have 'time' after death, the intervening time between a person's death and the general resurrection? "How are we to think of time and the temporality of a departed soul," Rahner asks, "if on the one hand the soul is already with God in its perfected state, but on the other hand has 'to wait' for the reassumption of its function toward its own body?"[8] To resort to the distinction between time and *aevum*[9] is a convenient device but hardly an illuminating one, since it still may be asked why in such an *aevum* change in freedom is no longer possible.

Secondly, the doctrine of the intermediate state presupposes the *anima separata*. But this notion of a disembodied soul is highly problematical if one adopts the Thomistic doctrine that the soul is *unica forma corporis*. If the informing act of the body by the soul is not an accidental determination of the soul but is identical with it, it would be difficult to see how the soul does not cease to exist when it is totally separated from the body.

Rahner recalls his earlier theory of the cosmic relation between the soul and the one matter of the world as a possible solution to this dilemma. As a result of the various criticisms of his novel theory of the pancosmicity of the soul[10] Rahner abandoned it and adopts a simpler and more familiar solution. Without postulating an intermediate state, he believes that the enduring relation between spirit and matter can be expressed in scholastic language by saying that the glorified body is permanently informed by the perfected spirit soul.[11] A possible objection may be urged against this solution on the ground that the identity between the earthly body and the glorified body is thereby destroyed, since there should be at least some material fragment of the earthly body present in the glorified body for them to remain identical. Rahner replies that such an identity does not remain even in the different stages of the same earthly body in its lifetime due to its radical metabolic processes. Further, it is extremely problematic, if not impossible, to split up mere matter into so many 'substances' and clearly divisible particles, as prescientific philosophy thought could be done. And, of course, it is no longer theologically possible to conceive of the resurrection of the body as the revitalizaton of some or all material particles that used to belong to the earthly body.

For Rahner, therefore, the identity between the earthly self and the glorified one does not come from the identity of the body; rather, "identity consists, now and in the future, much more in the identity of the free, spiritual subject, which we call the 'soul'."[12] That is why, for Rahner, even empirical experience of the corpse in the grave is not per se a proof against the fact of the resurrection. If this is so, there is no compelling argument for the intermediate state, and Rahner puts a tantalizing question: "So why should we not put the resurrection at that particular moment when the person's history of freedom is finally consummated, which is to say at his death?"[13]

Finally, Rahner takes into consideration some of the philosophical and theological objections against his view that the notion of the intermediate state is no more than a theological construct and not a defined doctrine. On the philosophical level, it may be suggested first of all that a real distinction between body and soul, which is still valid in a contemporary anthropology, seems to imply the notion of the intermediate state. Rahner points out, however, that, despite such a perennially valid distinction, the human being counts "empirically and ontologically, first and last as being *one*."[14] Body and soul are not complete and independent substances but *principia entis*. Even the most spiritual human act always has a material element and vice versa.

Secondly, it may be argued that the immortality of the soul, as distinct from the resurrection of the dead, can be proved rationally and implies the notion of the intermediate state. Rahner replies that even if the immortality of the soul can be established by means of rational proofs, it may mean no more than that the human person, as a being of transcendence and freedom, is one who through his or her history of freedom can achieve final validity before God. Further, the immortality of the soul must be grasped together with the resurrection of the dead as referring to the *one* human person. Consequently, says Rahner, "in view of its understanding of the unity of the human person, modern metaphysical anthropology can never (or only with the greatest reservations) consider that an intermediate state, or an absolutely non-corporeal mode of existence on the part of the spiritual subject, is possible."[15]

Thirdly, it may be argued that the scholastic doctrine of the soul as *forma in se subsistens* implies the doctrine of the intermediate state. Rahner answers that this concept, correct and meaningful in itself, means no more than that "through his death the individual is not destroyed, but arrives at perfection."[16] It does not mean that the soul can go on existing by itself, apart from the body. To take the doctrine to imply that there is an intermediate state is to go beyond the evidence.

On the theological level, against Rahner's view it may be pointed out that the definition of the dogma of the Assumption of Mary seems to indicate that apart from Jesus and Mary human beings are not given the privilege of immediate enjoyment of the eternal beatitude in 'body and soul'.[17] Rahner concedes that those involved in drawing up the Apostolic Constitution, *Munificentissimus Deus*, might have entertained this notion, but this is no cogent proof against this view. For nowhere in the definition is it explicitly stated that assumption, that is, a perfect and glorified corporeality which is even now a part of the total fulfillment, is a privilege reserved to Mary alone.

Already in his article, "The Interpretation of the Dogma of the Assumption," published less than a year after the promulgation of the dogma,[18] Rahner attempted to root the dogma of the Assumption in the articles of the Creed regarding Christ's descent into hell and resurrection from the dead. Because he descended into hell, Christ became the "heart of the world" and there liberated those who had died before him, and because he rose as the "first born among the dead," he did not and could not rise alone. That is why, says Rahner, "when the early Church defined her belief in Christ's descent, victorious over death, she had in mind other dead ones, who 'already' share in the definitive character of the total victory over death and sin."[19] Because of her divine motherhood and because of her position in the history of salvation, Mary was the perfectly redeemed and the representation of perfect redemption. That is why she must, *even now*, have achieved that perfect communion with God in the glorified totality of her real being, her body and soul: "She who by her faith received salvation in her body for herself and for us all, has received it entire. And this entire salvation is a salvation of the entire human being, a salvation which has already begun even in its fullness. Mary in her entire being is already where perfect redemption exists, entirely in that region of being which came to be through Christ's resurrection."[20]

For this reason, it is only natural that the Church singled out Mary's case and proclaimed it as a dogma. However, Rahner points out, the "privilege" implied here does not mean that she alone is enjoying it.[21] Because of Christ's resurrection and bodily ascent into heaven, "it is completely 'normal' (which is not to say 'general') that there should be men and women in whom sin and death have already been definitively overcome. Christ's victorious descent into the kingdom of death is precisely not just an event belonging to his private existence but a saving event, one which affects the dead. . . . And his entry into the eternal glory even of his body does not open up an 'empty space', but institutes a bodily community of the redeemed: however far from being complete the number of the brethren may be, and however little we may be able, with a single exception, to call them by name as those who have been redeemed even in their bodies."[22]

Rahner was quite aware that numerous texts could be selected from Scripture and tradition that would seem prima facie to affirm the existence of an intermediate state. He appealed, however, to the important hermeneutical distinction between the binding content of a statement and the temporally conditioned modes of expression belonging to a particular *Zeitgeist*: " . . . Do these texts really intend to expound an intermediate state as a truth binding on faith? Or do they merely presuppose it because at the time when they were formulated, in the aftermath of Platonism and under the influence of a naïvely empirical view of the corpse in the grave, nothing else could be said with regard to what they had to expound clearly as being a genuine part of actual Christian faith?"[23]

It is clear the Rahner opted for the second alternative. "In my view, the idea of the intermediate state contains a little harmless mythology, which is not dangerous as long as we do not take the idea too seriously and do not view it as binding on faith."[24]

In short, Rahner believes that it is not heretical to hold the following three theses regarding the final and definitive fulfillment of each human being without having to postulate the existence of an intermediate state: ". . . that the single and total perfecting of the human person in 'body' and 'soul' takes place immediately after death; that the resurrection of the flesh and the general judgment take place 'parallel' to the temporal history of the world; and that both coincide with the sum of the particular judgments of individual men and women."[25]

II. Purgatory as Integration of the Many Levels of the Person

1. Introduction: Sources and Interpretation

Rahner's ideas on the intermediate state that I have expounded above can be said to represent his more mature thinking. In an earlier article on the afterlife published in 1959, speaking of the difference between Catholic and Protestant theologies regarding the existence of purgatory, Rahner wrote:

> It [the Catholic doctrine] maintains firmly in the doctrine of purgatory that death does indeed make definitive the freely matured basic atti-tude of the human person, which again is purely by the grace of God, since this finality is good. But it also maintains that the many dimen-sions of the person do not at all attain their perfection simultaneously and hence that there is a full ripening of the whole individual 'after' death, as this basic decision penetrates the whole extent of his reality. Such a difference of phasing, which results from the plurality of the person's structure, is in fact to be seen in the contrast between the fulfillment of the individual in death and the universal consummation of the world, between the finality achieved by the individual in death and the clarification and perfection of this fulfillment which is still to come in the transfiguration of his bodily existence. Since it cannot be denied that there is an 'intermediate state' in the destiny of the person between death and bodily fulfillment, unless one holds that the person who is saved would no longer be the same as the one who was to be saved, there can be no decisive objection to the notion that the indi-vidual reaches personal maturity in this 'intermediate state'.[26]

As has been said above, the later Rahner did not deny the doctrine of an intermediate state as such but simply maintained that it cannot be regarded as a defined doctrine. Of course, writing in the late fifties, Rahner was merely following the current *sententia communis* regarding the existence of an intermediate state. However, with the benefit of biblical and historical studies, Rahner later came to the conclusion that the intermediate state is no more than a cultural amalgam, a little harmless piece of mythology, as he put it. Nevertheless, if a Catholic theologican holds that the intermediate state is but a cultural construct, it is incumbent upon him to show how his view is compatible with the Church's defined dogma of purgatory and its attendant practice of praying and gaining indulgences for the dead.

Rahner's discussion of purgatory, with the exception of an article published in 1980 in a Festschrift for Heinrich Stirnimann, was obiter dicta, mostly in his studies on indulgences.[27] It is of course not pertinent to the scope of our work to investigate Rahner's theology of indulgences as such, but only to the extent that they are conceived as spiritual aids to the dead and hence would seem to imply an intermediate state.[28] Before embarking upon an examination of Rahner's view of purgatory, it is perhaps necessary to say something about the literary genre of Rahner's only extended and explicit article on purgatory, referred to above.[29] It is not a straightforward exposition of the author's ideas on purgatory; rather, it is presented as a dialogue between two theologians on the subject. To my knowledge Rahner made use of this genre of "Platonic dialogue" only in one other essay, "A Spiritual Dialogue at Evening: On Sleep, Prayer, and Other Subjects," in which a priest and a doctor engage in a conversation on sundry topics.[30] Whereas it is possible to identify Rahner's views with those of the priest in this latter dialogue, it is not clear which of the two theologians in the former dialogue stands in for Rahner. On the basis of the contents of their discourses, I suggest that both theologians represent Rahner: the first theologian, whose views are somewhat conservative, conveys Rahner's more securely established positions on purgatory (pp. 183–87), whereas the second, whose ideas are liberal, represents Rahner's more tentative explorations into new theological theories (pp. 188–93). To differentiate these two series of views, whenever such distinction is important, I will use the expressions, Rahner "the first theologian" and Rahner "the second theologian."

2. Purgatory as a Theological Problem

The doctrine of purgatory,[31] formulated dogmatically for the first time in the Middle Ages,[32] was, as is well known, rejected by the Reformers, Luther, Calvin, and Zwingli. In reply, the Council of Trent, making a distinction between *reatus aeternae poenae* (*reatus culpae*) and the *reatus poenae temporalis*, taught that "there is a purgatory and that the souls detained there are helped by the acts of intercession of the faithful and especially the acceptable sacrifice of the altar."[33] Trent, however, remained silent on the nature of purgatory and the *reatus poenae temporalis*.

In general, official documents do not propose any dogmatically binding teaching as regards fire, a place of purification, or the duration, kind, and intrinsic nature of punishment.[34] It is on some of these issues that Rahner has contributed quite original reflections.

First of all, Rahner, at least as the "second theologian," is acutely aware that the doctrine of purgatory meets with a widespread skepticism, not least because the language used even by recent magisterial documents proves quite unintelligible and misleading. Expressions such as "expiation in the fire," "detention of souls," "penalty" are still being used in reference to purgatory. Further, if one searches for biblical and patristic foundations of the doctrine of purgatory, there is precious little to be found. Rahner puts it quite bluntly: "There is not much to be got out of Scripture, whether of the Old or the New Testament, particularly if we may hold the opinion that prayers for the dead do not necessarily imply a doctrine of purgatory. If we turn to the Fathers of the Church, there are certainly not a few whom we could name as upholding some kind of doctrine of purgatory. But does this mean *ipso facto* that such an idea is part of revealed doctrine and binding as such or might it not be merely an ideal type which in the last resort remains without binding force and which enables us to satisfy our curiosity by finding answers to questions which we ought to leave unanswered in the presence of the silent majesty of death?"[35]

This does not mean, however, that the doctrine of purgatory is to be rejected or that it is impossible to reformulate it in such a way that it may be intelligible, credible, and compatible with modern anthropology. This is what Rahner the "first theologian" attempts to do.

3. The Many Levels of the Human Person and Temporal Punishments Due to Sin

To achieve some understanding of the doctrine of purgatory and its related concepts of temporal punishments (*reatus poenae*, which still remains in the sinner even after the *reatus culpae* has been forgiven), satisfaction, purification, and indulgences, Rahner first of all recalls a fundamental feature of the human person, namely, that humans are complex beings with many levels in their ontological makeup: "The decisions man takes and the acts he initiates from the source and center of his personal freedom, from the innermost 'kernel' of his personhood, take shape in dimensions of his being which are not simply identical with the center of personhood in his being considered as the source and origin of everything else in his make-up. He acquires attitudes and habits. He gives his character its distinctive mould and he 'objectifies' the acts in which he exercises his freedom, imposing them upon his 'environment'. The initial 'environment' which receives the impress of the act arising from his original decision, and in which it is objectified, consists of his own self in the external levels of his make-up."[36]

Because of this multileveled structure of their personality, when human beings turn back to God in the act of conversion, the innermost center of their personhood *can* be made whole immediately by divine grace. However, Rahner points out, "*it can also be the case* that this interior transformation of the person is present in a certain sense like a glowing kernel at the center of his personhood, yet that it does not simply and at one blow do away with all the ingrained attitude, encrustations and after-effects of the earlier course of life led by the individual concerned. . . . This grace of conversion is, in fact, intended to draw the whole human nature into its sphere of influence, extending this to the physical side of the person's nature, to the unconscious movements of his nervous system, to the submerged impulses in it, in order that all may be healed and sanctified."[37] Such a transformation of the whole person physical, psychological, and spiritual, and the integration of all his or her levels of being cannot fail to be an arduous and painful process.

This painful process of transformation and integration, originating from sin and continuing after it, can be called the temporal punishments due to sin: "They are 'temporal' because they must be endured in a process of development over a period of time, and can only be overcome in this. They are punishment because they are the consequences of sin and a judgment upon it both at the same time."[38] It is therefore not necessary to view the temporal punishments due to sin as something that is extrinsically imposed upon humanity by the justice of God, conceived of as something purely vindictive. We are not required by the dogma of the Church to think of purgatory "as a purely passive endurance of vindictive punishments, which, when they are paid for in this sense, release the individual in exactly the same condition in which he commences this state of purification."[39]

On the contrary, the temporal punishments due to sin should be conceived as consequence intrinsic to sin itself. Sin gives birth to its own punishment. In sinning, human beings violate and destroy their own nature and experience an inner contradiction between what they sinfully choose to be and what God intends them to be. And this radical contradiction produces pain, the punishment of sin. Consequently, purgatory or the payment of these temporal punishments is nothing but a gradual and painful removal of this inner contradiction, "a maturing process of the person, through which, though gradually, all the powers of the human being become slowly integrated into the basic decision of the free person."[40]

This view of the temporal punishments and purgatory does not imply that there are no 'external' punishments for sin or that there are no punishments imposed by God. What is being denied is that they are simply extrinsic penalties imposed by the vindictive justice of God and unrelated to the nature of sin itself. On the contrary, there are external punishments for sin in the sense that the sinful actions, which are necessarily incarnated in the exterior of the sinner and his or her physical environment, cause a damage that can be repaired only by a slow process which may last much longer than the interior act of conversion in the center of the person. Repentant sinners cannot but experience this process of healing in their exterior and in their physical environment also as a punishment 'from without', an external penalty determined by God and provoked by their personal sin itself. Consequently, when it is said that God remits the temporal punishments on account of the prayers offered or indulgences gained, what is meant is not that God refrains from torturing the holy souls or from adding further penalties. Rather, what is meant is that "the process of painful integration of the whole of man's stratified being into the definitive decision about this life, taken under the grace of God, happens more quickly and intensively and therefore also less painfully."[41]

How is this tranformation and integration of all the multiple levels of the sinner's ontological structure achieved? The means that traditional theology suggests are penance, prayer, and good works. While denying none of these Rahner prefers to emphasize the role of love in the process of integration: "The subject wills to achieve, in this radical decision of his, that love in which God and his neighbor are loved 'with his *whole* heart and with *all* his powers'. And conversely it is also true to say that this love is itself made perfect in virtue of the fact that it integrates within itself all the dimension of human nature."[42] This is why classical theology maintains that the love of God and neighbor, when it has reached its perfection, blots out all the temporal punishments due to sin. But, consistent with his view of the punishment of sin, Rahner warns that we should not regard this blotting out of temporal punishments as an external 'reward' given by the remunerative justice of God. Rather this blotting out is the connatural consequence of love: "Perfect love is that which has oriented 'all the powers', i.e. all the manifold levels of reality in the complexity of the person's makeup purely to God, so that these, without themselves being suppressed or deprived of their true natures, become the 'material', the 'expression' and the 'manifestation' precisely of this love."[43] Indeed, love is the only way in which the temporal punishments for sin can be blotted out.

4. Purgatory as a Temporal Process?

A further question can be now raised: When is this process of purification, integration, and personal growth taking place? Of course, during this earthly life. But what if it is not completed at the end of this life? Is it to be continued and completed 'after' death? In this case, the existence of an intermediate state would seem to be necessary. But Rahner has already suggested that such a state is simply a cultural prop and not a defined dogma. Rahner is fully aware of the difficulty of this problem. On the one hand, one may not suppose that the unintegrated elements of a person's ontological and spiritual existence simply cease to exist and are no longer relevant to his or her eternal happiness. On the other hand, one cannot hypothesize that they are removed by a juridical decree of God as a deus ex machina. And yet, because death is the last and definitive act of human freedom, the dead are released from the flux of time and therefore can no longer undergo the process of integration 'after' death.

As solutions to his problem, Rahner "the first theologian" offers two possibilities. The first would suppose that the integration of the various levels of the person is completed in the last personal decision, which is a lengthy *process*, made definitive in death. This process is conceived in analogy to our earthly time, in a way that by and large corresponds to the traditional idea of purgatory. Since the dead are not cut off from the world, it is conceivable that they, although made definitive in their basic decision, can and must continue in their own way to participate in the fundamental temporality and historicity of the world, even if they have already reached their consummation in the beatific vision of God. This solution has the advantage not only of preserving the traditional representation of purgatory but also of appropriating the idea—widespread in the history of religion—that the lot of the dead person is a kind of process. However, Rahner is not sympathetic to it since it ultimately presupposes that there is a kind of an intermediate state.

The second solution proposes that the total integration of the person occurs in and through death itself. It is not a process that goes on after death but something which comes to prevail in the whole length and depth of a person's existence as the result of a final basic decision occurring in time. In this hypothesis, the notion of time, either empirical or analogous, in the traditional doctrine of purgatory does not refer to the nature of purgatory itself. Rather it is an imaginative device to emphasize the fact that humans are complex, endowed with several levels of being which cannot be integrated at one stroke and from the outset but only gradually and with great pains through their lives. Hence, Rahner believes that it can be said without contradicting the official teaching on purgatory that "everything happens in death itself, that the 'purification' in purgatory is an aspect of death itself and can be made intelligible in the light of the different characteristics of death itself."[44]

In this hypothesis the 'duration' of the person's purification is understood not in temporal terms but as the depth and intensity of the pains the person experiences in death itself. These pains are purifying and constitute the essence of 'purgatory'.

The prayers for the dead in 'purgatory' (the *suffragia*) could also be regarded as intercessions for their blessed death. One may object that these
prayers are offered for those who are already dead, and not for their even-
tual 'holy' deaths. Rahner replies that if in the traditional idea of purgatory
we still regard suffrages offered for a particular soul in purgatory as
appropriate even though we do not know whether that deceased person
need them or not, it would not be absurd to apply our intercessions for a
particular 'holy' death, no matter when precisely in our earthly time these
prayers are said. After all, Jesus' prayers on the cross were valid even for
those who had died before him. On these presuppositions Rahner sees no
difficulty in accepting the thesis that "purgatory takes place in death
itself."[45]

5. Purgatory in the Context of the History of Religions: The Possibility of
    Reincarnation?

Rahner "the second theologian" listens patiently to these lengthy explanations of purgatory, its nature as a painful process of integration of the
multileveled personhood, its duration as the intensity of the pains suffered
in death, the prayers for the dead as intercessions for their holy deaths, and
purgatory as taking place in death itself. Even Rahner "the first theologian" feels that his own explanations are perhaps not very illuminating,
that perhaps he was explicating the *obscurum per obscurius*. Rahner "the
second theologian" remarks that his partner in dialogue has done no more
than take the doctrine of purgatory straight out of Denzinger and interpret
it "speculatively."[46] If this doctrine was not simply "telephoned down from
heaven" but emerged out of a particular religious context prior to Christian
revelation, then it should be reexamined, Rahner "the second theologian"
suggests, in the light of that context. Now, in the history of religions, there
is a widespread conviction that the human person survives beyond death
and leads a life of a very definite kind. If this belief is taken into consideration, is it possible to elaborate the doctrine of purgatory anew, drawing
from the deepest insights common to many world religions? This is what
Rahner "the second theologian" sets out to do in his turn.

First of all, Rahner observes that the Christian doctrine that with death a
person's history comes to a definitive completion (the 'particular judgment') should not make us forget that his or her total consummation is not
yet realized (whether "not yet" is conceived in analogy to our earthly time
or not). On the other hand, things do not simply go on as before. What
happens in this state between a person's definitive completion and his or
her total consummation? The traditional doctrine of purgatory asserts that
the soul is purified through suffering during this "time." But this answer,
Rahner argues, is "first, terribly formal and abstract and, second, really

has no connection with what such a 'soul' inevitably is, what it has and does, since we cannot really imagine that its life and activity is nothing but 'suffering'."[47]

It is here that the insights of other world religions on life beyond the grave may prove helpful. These religions maintain that there is in the dead a further and even welcome development of an enduring and active relationship with their former world, both physical and personal. This further development is not identical with the beatific vision and may be taken as referring to the human dimension and to the human consummation affirmed, however abstractly and indirectly, by the doctrine of purgatory.

These insights, Rahner concedes, would not at first blush sound terribly exciting to an average Christian. But their significance for a dialogue between Christianity and other religions will be brought home in the light of further questions: Do the Christian eschatological doctrines apply in a binding way as statements of faith to all human beings, i.e., all those who belong to the human species? Or do they refer *only* to those who have disposed of themselves in a definitive way through free decision? Traditional Christian eschatology has of course always assumed the first alternative. For example, it takes for granted that the teaching of the Fifth Lateran Council on the immortality of the soul is true of any soul, irrespective of the situation in which it may find itself immediately before death. But is this obvious and certain? Rahner cautiously raises the question: "Is this doctrine of the final permanency of human spirit-persons and of their definitive destiny either in the immediate possession of God or in eternal perdition true and binding as a matter of faith with regard to those who never reached finality as a result of self-enactment in freedom?"[48]

If this question is answered in the affirmative, one would find oneself in the unenviable predicament of being compelled to hold the following discomforting theses: that the majority of heaven's inhabitants (at least if we allow the salvation of children who die unbaptized, against the Augustinian tradition) consists of people who never came to a personal decision and that eternal happiness is the result partly of a free act and partly of a purely natural happening. Would it not be more realistic, without postulating the hypothesis of limbo and the complicated theories to account for the salvation of those baptized who die before reaching maturity, to affirm that the statements about the hereafter are absolutely binding only with reference to the persons who have reached their definitive self-enactment in the realization of their radical freedom? "Would a midway solution," Rahner asks, "(in the light of the doctrine of purgatory) be conceivable here, by seeing an opportunity of free personal decision as open to these others within the confines of 'purgatory'?"[49]

One may object to the possibility of a free choice after death since death is the definitive termination of a person's history of freedom. Rahner agrees that with the death of a person his or her history of freedom comes to a definitive end. But he cautions against a too hasty application of this principle to cases where this history of freedom has not even begun and death is not by any means death in the full theological sense of freedom made definitive, freedom as final self-determination. "If there is such a state as purgatory," asserts Rahner, "which does not come into existence merely by an external decree and intervention of God, but is a connatural consequence of the nature of the plural human being, then I could imagine that it might offer opportunities and scope for a postmortal history of freedom to someone who had been denied such a history of freedom to someone who had been denied such a history of his earthly life."[50] If this suggestion sounds farfetched, at least it is not as dreadful, Rahner argues, as the idea that there are people whose eternal destiny God has refused for all eternity to permit to be also the finality of their act of freedom.

Finally, can the Christian idea of purgatory after death be understood in terms of the doctrine of reincarnation or migration of souls that is taught by several world religions and serious thinkers? Even Rahner the "second theologian" entertains little sympathy for the theory of a migration of souls as such, but he wonders whether a "modified" version of it from the standpoint of metaphysical and realistic anthropology might not be acceptable to the Christian faith. He emphasizes "modified," because, consistent with the Christian belief that with death comes the finality of human beings' basic option which permeates their history and in which they dispose of themselves vis-à-vis God, Rahner would find it impossible to accept that version of reincarnation doctrine in which reincarnation is represented merely as a continuous repetition of the suffering and misery of temporal existence. This version is tied in with the doctrine of cosmic eternal recurrence and the periodic disappearance and reappearance of humanity during which the soul transmigrates without end. Such endless metempsychosis would be equivalent to damnation itself. From the standpoint of Christian theology, too, Rahner feels himself obliged to reject any doctrine of reincarnation that presupposes that the human soul is to be understood as a substance independent of the body, surviving the decay of the human bodies which it successively inhabits, even though not unendingly.

In which context, then, can the doctrine of reincarnation in a modified form be accepted by the Christian? The doctrine, we may recall, was conceived as an answer to the philosophicoreligious question of justice in a world in which human lots are so unequally and unjustly assigned. It seeks to provide both an explanation for human beings about themselves, their origin and future, and a justification for God. If, however, instead of viewing reincarnation as a solution to the theodicy problem, we place it, as Rahner suggests, in the context of death as the termination of the human being's history of freedom, then it may be adopted as a plausible theory in those cases in which the physical death of a person does not necessarily coincide with the definitive end of his or her history of freedom. If clinical or physical death is not identical, chronologically and essentially, with death as the final and definitive consummation of the history of freedom, then where there is no *history* of freedom properly speaking, there is not 'death' in the sense of freedom made definitive, even though clinical or physical death has occurred.

Among these cases one can think first of all of infants who are stillborn or who die before reaching the age of reason. Rather than consigning them to eternal damnation (as, e.g., Augustine) or to limbo (as, e.g., Thomas Aquinas) or to eternal salvation (as, e.g., many contemporary theologians), one might very well opine that they are given the opportunity of another life in which they would be able to reach a personal decision about themselves. Other cases include people who because of psychological impairments are incapable of responsible decisions. Lastly, even "adults" in the general sense of the word may not always be capable of making *that* decision which engages the depths of the person and is rendered final by death.[51]

Of course, the Christian faith continues to presume, and rightly so, that such a definitive personal decision can certainly be and is made in the normal case of *one* human life. On the other hand it *may* accept the theory of reincarnation at least for those individuals whose lives do not possess a genuine history of freedom. However, it maintains that this reincarnation cannot be an eternal cycle of birth and death and therefore one's history of freedom must sooner or later be brought to definitive end, under the sign of either eternal blessedness or eternal damnation. Moreover, it must also reject a reincarnation in subhuman creatures as unnecessary and unworthy of the human person. In any case, says Rahner, "the Christian (despite the presumption just mentioned) and the advocate of a theory of migration of souls know nothing that is absolutely certain about how many cases there are of human beings for whom there is not an absolute decision for or against God in a particular life. The former cannot deny that there are such cases, according to traditional doctrine; the latter cannot know if such a case is normal in relation to the totality of human beings."[52]

III. Tradition and Openness

Rahner's discussion of the intermediate state and purgatory is fascinating not only in terms of the specific theses he finally comes to hold regarding these two thorny topics of eschatology, but also because of the method he employs in dealing with these subjects.

As is well known, the intermediate state and purgatory have been in traditional eschatology a fantastic playground for apocalyptic imagination, in Rahner's pejorative use of the word *apocalyptic*. One needs only to recall the medieval hairsplitting debates on the nature of fire in purgatory (material fire according to the Latins), the length of the stay in purgatory (according to Dominic Soto and Juan Maldonnato not more than ten years, an opinion condemned by Pope Alexander VII), the system of computation of indulgences (finally abolished by Pope Paul VI), and the abuses of the latter that provoked Luther's caustic sarcasm to realize how the lack of a correct hermeneutics of eschatological assertions can lead to frivolous speculation on the afterlife.

One may recall here Rahner's basic distinction between a genuine eschatology and a false one (which he terms "apocalyptic"). Consistent with his hermeneutical principles, in his discussion of the intermediate state and purgatory, Rahner refuses to give us an advance report on the state of the souls in purgatory. Rather, on the basis of his understanding of eschatology as anthropology read in terms of the future fulfillment, he reinterprets the intermediate state in light of the human being's substantial unity of body and soul and purgatory in light of the multiplicity of strata in the human ontological makeup. In this reinterpretation Rahner displays on the one hand a profound knowledge of and genuine respect for the tradition and, on the other hand, a sympathetic openness not only to modern philosophical anthropology (his view on the intermediate state), but also to ecumenical unity (his interpretation of purgatory) and interreligious dialogue (his receptiveness to a modified version of the doctrine of reincarnation). Of course, Rahner, perhaps more than his critics, is acutely aware of the obscurity of the problems and the tentativeness of his solutions. Hence his intriguing use of the genre of internal dialogue and his repeated protestations of ignorance. But, in spite of the intrinsic obscurity of these subjects, Rahner the theologian feels that he is in duty bound to offer an explanation which both preserves the mystery of these eschatological realities and presents them in a credible manner to modern hearers. His hypotheses regarding the intermediate state, purgatory, and the possibility of reincarnation display once again the marvelous and powerful cohesiveness of his transcendental theology of the human being as a unity-in-distinction of matter and spirit, of human freedom, and of death.

A discussion of the plausibility of Rahner's theses will be given in due course. Meanwhile, a few critical questions can be raised and should be kept in mind as we proceed to examine other parts of Rahner's eschatology.

First, is there not a measure of ambiguity in Rahner's position regarding the intermediate state? His declared purpose is not to deny this doctrine, yet he has shown beyond doubt that it is no more than a conceptual framework to express other Christian truths. This reluctance to do away with it altogether has prevented him from developing a full doctrine of an immediate resurrection after death as Boros has done.[53] Of course, he has raised the possibility of an immediate resurrection in death and affirms that the identity of the person does not consist in the identity of the earthly body with the glorified body but in the permanent "information" of the glorified body by the perfected spiritual soul ("bleibende Informiertheit des verklärten Leibes durch die vollendete Geistseele").[54] But when does this glorified body begin its existence? Is it anything more than the material world to which the corrupted body returns? In this case, Rahner would fall back upon his theory of the pancosmicity of the soul. Can one go further and say that since Christ in his death became the "heart of the world," and since the soul preserves its pancosmic relation, the soul has its embodiment in and from the body of the risen Christ, as Pierre Benoit has suggested?[55]

The rejection of the intermediate state, it may be noted in passing, need not be in conflict with the most recent pronouncement of the Roman Catholic magisterium on eschatology. The Letter of the Sacred Congregation for the Doctrine of the Faith, *Recentiores episcoporum Synodi* (17 May 1979), leaves open the possibility of an immediate resurrection of the whole person.[56] It is well known that there is a noteworthy discrepancy between the text given in the *Osservatore Romano* (23 July, 1979, pp. 7–8) and in the *Acta Apostolicae Sedis* (71 [1979]: 939). The former text says that "a spiritual element survives and subsists after death, an element endowed with consciousness and will, so that the 'human self' subsists" (no. 3), whereas in the latter text, there is an added phrase, "though deprived for the present of the compliment of its body" (*interim tamen complemento sui corporis carens*). This variance may indicate that there exists an uncertainty on the part of the magisterium regarding the dogmatic value of the doctrine of the intermediate state and therefore suggests, at least indirectly, that Rahner's thesis regarding the intermediate state is not untenable.

Secondly, is Rahner's explanation of the suffrages for the dead as retroactive prayers for their holy deaths fully credible? The above-mentioned letter, while remaining silent about the possibility of the human being's purification at the moment of death, affirms that "the Church excludes every way of thinking or speaking that would render meaningless or unintelligible her prayers, her funeral rites and the religious acts offered for the dead. All these are, in their substance, *loci theologici*" (no. 4). Is Rahner's appeal to the fact that Jesus's prayers were efficacious even for those who had died before him really to the point? Did Jesus pray for their holy deaths retroactively, or did he, with his prayers and his death, enable the dead to rise from their death? If so, should not prayers for the dead in purgatory be understood rather as prayers for the second coming of the Lord (Rev 22:17)?[57]

Finally, Rahner's attempt to correlate the doctrine of purgatory and the doctrine of reincarnation is highly commendable, and his bold proposal of a modified version of the doctrine of reincarnation as compatible with Christian faith is not devoid of plausibility, or at least is as plausible as any other hypotheses regarding the possibility of salvation for those who have not had the opportunity to exercise their freedom. Nevertheless, one may query about the situation of the 'soul' before it is reincarnated in another body, assuming that only the body of the person who has died without a genuine history of freedom has perished. Do we have here a case of a 'preexistent' soul? Of course this is not the same as the Origenist theory of the preexistence of the soul, since it does not maintain that the soul is sent down into its body as a punishment for the sins it committed in its previous existence and hence it does not fall under the condemnation by the Second Council of Constantinople.[58] However, if the soul, at least in this case, preexists the body, would its subsequent union with the body result in a substantial unity? Perhaps it would be inappropriate to press the issue to this detail, since the modified version of the doctrine of reincarnation is put forward as a very tentative proposal by Rahner the "second theologian." Nonetheless, it is a point worth noting in view of Rahner's emphatic affirmation of the intrinsic unity between the body and the soul.

6

Heaven and Hell

> These eschatological statements (i.e. about heaven and hell) are
> basically statements about humans existing *now* insofar as they
> face these two possibilities about their future. In this sense,
> however, the message of Christianity as the radical interpreta-
> tion of the subjective experience of freedom is absolutely and
> deadly serious. It says to each one of us, not to someone else, but
> to me personally: in and through yourself, in and through what
> you in your innermost depths are and definitively want to be, you
> can be a person who closes himself into the absolute, deadly and
> final loneliness of saying "no" to God. (*FCF*, 103–4)

In the last chapter we saw that Rahner made his own Pope Benedict
XII's teaching on the immediate retribution of the departed after their
death, in either blessedness in heaven (after due purgation if necessary) or
damnation in hell, although he did not consider the presumed notion of the
intermediate state of a disembodied soul as dogmatically binding.

Further, as has been made clear in our discussion of Rahner's hermeneutics of eschatological assertions, he maintains that the statements about
heaven and hell are not on the same level. Of course, in discoursing on
eschatology, Christians cannot avoid speaking about heaven and hell as the
twofold end of history, of the individual as well as the whole of humanity.
Since eschatology, contrary to 'apocalyptic', reads from the present out
into the future and interprets the present situation in terms of its future
mode of fulfillment, and since the present situation is one of grace and sin,
the possibilities of perfect communion with God *and* damnation must be
mentioned together.

However, Christian eschatology is not the parallel prolongation of a doctrine of the two ways as found, for example, in the first psalm or in the first
part of the *Didache*. Heaven and hell are not two equal alternatives God
offers to human freedom. The central affirmation of the Christian faith is
concerned only with the victorious grace of Christ. Hence, concludes
Rahner, on principle only *one* predestination will be spoken of in a Chris-

tian eschatology, and it contains only *one* theme, namely, the victory of grace consummated in redemption. Possible damnation may and must be spoken of, but only insofar as it is forbidden to assume that universal *apocatastasis* is a fact or that the salvation of the individual is certain *before* death.

In what follows, in accord with Rahner's basic insight regarding the priority of the message of God's victorious grace, we will focus first and foremost on heaven as the primary eschatological reality. Subsequently we will discuss hell, not as a fact, but as a serious *possibility* for every human being. Be it noted that what is said here refers primarily to the destiny of the individual. It will therefore remain fragmentary and incomplete until the consummation of universal history is discussed in the next part.[1]

I. The Christological Structure of Heaven

1. Heaven as Eternity, Absolute Future, and Uncreated Grace

Given the central importance of heaven in eschatology it would seem that Rahner's specific writings on the subject are scanty indeed.[2] This scarcity may partly be explained by the occasional nature of his eschatological essays. However, if one does not take heaven in its strict sense of the final and definitive salvation in God often described in terms of the beatific vision, but in the larger sense of the ontological communion with the Trinitarian God that is already a present reality in this life, then heaven is indisputably a pervasive theme of Rahner's theology. It is implicit in his theology of time and eternity, his theology of the Absolute Future, and above all in his theology of grace. Since I have already discussed at great length the eschatological implications of these themes, suffice it to give succinct summaries of them here and then proceed to examine the specific issue of the christological structure of heaven.

For Rahner, time is the mode of existence of finite beings who enact themselves successively, in freedom. Together with freedom, time and history are the conditions of possibility for the eschatological fulfillment of humankind and the cosmos. Human time has a genuine beginning, a definitive end, and an irreversible course. Eternity, on the other hand, is a characteristic of God who stands in radical contrast to humankind situated and living in time and contingency. God's eternity is essentially to be understood as continuance without any kind of succession. It not only has no beginning and no end but also is a present that has always been in absolute possession of itself and for which, subsisting in itself, there is no such thing as 'before' or 'after'.

The eternal God, however, in the act of Creation, shows that eternity is not a pure negation of time but the master of time. Above all, in the Incarnation of the eternal Logos, the eternal and immutable God himself has become subject to change in his other, his symbol, namely, his humanity. In accepting human temporality God raises it into his own eternal self-possession. Ultimately, therefore, eternity for us should not be conceived as an indefinite continuation of time after death, time running on into infinity on the other side of this world. Rather, eternity is time made definitive by human freedom and above all by freedom's final act, death. Eternity is in time as time's own mature fruit. Consequently, heaven, insofar as it is *eternal* life, is another name for human and cosmic history made definitive and final before God and by his grace.

In virtue of their historicity, humans are placed in a world that they must accept in freedom. They must become 'persons' by transcending their own nature, transforming physical time into their personal time, the mere environment into their real world, in the now of their responsible decisions. But this task can never be accomplished. Past and present human achievements always transcend themselves, reaching out toward absolute validity, which remains a future goal. This future goal, which must be distinguished from any inner-worldly, controllable, plannable, and calculable future human achievements, Rahner calls the Absolute Future. This Absolute Future, which cannot be reached by human beings but freely bestows itself to us, is a hermeneutically suitable term for God, God as God-with-humanity-and-world. In this context, heaven as a *future* reality is the *total* future yet to come, a future that is both humanity's achievement in freedom and God's gratuitous gift.

This Absolute Future, however, is already bestowing itself on humankind in the present as its 'supernatural existential' in the mode of offer and as Uncreated Grace if this self-donation is personally appropriated. This Uncreated Grace, of course, produces an ontological transformation of the person who accepts it (created grace). Uncreated Grace, however, remains the primary reality, by which the justified person enters into a proper, and not merely appropriated, relation with each of the divine persons. Heaven as grace, therefore, is nothing more than the absolute fulfillment of this ontological communion between the redeemed person and the Triune God. Indeed the very immanent relationship among the three divine persons (the Father as the unoriginated fullness of being, the Son as the self-expression of this fullness of being, and the Spirit as the unity of the fullness of being and its self-expression) are freely shared with humans so that they can live by them now in history and become children of the Father, sharing in the sonship of the Son by the unifying and sanctifying power of the Spirit. Human participation in these relationships is constantly under the threat of destruction as long as we are pilgrims in history. Heaven is the destination of our pilgrimage. In heaven humankind has finally arrived home, where our relationship with the Triune God is no longer precarious but made permanent and definitive.

Heaven as eternity, Absolute Future, and Uncreated Grace is, however, made possible by the Logos in his humanity, the one mediator between God and humans. Unfortunately, Rahner remarks, whereas the role of Christ's humanity in the work of redemption is widely recognized and emphasized, its significance for 'heaven', that is, for our permanent relationship with God, is not sufficiently appreciated. It is this aspect, namely, the christological structure of heaven, that Rahner has especially highlighted.

2. The Eternal Significance of the Humanity of Jesus for our Relationship with God

Rahner broaches the subject regarding the role the glorified humanity of Jesus plays in our eternal blessedness in the context of the veneration of the saints and the devotion to the Sacred Heart of Jesus. Rahner believes that the persons and objects with which we come into contact in our everyday experience can be divided into two categories: world and God. Two questions can then be raised. First, into which of these basic divisions do the saints, the angels, and, in particular, the glorified humanity of Christ and his heart belong? In a sense, they all belong to the world insofar as they form part of the created world. On the other hand, because they are encountered in the realm where God is and hence in our religious experience, they belong to God rather than to the world.

The second question is: Can we and do we encounter them in our experience of God as individuals in their autonomy, and not merely as many changing labels or names for the one and same reality, namely, God? Rahner aptly remarks that whereas it was natural for a polytheistic person to think of them as numinous powers and persons outside God, monotheistic believers tend to reduce them to no more than different names for God.[3]

More germane to the topic at hand is Rahner's pointed question regarding the glorified humanity of Christ: "Let us look at an average theological treatise on the Last Things, on eternal happiness. Does such a treatise mention even a single word about the Lord become man? Is not rather everything swallowed up by the *visio beatifica*, the beatific vision, the direct relationship to the very essence of God which is indeed determined historically by a past event—namely the event of Christ—but which is not *now* mediated by Jesus Christ?"[4]

Perhaps Rahner's point will be seen in its full force if it is recalled that for traditional eschatology the souls of the blessed, in the words of Benedict XII, "see the divine essence with an intuitive vision and even face to face, *without the mediation of any creature* by way of object of vision; rather the divine essence *immediately* manifests itself to them, plainly, clearly and openly and in this vision they enjoy the divine essence."[5] Have we not been too quick to assume that "without the mediation of any creature" and "immediately" imply that the created humanity of Christ has no role to play in the beatific vision which constitutes the essence of heaven?

Rahner rejects such an assumption, and to explain the role of the glorified humanity of Christ in the beatific vision of God in spite of its freedom from the mediation of any creature, he appeals first of all to the structure of the relation between created realities and God. As has already been pointed out on different occasions in previous chapters, the fundamental principle governing the relation between the creatures and God, according to Rahner, is that the creature's genuine autonomy and radical dependence on God are simply two sides of one and the same reality, and therefore they grow in direct and not in inverse proportion. This is so because the relation between the creatures and the Creator is a transcendental one. It is only in the realm of the categorical that the radical dependence of the effect on the cause and its independence and autonomy vary in inverse proportion.

On this showing, the creatures cannot be an obstacle or something that can be dispensed with in our approach to God. "No, precisely when we come face to face with the Absolute by a religious act in the course of our existential realization," says Rahner, ". . . we come face to face with that absolutely serious love of what has been created by that Love: the valid, eternal, living reality, that which truly is, precisely because—and not even though—it exists through this Love."[6] In our experience of God, therefore, we should carefully avoid stripping God of his world. Instead, "we must love everything loved by him with this love, and so must love it in that precise way—not as something provisional, as the cloud which, breaking up its contours, dissolves in the presence of the infinity opening up before us—but precisely as something valid in the sight of God, as something eternally justified and hence as something divinely and religiously significant before God."[7]

One may object at this point that the creatures, despite God's real love for them and the healing and elevating grace which he bestows upon them, are also sinful, and therefore there must be a Christian *aversio a creaturis* as the condition of possibility for the *conversio ad Deum*. Rahner readily concedes to the necessity of a flight from the world. The world can entrap human beings in its self-sufficiency and autonomy and is opposed to the God of revelation who comes to us with the message about the foolishness of the Cross and the command for us to renounce and flee from that world.

Nevertheless, for Rahner, the *fuga saeculi* is but the first stage of the human journey toward God. Christians in their flight from the world must recognize that their service to the creatures, their movement away from God back into the world, is the second necessary stage. Because their encounter with God is not a natural outcome of their ascetical renunciation of the world but God's gratuitous gift, Christians know that God can accept in grace also their service to the world, that they can encounter God not only in a radical opposition to the world but also *in* the world, the same God who is beyond the world.

There is, says, Rahner, a third stage, and this is pertinent to the question of the permanent significance of Christ's glorified humanity for our eternal blessedness, namely, "to find the very creature itself, in its independence and autonomy, in God, in the midst of the jealously burning inexorableness of his being-all-in-all; to find the creature even in the very midst of this—the small in the great, the circumscribed in the boundless, the creature (the very creature itself) in the Creator—this is only the third and highest phase of our relationship to God."[8]

There are then, three stages in the human journey toward God. The first two stages are carried out in history: the flight from the world into God and the return from God back to the world in order to find him in all things. The third stage—finding the created world in God—the stage of panentheism, to which the first two stages are raised and into which they are resolved, constitutes heaven itself. It is precisely here that the problem emerges: Do we find the created humanity of Christ at this stage of panentheism? What role does this glorified humanity play in the reconstitution of all things in God? Can we say that once the redemption has been achieved, we can bypass Jesus on our way to entering into an absolute immediacy with God? Are we still Christians if we think that we now no longer have to deal with anything except with God himself in our enjoyment of the divine essence which is manifested to us *nude, clare et aperte*? In Rahner's estimation, there is no doubt that theology explicitly worked out by teachers and preachers has paid far too little attention to this question, so that it almost appears as though the connection with the risen *humanity* of Jesus is a sort of adjunct within the total vision of the heavenly glory, supplementary to the vision of the Triune God.

In opposition to this widespread misconception, Rahner firmly maintains that "the humanity of Jesus is the medium through which our immediate relationship with God is achieved."[9] But is it not self-contradictory and contrary to the teaching of Benedict XII to hold that our immediate vision of God is mediated through the humanity of Christ? Rahner's answers are given on two levels, philosophical and theological. On the philosophical level, it must be recalled that humans enact themselves only by transcending toward the first otherness (spirit letting matter emanate from itself) and toward the second othernesses (other humans and God). Human beings can only come to know themselves in the act of knowing other things and other persons. Self-consciousness is achieved through the consciousness of the other. Sensation as going out of oneself to the other is the condition of possibility for abstraction as returning to oneself in self-presence. It is clear then that the immediate presence to oneself through the mediation of others is far from being an inconsistent notion; rather, the mediation of others is the condition of possibility for the immediate presence to oneself.

Nor is the notion of an immediacy to God as mediated immediacy self-contradictory. Because God is the transcendental ground of being, he does not need to remove something to make room for himself when he draws near to us. On the contrary, God's immediate presence to us takes place precisely in and through the finite existents. "Mediation and immediacy are not simply contradictory," affirms Rahner. "There is a genuine mediation of immediacy with regard to God. And when according to the understanding of Christian faith the most radical and absolutely immediate self-communication of God in his very own being is given to us, namely, in the immediate vision of God as the fulfillment of the finite spirit in grace, this most radical immediacy is still mediated in a certain sense by the finite subject experiencing it, and thereby also experiencing itself. The finite subject does not disappear in this most immediate manifestation of God and is not suppressed, but rather it reaches its fulfillment and hence its presupposition and the consequence of this absolute immediacy to God and from God."[10]

However, in Christianity the mediating agent for the immediacy of God is not only the finite subject itself but the historical Jesus. Therefore, on the theological level, Rahner argues that if the historical Jesus was in his earthly life the mediator between God and humanity, and if his history as the mediator is not something he left behind once he had accomplished it but continues to be effective and efficacious now that he is in 'eternity', since eternity is nothing but history in its definitive validity, then Christ's glorified humanity, by means of which he carried out his mediatorship, must continue to function eternally as the mediating agent for the immediate presence of God in beatific vision. "And thus the connection with the glorified Lord is the *anamnesis* of the crucified and dead Lord not merely in the sense that we 'know' that he whom we love 'once' had this history, but in the sense that he is loved in the eternal and enduring reality of his *history*, and, precisely as the one who has lived through this history, is the mediator who brings us into the immediate presence of God."[11]

There are, of course, other theological indications for the permanent significance of Jesus' humanity for the beatific vision. One can appeal, for instance, to Jesus' statements that no one knows the Father except through him and that the person who sees him sees the Father. These statements, in Rahner's judgment, retain their validity forever. Further, one can adduce the doctrine of the eternal liturgy and intercession of Christ in heaven as confirmation of the permanent role of the humanity of Christ. Finally, the doctrine that Christ's humanity is the *instrumentum conjunc-*

tum for the bestowal of all graces also bears out this continued function of Christ's humanity.

The structure of heaven is therefore clearly christological. Beatific vision is indeed an intuitive, immediate vision of God, as traditional theology holds. But this immediacy necessarily includes the mediation that the humanity of Christ performed in history. This mediation has now become definitively valid and remains effective for all eternity. In this way Rahner has brought christology and eschatology together in strictest unity: "Jesus, the Man, not merely *was* at one time of decisive importance for our salvation, i.e. for the real finding of the absolute God, by his historical and now past acts of the Cross, etc., but—as the one who became man and has remained a creature—he is *now* and for all eternity the *permanent openness* of our finite being to the living God of infinite, eternal life; he is, therefore, even in his humanity the created reality for us which stands in the act of our religion in such a way that, without this act toward his humanity and through it (implicitly or explicitly), the basic religious act toward God could never reach its goal. One always sees the Father only through Jesus. Just as immediately as this, for the directness of the vision of God is not a denial of the mediatorship of Christ as man."[12] It remains to be seen how Rahner understands the beatific vision itself.

II. Heaven as Beatific Vision

Taking a clue from 1 Cor 13:12 ("Now we see indistinctly, as in a mirror; then we shall see face to face. My knowledge is imperfect now; then I shall know even as I am known."), traditional Thomistic theology invariably describes heaven in terms of beatific vision. The nature and conditions of such vision were a subject of much dispute in the late Middle Ages. While it was generally agreed that essential heavenly beatitude consists in the beatific vision of God, the beatific love of God, and the unspeakable and indescribable joy, it was debated whether priority should be given to the vision of the divine essence through the *lumen gloriae* (the Thomists) or to the beatific love by which God as the supreme good is loved because of himself (the Scotists). Benedict XII in 1336, as we have seen, formally defined that the blessed see the divine essence "visione intuitiva et etiam faciali." The Council of Vienne in 1312 had laid down against the Beghards and Beguines that beatific vision transcends natural human capacities and that it is made possible through the divine gift of *lumen gloriae*. Such a light is necessary, Thomas had argued,[13] because the beatific vision, being a supernatural act, requires not only an increase in natural virtue in the created intellect but also the addition of a new disposition or habit inhering intrinsically in the intellect and elevating it for the purpose of beholding God intuitively. Finally, textbook eschatology often adds that such heavenly blessedness is not equal in all the elect but is proportioned in accord with the diversity of merits; that it renders the elect impeccable and therefore cannot be lost.

1. Beatific Vision as Vision of the Trinity

Rahner discussed the question of the beatific vision in a brief article, and much of it contains the traditional doctrine given above.[14] By beatific vision Rahner means "the full and definitive experience of the direct self-communication of God himself to the individual human being when by free grace God's will has become absolute and attained its full realization."[15] In accord with traditional teaching, he underscores its supernatural and hence totally gratuitous character. Despite its gratuitousness, however, it is the fulfillment of a 'natural desire' in human beings; it is the most perfect conceivable actuation of a spiritual creature inasmuch as such a creature is absolutely open to being, truth, and value. To balance its predominantly intellectualistic flavor, Rahner insists that beatific vision possesses "the personal character of the mutual reception and self-communication as compared to purely objectivating cognition."[16]

More important, however, is Rahner's emphasis on the Trinitarian structure of beatific vision and the permanence of the absolute mystery of God in such a vision. That the beatific vision is not an intuitive insight into some abstract divine essence but rather an eternal relationship of knowledge and love to the Father in the Son by the power of the Spirit is a corollary of Rahner's theologies of revelation, grace, and the Trinity. Revelation is not a communication of a doctrine about God but God's personal self-communication. Grace is not primarily a created, ontological reality produced in the human soul but the Uncreated Grace indwelling in the human being in virtue of which he or she possesses a proper, and not merely appropriated, relationship to each person of the Trinity. And, lastly, the immanent Trinity and the economic Trinity are not two separate realities; rather, the one is identical with the other.

In light of all this, it is clear that if the beatific vision is the eschatological fulfillment of God's self-communication in revelation and in Uncreated Grace and if the God of revelation is a Trinitarian God, then the beatific vision must be a vision of the Triune being of God. Rahner warns that "the doctrine of the beatific vision must, therefore, from the start make its Trinitarian aspect clear. When reference is made to a 'sharing in the divine nature,' it must not be overlooked that this participation is necessarily triune and is given for there to be a direct relation between God and the spiritual person of the creature. It is, therefore, implied that there is a direct relation of the creature to God precisely as Father, Son and Spirit."[17]

One may inquire further, what is the nature of this direct relation between the creature and God precisely as Father, Son, and Spirit and what makes such a relation possible? Rahner's answer to these questions shows how his Trinitarian theology, anthropology, and eschatology are indissolubly linked together. It is already adumbrated in our brief summary of Rahner's view of heaven as Uncreated Grace given above. What remains to be done is to draw out the implication of this view so that not only the christological but also the Trinitarian structure of the beatific vision may be brought to the fore.

It will be recalled that the basic principle of Rahner's Trinitarian theology is that the economic Trinity is the immanent Trinity and vice versa.[18] This axiom depends on Rahner's other principle that only the Son, not the Father nor the Spirit, could be incarnated, and that the descent of the Spirit presupposes the incarnation of the Son. The incarnation of the Son and the descent of the Spirit are not, however, two events merely externally connected with one another by the bond of a decree of God the Father or two functions of two divine hypostases that might be exchanged at will. Rather, they are two necessarily connected, although utterly free, moments of the *one* self-communication of God, hence as *one* economic Trinity.

Thus, for Rahner, when God freely steps outside of himself in self-communication, it is and must be the Son who appears historically in the flesh as man. Similarly, it is and must be the Spirit who brings about the acceptance by the world of this self-communication. To differentiate these two moments of the one self-communication of God the Father, Rahner uses four couplets of terms: origin and future, history and transcendence, invitation and acceptance, knowledge and love. The first series of four terms—origin, history, invitation, and knowledge—constitutes a unity and describes the first moment of God's self-communication, namely, the Incarnation of the Son. The second series of four terms—end, transcendence, acceptance, and love—also constitutes a unity and describes the second moment of God's self-communication, namely, the descent of the Spirit. Hence, God's one self-communication, insofar as it occurs as truth, happens in history, and insofar as it happens as love, it opens up this history in transcendence toward the absolute future. As Rahner puts it, *"The divine self-communication occurs in unity and distinction in history (of the truth) and in the spirit (of love)."*[19] Because of the identity of the economic Trinity and the immanent Trinity, these two temporal 'missions' are identical with the two intra-Trinitarian 'processions'.

As a result of this, the beatific vision, while historically grounded in the Incarnation of the Son (hence, the glorified humanity of Christ continues to exercise the mediating function in the beatific vision, as we have seen above), is primarily associated with the Spirit. The work of the Spirit is to bring the process of God's self-communication in history as truth to its absolute completion as love. In this way Rahner can be said to follow the tradition of Bonaventure and Suarez in the celebrated debate between Thomists and Scotists as to whether the heavenly beatitude consists formally in the intellectual vision of God or in beatific love. But rather than arguing that the ultimate perfection of the rational creature must consist essentially in an act of the intellect and an act of the will on the basis of rational human nature, Rahner urges that the beatific vision is both an act of the intellect and of the will on the basis of the twofold modality of God's self-communication as truth and as love. As a result, the Trinitarian structure of eternal blessedness is made manifest and the connection among eschatology, christology, and, above all, pneumatology is also made evident.

Further, Rahner points out, if in the beatific vision God himself fulfills in a quasi-formal way the necessary function of a *species impressa* for cognition and if, in addition, a created ontological specification of the mind, that is, the *lumen gloriae* as perfecting the *habitus* of faith, is required, then the relationship between this *lumen gloriae* and the quasi-formal self-communication of God for the beatific vision is analogous to the relation between created grace and Uncreated Grace. Moreover, if Uncreated Grace is not the abstract divine essence but the Spirit with whom the justified possesses a proper relationship, then the link between the Spirit and beatific vision, between pneumatology and eschatology, is made even stronger. Hence, Rahner concludes, ". . . the divine self-communication, which constitutes the supernatural order of salvation in contrast to the act of natural creation, cannot and should not be considered only as the communication of an abstract essence (a divine *physis*), but as the communication of God as he is, that is, as the triune God. For it is the triune God as such who 'dwells' in the justified and who is contemplated in the beatific vision."[20]

2. Beatific Vision as Vision of the Incomprehensibility of the Mystery

Traditional descriptions of the beatific vision as an intuitive insight of the divine essence *nude, clare et aperte* and the oft-repeated contrast between faith as indistinct knowledge as in a mirror and heaven as a face-to-face encounter with God may suggest to the average believer or even to the sophisticated semirationalist that the beatific vision finally dispels the mystery of God. Rahner, perhaps more than any other contemporary theologian, has frequently warned against such misunderstanding and has made the incomprehensible mystery of God his own distinctive theme. "The beatific vision does not of course annul God's incomprehensibility. It is rather the direct experience and loving affirmation of God as incomprehensible.

This mystery is not merely the limit of finite cognition, but its positive ground and final goal, the beatitude of which consists in the ecstatic raising and merging of cognition, without suppressing it, into the bliss of love."[21]

To clarify this statement a brief summary of Rahner's theology of mystery must be provided here.[22] In Rahner's view, mystery in neo-scholastic theology is taken as the property of a *statement*, as made up of *several* individual mysteries, and as *provisionally* incomprehensible, to be dissolved in heaven. This understanding of mystery is, in Rahner's judgment, defective for three reasons. First, it is based on an extremely narrow concept of *ratio* and therefore fails to see that mystery is the very goal at which reason arrives when it attains its perfection by becoming love. Secondly, it fails to show the religious and supernatural character of the strict mysteries of Christian revelation. And, thirdly, it is unable to exhibit the intrinsic connections of the Christian mysteries with each other in a coherent whole.

Rahner's own point of departure for a theology of mystery is the mystery of human beings as implied in their knowing and willing. As we have already seen, the 'whither' of human transcendence in knowledge and love is the nameless, the indefinable, the unattainable, or the Holy Mystery. This Holy Mystery, which can never be grasped as an object, is nevertheless the condition of possibility for every act of knowing and loving of the finite subject. Human beings, in our knowledge and love, are inescapably directed toward this distant and elusive mystery. Of course, in revelation and grace, this distant mystery has bestowed itself on humanity as nearness and accessibility. However, Rahner reminds us, it is near and accessible *as* an abidingly incomprehensible mystery. Grace makes God accessible in the form of the holy mystery and presents him thus as the incomprehensible.

Consequently, the beatific vision, for Rahner, is not and cannot be a dissipation of the mystery of God. On the contrary: "God remains incomprehensible, and the object of vision is this incomprehensibility, which we may not therefore think of as a sort of regrettably permanent limitation of our blessed comprehension of God. It must rather be thought of as the very substance of our vision and the very object of our blissful love. In other words, if God is directly seen as the infinite and incomprehensible, and if the *visio beatifica* must then be the permanent presence of the inexpressible and nameless: then, since to possess the absolutely simple in its immediate presence makes it impossible to distinguish between what one comprehends of it and what one does not comprehend, vision must mean grasping and being grasped by the mystery, and the supreme act of knowledge is not the abolition or diminution of the mystery but its final assertion, its eternal and total immediacy."[23]

The knowledge of the incomprehensibility of God is the positive element constituting the beatific vision. The contrast between the knowledge of faith and the beatific vision is not between a kind of vague and confused knowledge of God and a clear and perspicuous one. Rather, it is between the merely indirect presence of the mystery as distant and the radical and absolute proximity of this mystery, which is not eliminated by its proximity but really presented as mystery. Hence, concludes Rahner, "knowledge as clarity, sight and perception, and knowledge as possession of the incomprehensible mystery must be taken as the two facets of the same process: both grow in like and not in inverse proportion."[24] Indeed, it is only when the doctrine of the direct vision of God is placed in the context of the incomprehensibility of God that it can be properly understood. The incomprehensibility of God *is* the immediate object of the vision of God in heaven. This incomprehensibility of God is not to be taken as a 'part' or 'attribute' of God that remains hidden beyond what is communicated to the human being in the beatific vision. Rather, it is God as hidden and incomprehensible that is offered directly to human vision.

To understand how the beatific vision and the incomprehensibility of God do not contradict each other, Rahner suggests that one move beyond the neo-scholastic conception of human knowledge and God's incomprehensibility. For neo-scholastic theology, God's incomprehensibility is grounded in his infinity and his freedom. Knowledge, on the other hand, is seen as a process that leads to the penetration into and mastery of the object to be known. In this context, the incomprehensibility of God appears as an unfortunate limitation imposed upon the beatific vision by God's infinity and freedom. Rahner argues that this understanding of God's incomprehensibility is seriously defective. First, it leads to a kind of 'practical atheism', that is, indifference on the part of human beings toward the mystery of God since it is something that ultimately does not concern them, even in the beatific vision. Secondly, it does not show how the beatific vision can truly be a state of fulfillment and happiness for human beings since they are ultimately and forever trapped within their finite capacity of knowledge in the face of the incomprehensible God. Thirdly, it fails to preserve the incomprehensibility of God's freedom even though ostensibly it attempts to ground God's incomprehensibility in his freedom. For, if God's free decisions remain hidden only to the extent that they are not revealed in the history of salvation and if they are not related to his intrinsic incomprehensibility, then they seem to possess no special hiddenness beyond that belonging to any free personal decision before it is made known in history. Only if the actual content of God's free decisions in relation to us consists precisely in the presence of his incomprehensibility can God's freedom be the ground for his incomprehensibility.[25]

To overcome the deficiency of neo-scholastic theology of God's incomprehensibility, Rahner urges that one should reconsider the nature of knowledge in the context of mystery. Real knowledge is not mastery and comprehension of the object. Rather, "the essence of knowledge lies in the mystery which is the object of primary experience and is alone self-evident. The unlimited and transcendent human nature . . . directs the person rather to the incomprehensible mystery, in relation to which the openness of transcendence is experienced. . . . Transcendence grasped in its un-limited breadth is the a priori condition of objective and reflective knowl-edge and evaluation. . . . Thus the experience of the nameless mystery as both origin and goal is the a priori condition of all categorical knowledge and of all historical activity; it is not merely a marginal phenomenon at the end of the road."[26] The permanence of God's incomprehensibility in the beatific vision then is not an unfortunate limitation imposed upon the finite human intellect, which is unable to master a residue of the intelligible. In comparison with such unthematic knowledge of the over-whelming mys-tery of this *deus absconditus*, the categorical mastery and comprehension of the finite objects is but a secondary and derivative form of knowledge. Failure to understand this point will prevent one from ever grasping the nature of the beatific vision: "As long as we measure the loftiness of knowl-edge by its perspicuity, and think that we know what clarity and insight are, though we do not really know them as they truly are; as long as we imagine that analytical, co-ordinating, deductive and masterful reason is more and not less than experience of the divine incomprehensibility; as long as we think that comprehension is greater than being overwhelmed by light inaccessible, which shows itself as inaccessible in the very moment of giving itself: we have understood nothing of the mystery and of the true nature of grace and glory."[27]

Ultimately the apparent conflict between the abiding hiddenness of God and the beatific vision can be resolved only if knowledge is "raised up" (*aufhebt*) into love. It is not a matter here of the dispute between Thomists and Scotists as to whether the essence of beatitude consists in the vision of the intellect or the possession of the will or in both. Rather, Rahner argues, there exists a prior and more fundamental spiritual unity in the human being that finds subsequent expression in the duality of knowledge and love. In this essential unity we are unthematically but really referred to the *one* truth, which is also the *one* mystery for us. This one truth is "the primary event of the spirit; it is the mystery which endures and unfolds and establishes the essential human capacity for truth."[28] This orientation of humankind toward the mystery is, Rahner claims, what Thomas Aquinas refers to as the human *excessus* toward the unlimited being and the incom-prehensibility of God, which is the ground of all knowing. Only if we freely accept this "excessus" toward the Holy Mystery and surrender ourselves to it can we recognize divine incomprehensibility as our own blessed fulfill-ment.

On the basis of Thomas Aquinas's teaching on the *perichoresis* of the transcendentals of being (*ens*, *verum*, and *bonum*), of his notion of *excessus*, and of the original unity of the substance prior to its subsequent unfolding into a multiplicity of faculties, Rahner offers a novel explanation of how knowledge in the beatific vision does not come to grief or give up in despair when faced with the permanent incomprehensibility of God: "Freedom and love can be seen as identical in origin with the intellect (given the 'ordo' between them), and the intellect only achieves its own fullness of being when in hope and love, in a freedom which properly belongs to it, it surrenders itself to incomprehensibility as its own beatitude."[29]

III. Hell: The Possibility of Eternal Loss

As has been remarked at the beginning of this chapter, Rahner treats of heaven as a reality, whereas he treats of hell only as a *possibility*. Each human being, in the course of his or her still ongoing history, has to reckon absolutely and up to the very end with the real possibility of reaching his or her end in a radical rejection of God and hence in eternal loss. This, according to Rahner, is everything that can and should be said about hell, and the Christian does not need to know anything more than this regarding hell. It is not surprising that Rahner's explicit writings on hell are minimal.[30] In his summary of the official teachings of the Church on hell, he notes that the Church has declared that hell 'exists', that its punishment begins immediately after death (i.e., prior to the Last Judgment), and that it lasts forever. As regards the nature of the punishment of hell, he mentions the traditional affirmation of the *poena damni* (the loss of the vision of God) and the *poena sensus* (physical pains).[31]

1. The Interpretation of Eschatological Statements About Hell

More important, however, are Rahner's reflections on the hermeneutics of statements regarding hell. First of all, he recalls that eschatological assertions are not "advance coverage" of the beyond or what is going to happen at the end of time. Rather, they are statements about the possibilities of human life based upon the present experience of grace in Christ. Secondly, concerning the biblical assertions regarding eternal punishment, Rahner suggests that they be interpreted in keeping with their literary genre of "threat-discourse."[32] They do not provide a preview of future punishment but disclose the situation in which the persons addressed presently exist. The hearers are placed before a decision, the consequences of which are irreversible. They can be lost forever if they reject God's offer of salvation. Biblical eschatological discourses on hell, therefore, attempt to shed light on the present existence of men and women before God. They reveal that human life is threatened by the real possibility of eternal self-destruction because humans freely dispose of themselves and therefore can freely reject God.

Hence, for Rahner, the various metaphors (e.g., fire, worms, gnashing of teeth, darkness, etc.) that are the stock-in-trade of apocalyptic literature and are used in eschatological discourses to describe the eternal punishment all mean the same thing: "the possibility of the human person being finally lost and estranged from God in all the dimensions of his existence."[33] Consequently, all speculations regarding the nature of fire, the place of hell, and even eternal loss are misguided since the terms are metaphors for realities radically different from our empirical world. Further, it is not possible to deduce from Jesus' judgment discourses a clear indication as to whether people are actually lost and how many may be, since these discourses are not factual descriptions but a summons to personal decision for God. For this reason, Rahner reminds us, there are no binding declarations of the magisterium on the matter, since these pronouncements are to be read in the same way as the judgment discourses of Jesus. "The Christian message says nothing about whether in some people or in many people evil has become an absolute reality defining the *final end and result* of their lives."[34] Finally, the eternity of hell should be understood not as an additional punitive measure of God's vengeance but as the consequence of the inward obduracy of human beings. It is the rejection of God's grace made final and definitive in the human history of freedom, which is the capacity to posit the definitive. The eternity of hell is God's punishment only insofar as he does not release humankind from the reality of the definitive state that we have achieved for ourselves in our free choices. Hence, it is not appropriate to use the model of vindictive punishment inflicted by political society upon the offenders of the social order to explain the nature of hell. Whether the eternity of hell is compatible with God's mercy and omnipotence will be examined in the last part of this chapter where the doctrine of *apocatastasis* is discussed.

2. The Possibility of a Free Decision Against God as an Absolute Self-Contradiction

As we have seen in the second chapter, for Rahner human freedom as the freedom to dispose of oneself is a freedom vis-à-vis the subject as a whole, a freedom for something of final and definitive validity, and a freedom that is actualized in a free and absolute "yes" or "no" to that term and source of transcendence which is called "God." It is important to note here that God as the transcendental horizon of Absolute Value is not only the condition of possibility for every human act of freedom but also the real 'object' of human freedom. In other words, human freedom can and does intend God not only as the transcendental horizon of its acts but also as its categorical 'object'; it decides about God and with respect to God himself, although always in only a *mediated* way.

But precisely here a question arises. Even in a free decision against God as a categorical 'object', human freedom still must affirm God, necessarily and inescapably, as the condition of possibility for its act of denial. Consequently, there is in the act in which freedom says "no" to God a real and absolute contradiction by the fact that God is affirmed (transcendentally) and denied (categorically, although in a mediated way, by means of the realities of this world, especially our neighbor) at the same time. Is such a self-contradiction possible? An answer to this question is of course profoundly relevant to the theology of hell, if hell is nothing but this self-contradiction made absolute and definitive. Further, if this self-contradiction is real, then the punishment of hell affects the damned in a deeply personal way, since it is not something inflicted from the outside by the vindictive justice of God but an inner destruction of the self.

Rahner is well aware of the widespread view that an offense against a concrete and merely finite object can only be an offense against a finite reality willed by God and not against God's will itself. For, so the reasoning goes, if one assumed another offense over and above the one against finite reality, one would wrongly make God's will into an individual categorical reality alongside the reality that God wills. In this view, then, human freedom cannot fall into an existential self-contradiction because it does not intend God in or beyond the finite reality that it offends.

Rahner firmly rejects this popular opinion and affirms the real possibility of an absolute self-contradiction in freedom, and this for two reasons. First, if the possibility of offending against the ultimate term of human transcendence in the offense against a finite creature does not exist, then basically there would be no real subjectivity in freedom. As Rahner puts it, "If freedom is about the subject, because the subject is transcendentality; if the individual existents within the world which encounters us within the horizon of transcendence are not events within a horizon which itself remains untouched by what is within the horizon; if rather these concrete realities are the historical concreteness of the transcendence by which our subjectivity is borne, then freedom *vis-à-vis* the individual existents which encounter us is always and also a freedom *vis-à-vis* the horizon, the ground and the abyss which allows these realities to become an intrinsic element in our freedom."[35] In other words, if the subject is borne by his or her transcendental immediacy to God, then the freedom of the subject that disposes of the subject as a whole and in a final and definitive way can occur only in a "yes" or "no" to God, and hence an offense against a finite object is necessarily an offence against God.

Secondly, if, according to Christian revelation, the ultimate term of human freedom is not merely the distant and remote horizon of the actualization of existence but has given itself in the offer of grace as the near and accessible holy mystery, then human freedom receives an immediacy to God in and through which it becomes a capacity to say "yes" or "no" to God.

Consequently Rahner concludes: "As a being of freedom, therefore, the human person can deny himself in such a way that he really and truly says 'no' to God himself, and indeed to God himself and not merely to some distorted or childish notion of God. To God himself, not merely to some inner-wordly norm of action which we rightly or wrongly call 'God's law'."[36] Of course, because we cannot objectify with perfect clarity our original, transcendental, and subjective freedom, we cannot point out with certainty where and in what act the radical "yes" and "no" has been uttered for or against God. Even though we know that human freedom is inevitably and ultimately an answer to God as the source and term of our transcendence, our actual decision for or against God is always hidden. Because the Church proclaims the victory of Christ's grace, it can and must declare that the martyrs and those who have shown by miraculous signs that they have died in grace have attained salvation. But the Church, Rahner points out, is not allowed to make a parallel affirmation about the certain and actual damnation of others, since a person's ultimate decision against God is essentially hidden.

Finally, in order to understand the nature of hell, one should remember, as we have already intimated at the beginning of this chapter, that the "no" uttered against God is not an existential-ontological possibility parallel to the possibility of the "yes" to God. Because freedom's categorical "no" to God is made possible by a transcendental "yes" to God, it constitutes an absolute self-contradiction and entails a radical destruction of the subject. This "no," and hence hell, is, says Rahner, "one of freedom's possibilities, but this possibility of freedom is always at the same time something abortive, something which miscarries and fails, something which is self-destructive and self-contradictory."[37] Hell is therefore a serious threat, and its punishment is not an arbitrary penalty imposed from without that would make the damned suffer but would leave their being intact; rather, it is a contradiction and destruction of their very nature.

IV. Apocatastasis: An Object of Hope

It is well known that the possibility of hell and especially its eternity are widely questioned, if not downright rejected, not only by non-Christian thinkers but by Catholic and Protestant theologians as well.[38] Rahner himself was particularly sensitive to the difficulties that contemporary men and women experience with regard to the doctrine of hell, in particular its eternity. If hell is eternal, any hope of the reeducation of the damned is excluded. Consequently, the only logical conclusion seems to be that God wants to punish human beings, and so we are brought face to face with a God of revenge, not the God of forgiveness and love. Further, one may ask whether there can be human guilt so great as to justify the torment and suffering of an eternal separation from God.[39]

As we have seen above, despite these difficulties, Rahner maintains the serious possibility of eternal self-loss on the basis not only of biblical and magisterial teachings but also of the dynamics of human freedom. Eternal hell is the choice of human freedom to close itself to God, made definitive and irreversible in death. This failure is not a subsequent additional punishment imposed from the outside by an angry God on the real desire of human beings for freedom but belongs to the very essence of a definitive decision of freedom. A priori, therefore, one cannot expect in hell the possibility of a radical conversion of the human will toward God and hence divine forgiveness. That is not to say that human freedom's definitive turning away from God is not the sheerest absurdity that can be imagined.

Precisely because eternal hell is such an absolute self-contradiction, Rahner often reminds his readers that eternal salvation and eternal perdition are not two parallel choices. The Christian faith, he points out, professes that the world and the human race as a whole will *in fact* enter into eternal life with God. Heartened by this conviction, Rahner wonders whether the ancient doctrine of *apocatastasis*, although condemned by the Church, can be rehabilitated in an acceptable way. As is well known, the doctrine of the restoration of all creation—including sinners, the damned, and the devils—to a state of salvation and perfect happiness was defended probably by Origen, certainly by Gregory of Nazianzus, Gregory of Nyssa, Didymus the Blind, Evagrius Ponticus, Diodore of Tarsus, Theodore of Mopsuestia, John Scotus Erigena, and other theologians of medieval and modern times. The Church's magisterium has condemned the *positive* assertion of an apocatastasis as heretical.[40] Asked by Leo J. O'Donovan what he would still like to work on at the age of seventy-five, Rahner replied: ". . . I would still really like to have written something about such a teaching on apocatastasis that would be orthodox and acceptable. But it is a very difficult matter. You would probably have to study and answer once again new questions in the history of dogma and especially also in exegesis, you would also have to consider question of exegetical and philosophical interpretation. For all that, my time and strength may not be sufficient any more."[41]

Because of these personal limitations Rahner was not able to fulfill his wish. Nevertheless, he has provided us with a few helpful insights on the question of *apocatastasis*. Fundamental to an orthodox formulation of the doctrine of universal restoration is the principle that several doctrines must be dialectically maintained at the same time. On the one hand, the universal salvific will of God (e.g., 1 Tim 2:1–6) must be upheld. On the other hand, God's justice must also be affirmed. Furthermore, genuine human freedom, even in relation to this God, must also be asserted, and therefore every human being must reckon with a real possibility of refusing assent to this God.

How these propositions can be positively reconciled is not immediately clear to us. However, to claim the right to deny any one of them on the ground that this reconciliability is not obvious cannot be justified. To affirm *apocatastasis* absolutely as a fact would be to fail to take seriously human freedom as a created capacity for definitive self-determination. A person, says Rahner, "may not abolish indiscriminately the ambiguity of his own individual history of salvation by anticipation and by holding a positive, theoretical doctrine about an apocatastasis, that is, the salvation of absolutely everybody."[42]

Moreover, God's universal salvific will is not identical with his metaphysically necessary goodness and holiness, nor is it an attribute strictly derived from this. It is rather a free attitude that is directed toward the salvation of every being and has become a manifest principle, definitively and irrevocably, in Jesus Christ. Because it is a free attitude that a person must freely accept, no one can say with certainty that he or she as an individual will freely accept it in fact.

The unavoidable uncertainty of human freedom in the matter of ultimate salvation is rooted, according to Rahner, in two factors. First, created freedom in its basic decision remains impenetrable even for the person reflecting upon it. No one can say with absolute certainty whether he or she is in the state of grace or that of mortal sin. Secondly, a person, even in his or her freedom, remains at the sovereign disposition of God. Whether and when and where human freedom accepts God's offer of salvation, this acceptance is itself an effect of the gratuitous grace of God. This is the basis of the theological distinction between merely sufficient and efficacious grace. And so the ultimate decision of each human freedom vis-à-vis God remains a mystery.[43]

On the other hand, to deny a priori the *possibility* of *apocatastasis* would be to impose arbitrary limits upon the supreme sovereignty of God's will. Human freedom is embraced by God's more powerful freedom and mercy. Although there is in the Scripture no theory of an *apocatastasis* and although no affirmation is possible on the *theoretical* plane that the antecedent will of God is in fact such that it establishes final salvation for the individual, nevertheless it is possible to hope for an *apocatastasis*. So, says Rahner, ". . . there is nothing to prevent a Christian's hoping (not knowing) that in practice the final fate of every human being, as a result of the exercise of his or her freedom by the power of God's grace, which dwarfs and also redeems all evil, will be such that hell will not in the end exist.

Christians may have this hope (first for others and therefore also for themselves) if, within their histories of freedom, they seriously consider the opposite: final damnation. In having to consider this, Christians are doubtless doing something essential to Christian existence."[44]

The ground for such hope is God's universal salvific will, which is real and efficacious. Rahner recalls that Christ died for all; that, according to Church teaching, all receive sufficient grace to avoid every formally grave sin and to attain their salvation; that it is heretical to affirm that Christ died only for the predestined or only for the believers, or that pagans, heretics, and others, outside the Church do not receive sufficient grace for salvation, or that there is positive predestination to damnation, or to sin, antecedent to the human being's own guilt.[45]

The doctrine of *apocatastasis* is then indissolubly linked with the theology of hope. Humanity encounters God's saving will not in theoretical certainty but in hope. But we can never tell ourselves with certainty whether we are really hoping except by *hoping*, that is, by taking refuge in what is beyond our control. For Rahner, hope is not a transient mode or provisional form of faith and charity but a prior medium or common factor between knowledge and will, between faith and love. Further, it is the virtue of hope that makes *apocatastasis* an acceptable and orthodox doctrine. Faith, Rahner points out, can only proclaim God's universal salvific will as a *general* principle. *This* faith as such cannot tell me as an *individual* whether God has conferred efficacious grace precisely on *me* in particular and in thus bringing about my salvation in the concrete.

Since the distinction between 'sufficient' and 'efficacious' grace is established *by God himself* prior to an individual's fault, the presence or absence of this efficacious grace does not simply depend on his or her guilt. Hence, faith in its theoretical aspects cannot by itself overcome and remove the distinction between the universal promise of salvation (sufficient grace) and the concrete and particular application of that promise to me as an individual (efficacious grace). The transformation of sufficient grace into efficacious grace occurs when God's offer of grace is personally accepted, and this happens precisely in hope. "Hope, then," says Rahner, "is the act in which we base ourselves in the concrete upon that which cannot be pointed to in any adequate sense at the theoretical level, that which ultimately speaking is absolutely beyond our power to control, namely, upon God who, in himself, can be the God of grace *or* the God of anger, but who in this case is apprehended as the God of grace and under no other aspect."[46] Hope, in this sense, is not a mere consequence of faith; the basis for such hope is not something that faith can provide, but rather something that is grasped solely by hope as such.

But if this hope for salvation is possible for me as an individual, there is no reason why it should not be extended to others, and indeed to all beings. On the contrary, Rahner argues, it is the Christian's duty to extend it first to others and then to oneself. Hence, the doctrine of *apocatastasis* is justified by the virtue of hope, not as a statement of fact, but as an object of hope and prayer.

V. Overview and Critical Questions

A retrospective glance at Rahner's theology of heaven and hell will disclose an admirable coherence between it and his hermeneutics of eschatological assertions as well as his basic theological positions. Consistent with his hermeneutics Rahner focuses on heaven as the primary reality and treats of hell only to the extent that it is a serious threat for each individual. He correctly interprets the New Testament eschatological discourses as threat-speeches illustrating the seriousness of the situation of human freedom here and now and not as descriptions of future punishments. His optimism regarding the reality of heaven mirrors his fundamental theological position, as he candidly admitted in a speech given on the occasion of his eightieth birthday: ". . . let it be admitted here, even if with some anxiety, that in my theology the topic of sin and the forgiveness of sins stands, in what is certainly a problematic way, somewhat in the background in comparison with the topic of the self-communication of God."[47]

In his discussion of the beatific vision Rahner has done a great service to theology by stressing the permanent role of Christ's glorified humanity as the medium through which the blessed enjoy the vision of God despite God's immediate self-communication to them. Also of profound importance is his insistence on the beatific vision as vision of the Trinity and as vision of the incomprehensibility of the divine mystery. In this way not only does he succeed in preserving the original unity of knowledge and love, of faith and charity, but also in maintaining the uniqueness and the abiding validity of the theological virtue of hope in heaven. Finally, on the basis of such hope Rahner is able to retrieve and reformulate the ancient doctrine of *apocatastasis* without jeopardizing the definitive character of human freedom or the seriousness of the possibility of eternal self-loss.

Despite the compact unity, tight cohesiveness, and marvelous richness of Rahner's theology of heaven and hell, a few critical questions can be asked, although not answered here. First of all, one certainly can and should share Rahner's view that contemporary men and women encounter tremendous difficulties in accepting the existence of hell and in particular its eternity. Obviously the contemporary Western mentality, nourished by the rationalism of the Enlightenment; the depreciation of the sense of personal guilt in favor of the sinfulness of social groups, classes, or structures; the radical secularization of religious eschatology in favor of an intramundance eschatology, all of these militate against the existence of hell as the punishment for personal mortal sins. Moreover, the misinterpretation of biblical texts on hell as descriptive accounts of the beyond, the cosmologization of the *eschata*, and the use of eternal damnation as a threat to control and manipulate consciences, all of these rob hell of its credibility. Finally, hell as an eternal punishment does not seem on the one hand to be compatible with God's omnipotence and infinite love; on the other hand, if one says that hell is not imposed by God but created by human freedom, hell with its absoluteness does not appear to be a proportionate product of that fragile and precarious freedom.

One cannot but admire and concur with Rahner's attempt to overcome these objections by placing the Christian discourse on hell within the context of Christ's definitive victory, of the absolute validity of human freedom, and of the importance of Christian hope. Nevertheless, one may wonder whether the scarce attention and space Rahner has dedicated to sin and hell, on the one hand, and, on the other, the strong emphasis he placed on the certainty of the salvation of the world *as a whole* as well as his speculation on *apocatastasis* (even only as an object of hope) do not lead one to make light of the threat of eternal self-loss. His repeated protests against the calculation of the number of the damned and his insistence on our ignorance of whether anyone will actually be lost at all may ironically produce another surreptitious calculation that affirms that there is and there will be no one in hell. Barth has expressed the issue with particular vigor: "The Church will not then preach an apocatastasis, nor will it preach a powerless grace of Jesus Christ or a wickedness of men which is too powerful for it. But without any weakening of the contrast, and also without any arbitrary dualism, it will preach the overwhelming power of weakness of human wickedness in face of it."[48] Has Rahner preserved this delicate balance?

Further, Rahner's interpretation of the eschatological discourse on hell as threat-speech could have been enriched by a fuller discussion of language as 'performative'. It is true that biblical statements on hell do not intend to provide information on the beyond but to urge the hearers to create something new, to accept the responsibility of their freedom before God here and now. Nevertheless, performative language does give information, not directly on the other side of life for the purpose of gratifying idle curiosity or providing mere knowledge, but indirectly insofar as it gives direct information on this side of life in the hope of provoking, confirming, or maturing a fundamental option for God. Has Rahner not down-played the indirectly informative character of the threat-speeches about hell? Does not the emphasis on the purely performative purpose of these speeches run the risk of turning them into empty play of words?

Finally, the social character of heaven and hell seems to have been left in the background. The focus of heaven appears to be on the individual's contemplation of the Trinitarian mystery in its incomprehensibility. Again, hell remains almost exclusively the threat of eternal damnation for the individual. Does the belief in hell not consist in the decision to struggle with God and in his name against every form of evil, internal and external, personal and social, individual and political?

Part III

The One Categorical Eschatology as Collective Eschatology

The Resurrection of Jesus and the
Resurrection of the Dead

> Theologically, therefore, the resurrection of Jesus is ultimately
> not an instance of a general resurrection that is intelligible in
> itself, but the unique event consequent upon Jesus' very being
> and death, an event which alone is the ground of the resurrection
> of those redeemed by him. ("Resurrection," *SM* 5:332)

With this chapter we begin our examination of Rahner's collective eschatology, that is, the final destiny of the human person as a social being, of
human history, and of the cosmos. We will focus on Rahner's understanding of the fulfillment of the whole person, namely, the resurrection of the
dead. Applying the twin canons of the transcendental method, Rahner
starts from the fact of Jesus' Resurrection as the event in the light of which
the general resurrection is to be understood. Against this backdrop he in-
vestigates the conditions of possibility for the belief in the resurrection. In
what follows we will first of all consider Rahner's transcendental reflections
on the resurrection, next his theology of the Resurrection of Jesus, and
lastly his understanding of the general resurrection of the dead.

I. Transcendental Hope in the Resurrection as the Horizon for
Experiencing the Resurrection of Jesus and the Resurrection of the Dead

If the Resurrection of Jesus and our own resurrection are to be proclaimed credibly as fundamental truths of Christianity, one must first of all
establish the a priori horizon within which these truths can become intelligible and meaningful. This horizon includes an anthropology that grasps
the human being in *totality* and does not exclude from the outset any particular element of being as of no consequence for final fulfillment.

This quest for the transcendental conditions of possibility for the belief
in the resurrection is not invalidated or rendered superfluous by the fact
that it arises only *after* the historical experience of the Resurrection of

Jesus and that a transcendental anthropology is more successfully articulated in the light of such experience. Transcendental reflections on the conditions of possibility for the belief in the resurrection, although made possible by the historical fact of the Resurrection of Jesus, will in turn illumine and deepen our understanding of the Resurrection of Jesus itself. The reciprocal hermeneutics between transcendental and categorical experience is also operative here.

If it can be established that humans possess a transcendental hope in the resurrection, then this hope is the horizon for experiencing the Resurrection of Jesus in faith and for accepting the truth of the resurrection of the dead. For when this transcendental hope is not denied or suppressed, it necessarily seeks the mediation in and confirmation by historical events in which it becomes explicit. Then it acquires the precise characteristic of an *eschatological* hope that is aroused by a fulfilled hope. Basically, then, says Rahner, "it can only be a question of whether this transcendental hope in resurrection is still simply *looking* in history to see whether it can encounter a risen one, or whether he 'already' exists and as such can be experienced in faith."[1]

But, first of all, what is meant by "body" and by the "resurrection" of the body? Body for Rahner means "the whole person in his or her proper embodied reality."[2] Resurrection, on the other hand, is "the termination and perfection of the *whole* person before God, which gives him or her 'eternal life'."[3] If this is what the resurrection of the body means, then, Rahner suggests, an act of hope in one's own resurrection is something that takes place in every person by transcendetal necessity in the mode either of free acceptance or of free rejection. This transcendental hope is grounded in the fact that every person wants to survive in some final and definitive sense and experiences this claim in his or her acts of freedom and responsibility. Freedom, we may recall, is the capacity for final and definitive self-determination before God. The hope for resurrection is the practical consequence of the nature of human freedom. In this sense resurrection is not an event that occurs in some part of human beings, that is, their bodily reality, which has been corrupted and is now restored to life. Rather, it is the abiding validity of a person's historical existence.

How can this transcendental hope be established? Rahner recalls his basic anthropology and his reflections on death and eternity. Humans look forward to a future that is their fulfillment. Because they are a unity of matter and spirit, this fulfillment cannot be simply a fulfillment of their 'soul'. Rather it must be a fulfillment of their *whole* self, as a unity of body and soul. The "resurrection of the flesh" precisely implies that "the substantial and actual unity of the human person forbids us for our part to exclude on principle certain domains of human existence, as being merely provisional, from the human fulfillment which is asymptotically striven for."[4]

When this striving toward the future fulfillment is further specified by the notion of death as the supreme act of freedom in which a person comes to a final and definitive self-determination, then it may be interpreted as the desire and hope for the eternal validity of one's historical existence. For eternity does not, as we have seen, come after the experienced time of our biological life in time and space and continue this time indefinitely. Rather, it subsumes time by being released from the time that has come to be temporarily so that the final and definitive can be achieved in freedom. In other words, eternity comes to be in time as its own mature fruit.

This desire for the eternal validity of one's entire temporal existence in freedom, which is brought about in death, is precisely the transcendental hope for the resurrection. So affirms Rahner: "If, however, despite all possible distinctions between body and soul, the fundamental premise for me and my existential experience of myself is the unity of my physical and mental existence, then for me the irrevocable claim that my existence shall be saved and acquire definitive form implies a claim to resurrection. In this connection it makes no difference in the end that I cannot imagine or portray the definitiveness of this existence as it also includes bodiliness."[5]

This transcendental hope for the resurrection, however, occurs within the history of God's self-communication in grace. Prior to any acts of knowing and willing, human subjects possess a supernatural existential that directs their acts toward the God of grace and hence toward supernatural salvation which they accept or reject. Consequently, in the historical unfolding of this supernaturally constituted hope, the possibility has to be envisaged in which the whole existence of a certain human being is perfectly fulfilled as the beginning and the ground of the fulfillment of history and is grasped in faith as such. This being can be called the "Absolute Savior" and, according to the Christian faith, is identical with Jesus of Nazareth. In his death and above all in his Resurrection, the Absolute Savior showed that his definitive identity, the identity of his bodily history, has victoriously and irreversibly reached perfection in God. At the same time, he also showed that humankind's transcendental hope for the resurrection is not an empty one since it was in fact realized in him.

On the other hand, this transcendental hope provides the context in which Jesus' Resurrection is made credible: "The transcendental experience of the expectation of one's own resurrection, an experience man can reach by his very essence, is the horizon of understanding within which and within which alone something like a resurrection of Jesus can be expected and experienced at all. These two elements of our existence, of course, the transcendental experience of the expectation of one's own resurrection, and the experience in faith of the resurrection of Jesus in salvation history, mutually condition each other."[6]

II. Jesus' Resurrection and Parousia

My intention here is not to discuss the Resurrection of Jesus or Rahner's understanding of it in general.[7] Rather it is to examine whether, in Rahner's judgment, the Resurrection of Jesus helps us understand the resurrection of the dead and, if so, why and how. Further, together with Jesus' Resurrection, I shall also consider the eschatological events that traditional textbooks on eschatology often associate with the general resurrection, namely, the Parousia and the Last Judgment, since these acts are said to be performed by the risen Christ himself.

1. The Resurrection of Jesus as the Foundation of the General Resurrection of the Dead

A. JESUS' RESURRECTION AND APOLOGETICS

Just as the transcendental hope in the resurrection is the only context for understanding Jesus' Resurrection, the latter is in its turn the only context for understanding the general resurrection of the dead. However, before explaining how Jesus' Resurrection grounds the resurrection of the dead, Rahner must contend with the apologetical question of its historicity. With the majority of contemporary biblical scholars, he points out that the primary concern of the Easter message of the New Testament is not to offer an apologetical proof of the historical fact of Jesus' Resurrection in his total and hence physical reality into glory. Nevertheless, there is no doubt that for the first disciples Jesus' Resurrection was a solid historical reality based on two experiences which fortify and illuminate one another and, even when subjected to critical exegesis, defy serious contestation: the empty tomb and Jesus' repeated appearances.

Rahner was aware, however, that an empty tomb as such and by itself can never be a conclusive proof for the fact or the meaning of Jesus' Resurrection. For resurrection, he is careful to note, is neither resuscitation of a physical, material body nor a salvifically neutral survival of human existence but "the final and definitive salvation of a concrete human existence by God and in the presence of God, the abiding and real validity of human history, which neither moves further and further in emptiness, nor perishes altogether."[8] In this sense Rahner concedes that Jesus' Resurrection can be taken to mean that his "cause" (*sache*), to use Willi Marxsen's expression, goes on after his death, provided that "cause" is not interpreted idealistically as an idea or ideology but in conjunction with Jesus' concrete existence, which has been given definitive and abiding validity before God.[9]

Furthermore, if Jesus' Resurrection is the permanent validity of his person and his cause, and if his person and cause do not simply mean that some man or other and his history go on existing but that his claim to be the Absolute Savior is victoriously vindicated and accepted once and for all, then, Rahner argues, *faith* in his Resurrection is an intrinsic element of this Resurrection itself. If Jesus' Resurrection is the eschatological victory of God's grace in the world, it cannot be conceived of without the actual free faith of the disciples in it, for it is only in this faith that it is full realized. In this sense Rahner agrees with Bultmann that "Jesus is risen into the faith of his disciples,"[10] not in the sense that the disciples' faith projects Jesus' Resurrection as its own object, but in the sense that Jesus' Resurrection would not be understood and accepted without the "faith which knows itself to be a divinely effected liberation from all the powers of finiteness, of guilt and of death, and knows itself to be empowered for this by the fact that this liberation has taken place in Jesus himself and has become manifest for us."[11]

Consequently, for Rahner, the reality of Jesus' Resurrection cannot ultimately be proved by historical facts. Indeed, the knowledge of this event is sui generis. By the very nature of the case this is the most radical instance of reciprocal conditioning of faith and motive of faith. As the fundamental eschatological event, Jesus' Resurrection is essentially an object of faith and hence is attained only in faith itself. It is not an ordinary object of experience, such as the return of a dead man to his previous biological life in time and space, which would be amenable to empirical verification by anyone endowed with adequate intelligence and good will. At the same time it is precisely in this historical event that faith finds its ground and justification. The Easter faith and the Easter experience (faith and its ground) were inseparable for Jesus' disciples themselves; the ground of faith, that is, the fact of Jesus' Resurrection, is experienced only in faith itself.

Of course, Rahner does not intend to deny that this experience had a structure nor to suggest that the disciples could distinguish the actual ground of experience from the process of experience itself or that we can somehow establish a distinction between the cause of the experience (e.g., the number of witnesses, their reliability and disinterestedness, their personal transformation, etc.) and the experience itself. Nevertheless, Rahner maintains that "the Easter experience had a unique special character absolutely incommensurable with man's other experiences, and that for this reason our relation to it cannot be classed with reports of eyewitnesses in secular matters. Without the experience of the Spirit, i.e., in this case without acceptance in faith of the meaningfulness of existence . . . trustful reliance on the Easter testimony of the disciples will not come about even though the former can in many case draw its real strength from the latter and in any case only fully attains its own nature through the latter."[12]

As a result, we believers of today have to rely on the testimony of the disciples regarding Easter in an essentially more radical way than when we accept other eyewitness accounts. We must already possess a transcendental hope in our own resurrection in order to make sense of and accept Jesus' Resurrection. What is required of us, says Rahner, is "to venture our whole existence on its being wholly directed towards God, on its having a definite meaning, on its being capable of being saved and delivered, and on precisely this having occurred in Jesus. . ., so that it is possible to believe that with regard to ourselves as the first disciples did."[13]

B. THE CHRISTOLOGICAL AND SOTERIOLOGICAL ASPECTS OF JESUS' RESURRECTION

The Resurrection has both christological and soteriological aspects. Christologically, it means that "Jesus with his whole, and therefore his corporeal, reality rose to perfect fulfillment in glory and immortality (in contradistinction to bringing back a dead man to life: Lazarus)."[14] Rahner takes care to emphasize the unity between Jesus' death and his resurrection. Although the 'temporal' interval between the two events is not to be denied, nevertheless Jesus' death and Resurrection form a single event: "The death of Jesus is such that by its very nature it is subsumed into the resurrection. It is a death into the resurrection."[15] This is so because it is precisely in and through his death in freedom and obedience that Jesus achieved the definitive, final, and permanent validity of his historical existence, that is Resurrection. Otherwise, the Resurrection would simply be a new phase following the preceding one and therefore itself temporal and transitory, and not the final fulfillment of time and history.

Furthermore, Rahner emphasizes that Jesus' Resurrection was not only an action of God the Father upon him and hence an object of his merit but also Jesus' own act, which he performed by his own power. Consequently, in his Resurrection Jesus is vindicated as the Absolute Savior or, more cautiously, as the final prophet, that is, the historical presence of the final and unsurpassable word of God's self-disclosure.

Moreover, since Jesus' bodily humanity is a permanent part of the world, his Resurrection is soteriologically and objectively the beginning of the glorification of the world: the final consummation of the world has been decided in principle and has already begun. Rahner objects to the common notion that Jesus' Resurrection is not a morally meritorious cause of our redemption because, it is alleged, in itself it is not a free moral action of the man Jesus. He points out that Jesus' Resurrection is an element in a single event in which his death, as we have seen above, is the first phase constituting the actual Resurrection itself. Furthermore, even if one does not consider Jesus' Resurrection as the meritorious cause of our redemption, still it is possible to regard his humanity, including his corporeal nature, as the instrumental cause of our salvation.[16] On this basis the soteriological significance of Jesus' Resurrection and of the risen Lord would have to be rethought afresh. Indeed, since Jesus' corporeal humanity is a permanent part of the world with its single dynamism, Rahner maintains that Jesus' Resurrection is not only in the ideal order an 'exemplary cause' of the resurrection of all but objectively is the beginning of the ontological transfiguration of the world.

Further, if every supernatural communication of God to a created spirit in grace and vision is an element of God's personal self-communication to the world in the hypostatic union, and if such process of divine self-communication in history is only fully accomplished in the definitive fulfillment of Jesus' existence, namely, in his Resurrection, then, Rahner argues, one can understand why Jesus not only de facto and by a certain extrinsic suitability is the first to rise from the dead to the definitive state of glory but must necessarily be the first to do so.

By his Resurrection and Ascension Jesus did not merely enter into a preexistent heaven; rather, his Resurrection created heaven for us. In this way, it is clear that by his Resurrection Jesus became the pledge and the beginning of the fulfillment of the world, the representative of the new cosmos, the bestower of the Spirit, the head of the Church, the dispenser of the sacraments, and the heavenly mediator of the beatific vision.[17] In other words, Jesus' Resurrection is the meritorious, exemplary, and instrumental cause of our own resurrection from the dead.

2. *Christ's Parousia and the General Judgment*

The Hellenistic term *Parousia* means the arrival, visit, and presence of armies, officials, rulers, and gods. In the New Testament the word is sometimes used to designate the eschatological coming of Jesus. Here we are concerned only with what has been inappropriately referred to as the "Second Coming" of Christ or what the Creed professes when it says that Jesus "shall come again in glory to judge the living and the dead."

In the Synoptic Gospels the Parousia is described as the coming of the Son of Man in glory (the glory of the Father) with the angels (Mt 16:27; 25:31; Mk 8:38; Lk 9:26), as a coming on the clouds with power and glory (Mt 24:30; 26:64; Mk 13:26; 14:62; Lk 21:27). The time of the Parousia is said to be indefinite and is known to no one, not even to the Son of Man himself (Mt 24:36; Mk 13:32). Therefore, continuous vigilance is urged upon the disciples.

In Paul, the Parousia or the Day of our Lord Jesus Christ is the hour of the resurrection of the dead; the righteous will join him in glory in the clouds and the living will be snatched up in glory (1 Co 15:23; 1 Th 4:13; Col 3:4). The same conception appears in the Catholic letters, although less frequently (Js 5:7–9; 1 Pt 4:7). The Parousia is also called the revelation (*apokalypsis*) and the appearance (*epiphaneia*) of Jesus Christ. It is the time of judgment, a revelation of the glory of Jesus.[18] How does Rahner understand Christ's Parousia and the universal judgment?

A. CHRIST'S PAROUSIA

For Rahner, Christ's Parousia is "the permanent blessed presence of Christ in the manifest finality of the history of the world and of salvation which is perfected and ended in the destiny of Jesus Christ. It is the fullness and the ending of the history of humankind and of the world with the glorified humanity of Christ—now directly manifest in his glory—in God."[19] Of course, with the Ascension, Christ's physical presence is no longer accessible to us as it was for his disciples before his death.[20] Nevertheless, because Christ, freed by his Resurrection from the limiting individuality of his unglorified body, has in truth become present to the world, his Parousia will only be the public disclosure of this relation to the world that he obtained by his Resurrection. It is "the consummation of history (Jesus Christ's and the world's) in God, who will be directly revealed in his glory."[21] In his Parousia, Christ is revealed as the source and support, the central meaning and climax of the process of God's transfiguring self-communication, which human beings definitively either accept or reject and hence are saved or damned. As a consequence, Christ's Parousia is also his act of judgment upon human history, the definitive crystallization and manifestation of the eternal results of history.

Since Christ's Parousia as the consummation of the whole history of humanity and of the world is still lying in the future in a genuine, even 'worldly' temporal order, Rahner suggests that the belief in the Parousia must affect the nature and mission of the Church. The Church must be "the community, called together by God's grace in Jesus Christ, of those who in hope and love believe in the Parousia of Christ as still to come."[22] The faith that hopefully awaits Christ's return is not merely something which the Church teaches and mediates to individual Christians for their individual salvation but is a constitutive element of the Church as such. It makes the Church essentially eschatological, that is, a community of those who hope, of pilgrims who are still marching toward their home-land, of those who understand their present in terms of the future fulfillment.

Hence, the Church must always understand itself as still provisional, as still looking for its fulfillment, which does not lie in itself but in the kingdom of God. Rahner warns that the Church ought never to misunderstand itself to the extent of thinking that its present form is the ultimate one, or that its historical dimension affects in the last analysis only the individual for whom it is the means of salvation, or that while its present form will one day pass away, namely, at the Parousia, yet between Pentecost and Parousia it has no history. Of the relationship between this eschatological community and this-worldly future hope and utopias we will speak at greater length in the next chapter.

B. THE LAST JUDGMENT

As has been mentioned above, for Rahner Christ's Parousia includes as its intrinsic moments both the resurrection of the flesh and the universal judgment. In Christ's Parousia the completion of the whole history of the world's freedom is made radically manifest. This consummation is called the judgment of *God* because it is not simply the result of a development immanent in the world but depends on the sovereign discretion of God who determines its end. It is called the judgment of *Christ* because its ultimate character is essentially determined by the nature and work of Jesus Christ owing to the christocentrism of all reality in all its dimensions. It is called the *general* judgment because it embraces all humans, good and evil, in their mutual relationships and their ultimate destinies. And, finally, it is called the *last* judgment because it is the definitive consummation that concludes history.[23]

Rahner is concerned to stress the unity between the general and particular judgment. The human being is both spirit and matter, a unique individual and a social being, and not reducible to any of his or her two components (body and soul). Hence, in principle the consummation of this one human being can only be expressed in two series of indissociable dialectical affirmations corresponding to the indissoluble dialectical unity of the two constitutive elements in the human being. These affirmations constitute individual eschatology and collective eschatology. Consequently one has to speak of both particular judgment *and* general judgment.

Rahner rejects both the modern trend to retain only an individualistic eschatology through demythologization and the tendency to pass over personal eschatology in favor of the cosmic one. Neither attempt does justice to the unity of human beings and our consummation since we are not divisible into parts even though we are multidimensional. As regards the two judgments, Rahner holds that there can be no justifiable attempt—or demand—to indicate neatly and clearly which particular elements in the consummation of the individual belong to one or the other of two definitely distinct events, separable in time and unrelated to one another. The consummation of the human being as a social being and part of the world (the 'resurrection of the flesh', for instance) is a moment of the consummation of his or her uniqueness. Even as spirit the individual is only fulfilled in this event. And the consummation of the individual as his or her own very self (the vision of God, for instance) is a moment of the history of the cosmos. This fundamental relationship between what is distinct and still not adequately divisible in the statements of universal and individual eschatology also holds true for the general and particular judgment.[24]

Lastly, according to Rahner, Christ's Parousia to judge the living and the dead is the revelation of God's love. Rahner recalls the important hermeneutical principle according to which eschatological assertions are not anticipatory reports of future events, but the reading from the present out into its mode of future fulfillment. Hence hardly anything more concrete can be said with certainty about Christ's Parousia and the universal judgment than what Rahner has already said about them above. What can be held certain is that "God judges the world in an act of love which fetches home all that will let itself be fetched home, and which bestows this very will according to a disposition as yet unknown to us but revealed at the Parousia of Christ, with its purpose again centered on Jesus Christ."[25]

III. Immortality of the Soul and/or Resurrection of the Body?

1. Immortality of the Soul and Resurrection of the Body: Two Complementary Truths

Together with Christ's Parousia and the universal judgment, the resurrection of the dead is an article of Christian creed. It is well known, as the work of Cullmann has shown, how this belief in the resurrection of the flesh was obscured for centuries by Greek depreciation of the body and individualistic concern for the salvation of the soul. The emphasis was shifted from the resurrection of the body to the immortality of the soul. In Cullmann's judgment, the biblical belief in resurrection, based upon the concept of salvation history, is just as different from the Greek notion of the immortality of the soul as is the death of Christ from the death of Socrates. For the first Christians, the soul was not immortal by nature but became so only in virtue of the Resurrection of Christ, "the first-born from the dead."[26] How does Rahner understand these two distinct strands of thought, Hebrew-Christian and Greek? Are they mutually incompatible, as Cullmann says, or are they different formulations of the same truth, the resurrection of the body logically implying the immortality of the soul, as Harry A. Wolfson and Joseph Ratzinger seem to think?[27]

In our discussion of Rahner's theology of death, mention was made of his theory of the pancosmicity of the soul as his attempt to overcome the Platonic dualism between body and soul. With it Rahner also intends on the one hand to retain the doctrine of the immortality of the soul, which was defined by the Fifth Lateran Council in 1513, and on the other hand to give due recognition to the dogma of the resurrection of the flesh.[28] Precisely because the human soul is immortal it survives death and continues to be related to the cosmos. Further, because it continues to be pancosmic it does not lead a separated existence (the *anima separata* in the intermediate state) but already begins to exist in the risen state. One of the fundamental assertions of Rahner's anthropology is the substantial unity of body and soul, the soul being the *forma corporis*. He points out that "flesh" in Scripture does not mean the body as distinct from the soul, but the whole human being in its entire, bodily and spiritual, reality. Hence, the resurrection of the flesh is not understood as the final destiny of the body as such but "the destiny of the one and total person who as such *is* "flesh'."[29]

As we have seen in the first part of this chapter, Rahner holds that there exists in every human spirit a transcendental hope for the resurrection. He also indicates some concrete experiences in which this transcendental hope is realized. In his interpretation of eternity he has already singled out three ways in which we can have an inkling of eternity in time: the experience of change in which the changing phenomena replacing one another are manifestations of a permanent, persisting reality; the mental experience that combines past, present, and future into a unity; and the experience of free decision.[30]

These experiences of eternity are also for Rahner confirmation of the immortality of the soul, for the latter is simply another term for the human capacity for definitive self-determination: "Humans are immortal, not as though their biological life had no finite temporal form ending in death, but because within this very biological time they freely perfect themselves as spiritual persons and for this reason give up their spatio-temporal form (of their own accord, even though this task is accomplished against the resistance of biological life and by eternal causes)."[31] Of course, human immortality is rooted in the 'soul', which is a substantial, 'supramaterial' principle whose function is for Rahner more than that of merely shaping and informing a temporal and material being. Rather, its function is to fashion in freedom the human being's eternal destiny, either in salvation or in damnation, or, to put it in another way, to enable humans to share in the absolute, i.e., metaphysically necessary immortality proper to God alone.

Having identified immortality with eternity and resurrection of the flesh, Rahner goes on to inquire whether the experiences of immortality belong to nature or grace. His view is that it is not necessary to differentiate too sharply in reflection between what in these experiences belongs to the human being's spiritual and immortal nature, and what to grace. One can simply assume that "the experience [of immortality] draws its power and its life from that supernatural self-communication of God in grace which gives the eternity-making act of moral freedom its ultimate and radical depths."[32] Here the mutually conditioning relationship between the transcendental experience of grace and the experience of salvation history applies. Once the transcendental experience of our eternal validity as moral persons has occurred, it is natural for us to inquire whether it has not become concrete in and confirmed by the categorical experience of salvation history. And, of course, since we ourselves still have to die, this confirmation cannot be obtained except in the experience of the final and definitive fulfillment of another person.

As to the specific question of whether one should maintain either the immortality of the soul or the resurrection of the body, Rahner, on the basis of his integral anthropology, holds that we are neither justified nor obliged to split human beings into two components, 'soul' and 'body', and affirm a definitive fulfillment only for one of them. Hence, says Rahner, "our question about man's definitive validity is completely identical with the question of his resurrection, whether the Greek and Platonic tradition in Church teaching see this clearly or not."[33] This presupposes, of course, that the resurrection of the body is not taken to mean a return to space and time, which by definition is the realm where personal freedom comes to be and not the arena for the final achievement of such freedom.

On the basis of the fundamental unity of matter and spirit in human beings Rahner defends both the Greek doctrine of the immortality of the soul and the biblical teaching on the resurrection of the body. Unlike Oscar Cullmann and Philippe H. Menoud, he does not see them as incompatible with each other but as mutually illuminating: "In the Christian doctrine proposed by the Church of the 'immortality of the soul' and of the 'resurrection of the flesh' the whole man in his unity is always envisaged. This affirmation does not deny or call into doubt that there is a differentiation intrinsic to the definitive state of man which corresponds to the justifiable distinction of 'body' and 'soul' in his make-up. But if, as cannot be doubted, the 'resurrection of the flesh' in the creed of the Church means the definitive salvation of man as a whole, then the doctrine of the immortality of the soul, being a truth of faith and not just a philosophical tenet, is also concerned in fact with such a life, such a 'soul' as for instance Jesus placed in the hands of his Father as he died. Hence this assertion is also directed to the *whole* reality and meaning of man as he depends on the creative and life-giving power of God, *whereby* of course it refers also to what the philosophers as such may call soul in contrast to body, not a destiny which he may try to trace after death."[34]

This identification between the immortality of the soul and resurrection of the body on the basis of the definitive character of human freedom does not imply that both doctrines have the same connotations. Rather, they have distinct but complementary meanings. The doctrine of the immortality of the soul affirms that our existence possesses a destiny that goes beyond biological life, whereas the resurrection of the flesh emphasizes that such destiny involves human existence in its wholeness, including its bodily and material dimension. As has been shown in chapter 5, Rahner maintains that the doctrine of the intermediate state is not a defined dogma but a cultural amalgam to express the immediacy of eternal retribution after death and the future glorification of human beings in their entire reality, body and soul.

As a corollary Rahner suggests the possibility of an immediate resurrection after death.[35] This theory has been proposed by a number of theologians, e.g., Joseph M. Shaw, Russell Aldwinckle and Ladislaus Boros.[36] Rahner has not elaborated a detailed defense of this theory; he simply put it forward as a nonheretical possibility. But in this connection there are at least two issues that Rahner must deal with: what is the nature of the risen body and what is the purpose of the general resurrection of the dead if there is already an immediate resurrection of each person after death?

2. The Risen Body and The General Resurrection

A. THE RISEN BODY AND ITS LOCATION

Textbook eschatology often revels in speculating on the relationship between the present body and the risen body: Are they different or identical, and, if identical, is this identity specific or numerical or both? And in what does this identity consist? Is the identity of the soul or form sufficient, as Durandus or Billot opine? Or should the risen body be composed partly at least of the same matter collectively that it formerly consisted of, as many theologians think along with Thomas Aquinas? Furthermore, traditional eschatology takes delight in supplying explicit descriptions of the qualities of the risen body; these descriptions speak of its impassibility, splendor, agility, and subtility.

Rahner was of course aware of all these theological discussions, yet in dealing with these issues he showed remarkable moderation and restraint. This is so because methodologically eschatology for him is not a reportorial description of the afterlife but a reading from the present condition of salvation into its future mode of fulfillment on the basis of what has occurred in Jesus Christ.

Regarding the question of the identity between the present body and the risen body and in what this identity consists, Rahner maintains that there should be an identity between the present body and the risen, glorified body, but that such an identity cannot consist in having some material fragment or particle of the earthly body found again in the glorified body. Such identity is impossible for two reasons. First, there is no identity of particles

or cells even in the physical body during its lifetime due to its radical metabolic processes. Secondly, this kind of identity presupposes a conception of
matter according to which it can be split up into so many 'substantial' or
clearly divisible particles, a notion no longer acceptable to modern physics.
For Rahner the identity of the form consists, now and in the future, "of the
identity of the free, spiritual subject, which we call 'the soul'. That is why
even empirical experience of the corpse in the grave can no longer provide
an argument for there having been no 'resurrection'."[37]

What Rahner intends to affirm in the last, somewhat provocative statement, is not that risen persons have no bodies or exist in a bodiless, im-
material state. Rather he wants to emphasize that the resurrection is not a
revivification of the body and a return to the former life but the definitive
validity of one's history of freedom (the 'soul') before God. Such history of
freedom includes, of course, the body, but the identity of the person does
not consist in having the same earthly body or some part of it but in the
same history of freedom now made definitive and eternal by death.

Because the earthly body is part of the history of freedom that is made
definitive, it too participates in the resurrection. Pressed to describe more
exactly the nature of the risen body and its location, Rahner notes that it is
impossible for us who are still imperfect to form an idea of what has been
brought to perfection. For even the risen Christ, he points out, did not
show his glorified bodily condition "as it is in itself" but only "as it is for
us": "what the Apostles saw and touched of the Risen One himself is his
'flesh and bone,' as he himself said; and yet this was necessarily in the
manner in which something glorified can appear to the unglorified, it was
an appearance 'for us' which permits us to say little about him 'as he is in
himself.'"[38] This inability to form an idea of the glorified body was already
intimated by Paul when he insisted that an absolutely radical transformation of our bodily condition (our 'flesh and blood') is necessary so that we
may be able to inherit the Kingdom of God.

In the last analysis, Rahner remarks, all we really know of the risen body
can be stated only from the 'outside', from two points of view: "We
ourselves shall be in this condition, we with all the reality we had and all
our experience; and again, we shall be transformed, be quite different."[39]
In describing therefore the nature of the risen body one cannot but use
the language of paradox, which Paul himself has employed: "It will be a
spiritual body (1 Cor 15:44), i.e. a true bodily nature which, however, is
pure expression of the spirit become one with the *presence* of God and its
bodily existence, and is no longer its restricting and abasing element and its
emptiness. It will be a bodily nature which does not cancel again the freedom from the earthly here-and-now gained with death, but will, on the
contrary, bring it out in its pure form."[40]

As to the location of the risen body, it is well known that it has often been represented in popular imagination as a superior region ("heaven"), a spatial setting of the cosmos which existed even before Jesus' Resurrection and toward which the glorified bodies ascend (the "ascent into heaven"). Since this imaginative representation is no longer credible, contemporary theologians prefer to speak of heaven as a state. But because eternal happiness includes also the bodily dimension, although in its glorified condition, theologians are forced to speak of heaven as some kind of spatial location, although they insist that it is impossible to say 'where' it is.

Rahner finds this reticence commendable but unfortunate, because it tacitly suggests that heaven, however indefinite its location, is still a portion of this physical world of space, something infinite and in itself homogeneous with which we are acquainted as the space of our experience. To gain a better idea of the location of the risen body Rahner suggests that we conceive of space as a function of time rather than the reverse as the ancients did when they imagined that space is something *in* which a historical event happens.

Today, on the contrary, we think of 'space' and 'place' as arising through the happening of historical events in time; space is rather a function of time. Because of the radical event of transforming glorification of the body, a new kind of space emerges that is no longer a portion, however unlocalizable, of space as we know it but is incommensurable with it. Hence we cannot imagine it but have to postulate it as the necessary condition of the bodily resurrection, which cannot be dissipated by a false spiritualization. So, says Rahner, "the new 'spatiality' is a function of having history, of the time which *shapes* this space; it comes to be by the face of Christ's rising from the dead, and it is not given in advance as the possibility and the plea of this glorified state."[41]

It is the Resurrection of Jesus that created a new 'space', namely, heaven. In this way, one does not, on the one hand, ask the senseless question of 'where' heaven is (if by this 'where' we understand a location in our physical spatial world), and, on the other hand, one does not deprive heaven of 'place' by the mere fact that one is unable to accommodate it in a '*caelum empyreum*' by a homogeneous extension of the world of our experience. This new 'place' was created by Christ's glorified body; in Christ's Resurrection the world acquired a new mode of being, a new 'heavenly' dimension: not a 'fourth' dimension added to the three previous ones, but one that is incommensurable with the world and yet ontologically connected with it.

Two consequences, in Rahner's judgment, follow from this: First, there will be not only a new heaven but also a new earth, and the new earth will be no other than the perfection of the 'heaven' that will have wholly and exhaustively transformed into itself and its mode of being the reality of the world. Secondly, we may grant that the new heaven and the old earth are radically and necessarily connected. The heavenly form of existence does indeed involve a migration from the mode of being proper to 'flesh and blood', the earthly perishable manner of being characteristic of the body and its environment, under the sentence of death; but it does not involve a migration from the world itself.[42] And if the new heaven does not mean a movement away from this world, then it cannot be conceived as lacking all cosmic bonds with this as yet unglorified world, which objectively coheres with the glorified reality and is really capable of being used to express it, even though not by means of the same limited spatial categories.

B. THE GENERAL RESURRECTION OF THE DEAD

If the immediate resurrection after death can be entertained as at least a nonheretical possibility, must one still hold that there will be a general resurrection of the dead at the end of time? If so, what is its purpose and meaning? Is it not made redundant by an immediate or initial resurrection right after death? Rahner believes that it is not and suggests that its possibility be seen in the context of the plural or multidimensional character of human nature, and especially of humankind's historicity and permanent relation to the cosmos (his pancosmicity).

It is true that humans achieve an immediate and definitive union with or separation from God in death and *in this sense* are already risen from death. Nevertheless, human beings in their unity are yet something plural, existing in various dimensions (matter-spirit, individual-social, etc.) and therefore do not achieve their perfection in all dimensions at once. Further, the world to which the dead are permanently related owing to the pancosmicity of their souls still pursues its course so that their perfection cannot be said to be complete until the world and all the history of human freedom come to an end. Rahner recalls that the personal spirit, which constitutes the meaning of the world, is not a strange guest in the world; rather, precisely as human spirit, it is a material, incarnate, and intramundane spirit. Consequently, the physical world is the connatural surrounding of the fulfilled spirit whose perfection coincides with that of the world itself. "The end of the world," says Rahner, "is, therefore, the perfection and total achievement of saving history which had already come into full operation and gained its decisive victory in Jesus Christ and in his resurrection."[43]

The general resurrection of the dead is not therefore made superfluous by the immediate resurrection of each individual person after death, since this immediate resurrection only attains its fullness at the end of the world and especially at Christ's Parousia. The general resurrection does not mean another resurrection for each individual person; rather, it is the vindication and glorious manifestation of Christ's lordship over history and the cosmos. His "Second Coming" coincides with the total achievement of human beings, in their body and soul, and their perfection, already begun in death, becomes itself perfected, tangible in the world, embodied: "His Second Coming takes place at the moment of the perfecting of the world into the reality which he already possesses now, in such a way that he, the Godman, will be revealed to all reality and, within it, to every one of its parts in its own way, as the innermost secret and center of all the world and of all history."[44] Of the relationship between this eschatological, transcendent consummation of the world and the intramundane, temporal achievements and utopias of human beings we will speak at greater length in the next chapter.

IV. Recapitulation and Evaluation

Rahner's theology of the Resurrection of Jesus and the general resurrection of the dead is the result of a brilliant deployment of the transcendental method. Starting from a deep-rooted faith in the historical event of Jesus' Resurrection, Rahner seeks to correlate that object and ground of faith with the human experience of time, freedom, death, and eternity. Human beings experience time as the opportunity for freedom and responsibility, which in turn demand definitiveness and eternal validity. There is therefore in every act of freedom a transcendental hope not only for the immortality of the soul but also for total personal permanence, including the bodily dimension of personhood. This hope for eternal validity of one's history can be called the transcendental hope for the resurrection. But if definitiveness and eternal validity are achieved only in death, then there is an intrinsic connection between death and resurrection. In this way Rahner has accomplished several important things and contributed valuable insights to the theology of Jesus' Resurrection.

First, he has offered a new and valuable apologetical approach to the Resurrection of Jesus. In neo-scholastic apologetics the Resurrection of Jesus became almost exclusively the ground for faith supported by the extrinsic proofs of the appearances and above all of the empty tomb. But since modern historical-critical method has shown that the empty tomb did not in itself cause the disciples' belief in the Resurrection and that the traditions regarding the early discovery of the empty tomb are later literary texts (even though these probably contain historically reliable information), the edifice of traditional fundamental theology was deprived of its supporting pillar.[45] It is here that Rahner comes to the rescue by showing that the Resurrection of Jesus is not only the ground of faith (the basis or proof of what is believed) but also the object of faith (what is to be believed) or, more precisely, that it grounds faith primarily as an object of faith, grounding it not apart from faith but only *in* faith.

With this existential approach to the Resurrection of Jesus, i.e., placing it within the wider context of the transcendental hope for the resurrection, Rahner radically shifted the focus and probative force of the empty tomb and the appearances to the disciples. Whereas in traditional fundamental theology these were the main argument for the claim of Christianity, now they possess only a secondary function. Even for the disciples themselves, Jesus' Resurrection was both the ground and object of faith, just as it is for us, although it must be admitted that their faith in Jesus' Resurrection is a ground for our faith because their witness is prior to and the condition of possibility for our experience of Jesus' Resurrection. With this indirect method Rahner is thus able to circumvent the difficulties presented by the historical-critical method.

Secondly, by emphasizing that Jesus' Resurrection is an object of faith Rahner was able to retrieve the patristic or medieval conviction (e.g., that of Thomas Aquinas) that Jesus' Resurrection is not primarily the miracle demonstrating the truth of Christianity but the basic mystery of faith. He could therefore develop at great depth the christological and soteriological aspects of Jesus' Resurrection, which were almost totally neglected in neo-scholastic theology.

Thirdly, Rahner has drawn out more explicitly than his predecessors the intimate connection between Jesus' Resurrection (and Parousia and Last Judgment) and the general resurrection of the dead. In his brilliant and original interpretation of heaven as 'place', he shows that heaven is not something existing prior to Jesus' Resurrection and into which he ascended; rather, it is a 'space' created by Jesus' Resurrection itself. If this is so, then it becomes much clearer how and why Jesus did not happen as it were by accident to be the first being to rise from the dead but *must* be the first so that all other human beings can rise from the dead. In this matter Rahner closely follows the early church fathers, who insisted on relating Jesus' Resurrection to the Christian belief in the future resurrection from the dead.

Finally, by interpreting the resurrection of the body as the definitive and final validity of a person's history of freedom (and hence Jesus' Resurrection not so much as a physical fact as his entry into the permanent fulfillment and culmination of his life), Rahner is able to provide a unifying and tightly coherent view of temporality, freedom, death, eternity, immortality of the soul, and resurrection of the body. In particular, he is able to perform a rapprochement between the Greek conception of the immortality of the soul and the biblical belief in the resurrection of the body without jeopardizing and richness of either.

These achievements, besides many others that must go unmentioned here, are certainly impressive. But there is a nagging question of whether Rahner could achieve such a coherent and brilliantly executed synthesis precisely because he had made matters too easy for himself by giving an existential interpretation of the resurrection. In other words, is his understanding of the resurrection as the permanent validity of one's historical freedom fully adequate? How does it differ from death? Does the resurrection of the *flesh* add anything new to Rahner's notion of death as we have expounded it? Is Pannenberg right in reproaching Rahner for being too close to Bultmann in connecting Jesus' death and Resurrection?[46]

Another way of expressing this objection is to ask whether Rahner has distinguished with sufficient clarity between truth and meaning. In contrast to traditional fundamental theology, which insisted on the historical fact of the empty tomb as the proof for the truth of Jesus' Resurrection and hence of Christianity, Rahner underscores the meaningfulness of the Resurrection in its intrinsic revelatory significance. The Resurrection is meaningful as an existential affirmation and as a historical manifestation of the achievement of decisive and eternal validity of one's life. Of course, this approach does not deny the facticity of the Resurrection, but it certainly leaves it in the background.

Hermeneutically, it may be asked, as we have asked in chapter 3, whether Rahner has not favored *Sinngebung* over *Auslegung*. Despite the fact that Rahner repeatedly reminds us that the resurrection is the fulfillment of human beings in their entirety, including their bodily dimension, and despite his valiant attempt to retain heaven as a space (not commensurable with our physical space), one can hardly overcome the impression that his interpretation of the resurrection does not allow him to give a full account of the corporeal quality of the risen body. In this connection his obiter dictum that the presence of a corpse in the tomb does not of itself disprove the resurrection is a significant clue to his conception of the nature of the glorified body. And one may wonder whether his refusal to describe the risen body stems more from his inability to conceive the full bodiliness of the risen people than from his hermeneutics of eschatological assertions.

This criticism seems a bit odd when directed against a thinker like Rahner who continually insists on human beings as a unity of matter and spirit. My point is not to question his integral anthropology; rather, my concern is whether his understanding of the resurrection fully embodies his anthropology.

The Immanent and Transcendent
Consummation of the World

Christian eschatology must also develop a theology of the relationship between Christian existence and projected this-worldly
utopias. Just as Christianity, as a result of its unique understanding of the world, has emancipated from itself a secular world so
that the latter may grasp its freedom and its own significance,
so too, from the position of its own eschatological view of the
future, Christianity must allow a this-worldly vision of the future
to emerge legitimately from within. ("The Historicity of Theology," *TI* 9:74)

The title of this chapter, borrowed from one of Rahner's articles on the
relationship between Christian eschatology and inner-worldly utopias,
indicates the main themes to be treated in the following pages.[1] As the
exergue makes clear, it is appropriate in a discussion of collective eschatology to raise the question regarding the exact relationship between
Christianity's expectation of the Kingdom of God—that is, Christians'
awaiting of the Absolute Future which is God himself—and the inner-
worldly tasks and achievements of individuals, peoples, nations, historical
epochs, and, finally, of the human race as a whole.

As has been shown in chapter 1, there was in Rahner's eschatology a
homogeneous and gradual movement from a transcendental, interpersonal, and existential perspective to a more sociopolitical viewpoint. Rahner's
later writings, especially those written after the Second Vatican Council
and under the impact of political and liberation theologies, returned insis-
tently to the themes of the relationship between Church and world and of
the mission of Christians in the increasingly secularized and militantly
atheistic world. My intention here is not to examine Rahner's theology of
the Church and of the world in general;[2] rather, the focus is on the relationship between these two realities and especially the interplay between
their eschatological fulfillments. We will first of all study Rahner's view of
the relation between Church and world and secondly the relation between
the immanent and the transcendent consummation of human history.

180

I. Kingdom of God, Church, and World

The controlling metaphor of biblical eschatology, in both the Old and New Testaments, is neither Church nor world, but the Kingdom or reign of God (or "Kingdom of heaven"). It is therefore only against the background of the biblical notion of the Kingdom of God that the eschatological consummation of Church and world can rightly be understood.[3] By the same token, in order to grasp Rahner's view of the relationship between Church and world it is necessary to investigate his understanding of the Kingdom of God.

1. The Kingdom of God: God as the Absolute Future

By "Kingdom of God" Rahner understands, as most Christian theologians do, the full and perfect manifestation of "a free, unmerited and forgiving and absolute self-communication of God."[4] This divine self-communication takes place in history; by participating in it, all beings are healed and transformed by Jesus Christ through the power of the Holy Spirit.

This Kingdom of God is transcendentally present in the mode of offer throughout human history and constitutes a 'supernatural existential' in human beings.[5] In other words, antecedent to their entrance into the Kingdom of God by means of justifying grace, received sacramentally or extra sacramentally, or to their exclusion from it through culpable denial of grace, human beings are already inescapably subject to the universal, efficacious saving will of God. This offer of God's self-communication is supernatural because it is unmerited and absolutely gratuitous, and it is an existential because it is not an extrinsic but an intrinsic and real modification of human beings and their consciousness. In terms of revelation, it can be called *transcendental* revelation. But because humans are historical beings, this transcendental revelation cannot and does not exist apart from history; rather, it must necessarily be expressed in and mediated by history.[6]

Throughout history humanity has attempted to objectify this unthematic, indirect self-revelation of God in propositions and rituals of various religions. This history of reflection forms an intrinsic part of the historical process of God's self-disclosure in grace, of the history of the coming of his Kingdom. This reflection can be called (historical) *general* revelation and is carried out by those we call prophets, bearers and interpreters to others of God's revelation.[7] However, because of sin, which obscures and corrupts human understanding and actions, this interpretation is marred by errors and culpable ignorance and is therefore only partially successful.

In this history, which is coexistent, although not identical with, the history of salvation, above and beyond humankind's religious self-interpretation in various religions, God also directed, in a particular segment of universal history, a specific interpretation of his offer of grace. Through "prophets" authenticated by him by means of "signs and wonders," this interpretation is assured to be infallibly correct and unfailingly accpted, not only by individuals as such but also by a community of people. In this way his Kingdom is guaranteed of ultimate victory. In terms of revelation, this self-communication of God can be called (historical) *categorical* or *special* revelation.[8]

This special revelation is acknowledged by Christians to have occurred in the history of Israel and to have been recorded in its writings that they call Old Testament. The Kingdom of God is already present in the history of Israel in a tangible and visible manner, interpreted mostly in terms of a covenant between God and his people. This history is permanently valid for Christians, because on the one hand this history and no other is the immediate, concrete prehistory of the Incarnation of the Logos as the history of revelation, and because on the other hand the New Testament revelation is already to be discerned in it. However, this phase of salvation, considered in itself, was not yet concluded; it still hovered between judgment and grace. It was not yet shown that the merciful Word of God, and not the deeds of humans, will have the last word. It was only a promise, and not yet the unambiguous proclamation that God's Kingdom will definitively triumph.

The Christian faith professes that the Kingdom of God, searched for in general revelation and promised in the history of Israel, has definitively arrived in Jesus of Nazareth. With Jesus, especially in his death and Resurrection, as Rahner repeatedly points out, God no longer shows himself as the possibility of salvation *or* damnation, but unambiguously as the God of salvation and forgiveness: "Jesus proclaims the victorious coming of the Kingdom of God, which is addressed to the 'just' and sinners. . . . Its fundamental characteristics are that it comes from God, that it comes in inevitable victory and transcends (without destroying) human freedom in the power of divine compassion, by which God approaches the sinful world. The uniqueness of Jesus' preaching of the coming Kingdom consists in the fact that Jesus has the courage to know how the enormous drama of world history . . . will finally end . . . that history as a whole will have a victorious and happy ending, that the Kingdom of God, by the power of God, will irrevocably and remorselessly come. . . ."[9]

The victorious outcome of the Kingdom of God is definitively assured because in Jesus God has given, not simply a prophetical word, but an *eschatological* one: "A *prophetic* word of revelation is always essentially provisional. The *eschatological* word of revelation can consist only in the self-promise of God as the absolute future of the world. . . . The eschatological Word of God's self-promise to the world must be the irreversible victoriousness of this offering by God himself of God to the world."[10]

This Kingdom of God, which is already inaugurated by and present in Christ, is also a future reality. As we have seen, Rahner holds with Dodd and Bultmann that the Kingdom of God is a realized and existential reality which the believer must accept in faith here and now. But he also maintains with Cullmann that it is a future, yet-to-come reality as well, in the chronological sense. With Pannenberg and Moltmann the later Rahner increasingly and forcefully speaks of the Kingdom of God and eternity as the Absolute Future. In contrast to the intramundance future (or Moltmann's *Futurum* or *Futur*) the Absolute Future (or Moltmann's *Adventus* or *Zukunft*) cannot be known in advance nor planned nor controlled. Whereas the intramundance future, both that which comes about because of a predetermined evolutionary pattern and that which results from human creativity and freedom, producing the genuinely and radically new (the 'utopian future'), is achieved within time and space by human efforts, the Absolute Future bestows itself, freely and unexpectedly, as the incomprehensible and infinite mystery.

This outstanding *total* future, a future which is both humanity's achievement and God's gift, is the Kingdom of God. This Absolute Future is God himself, that is, God-with-humanity-and-world. This God as the Absolute Future, Rahner suggests, is specifically God the Spirit: "The absolute future of humanity bestowing itself of its free and sovereign power over history which is God is, however, in a special sense the 'Spirit' of God, because it can be characterized as love, freedom, and a newness that constantly takes us by surprise."[11] The presence of the Kingdom of God and of the Absolute Future as opposed to the intramundance future already anticipates the reality of the Church and its mission vis-à-vis the world.

2. Church and World

For Rahner the Church is essentially an eschatological community where the culmination and final form of God's eschatological self-communication and revelation in Christ is present explicitly and in a socially constituted form. It is both the fruit and the means of salvation, the community of the justified and the sacrament, that is, the efficacious sign and instrument of the Kingdom of God. However, Rahner cautions us, the Church is not identical with the Kingdom of God, because, although holy, it is also sinful.[12] Although it is already the guarantee of the victory of God's love, it is the pilgrim people journeying toward the Kingdom of God. It constantly proclaims its provisional status, that is, its being continuously eliminated in favor of the Kingdom of God.

Although the Kingdom of God, which is not yet fully attained, is a pure gift of God, it is also, Rahner insists, a task given to the Church. This task the Church must accomplish not only in the intraecclesial sphere through word and sacrament for the benefit of its members but also in and for the world, because the Kingdom of God comes to be not merely in the Church but in the world as well. Hence, Rahner also defines the Church as "*sacramentum salutis totius mundi*: sacrament-sign of the salvation of the world."[13] The important point here is that Rahner brings Church and world into an intimate unity: the Church is the *sacramentum mundi*; it has an intrinsic orientation to the world and vice versa.

Of course, Rahner does not deny that the Church is the sign of salvation, but it is the sacrament of the world precisely in its role as sign of salvation: "The Church is the sacrament of salvation of the world even where the latter is not and perhaps never will be the Church. It is the tangible, historical manifestation of the grace in which God communicates himself as absolutely present, close and forgiving, of the grace which is at work everywhere, offers God to each and gives to every reality in the world a secret purposeful orientation towards the intrinsic glory of God."[14]

It is therefore possible to establish a positive relationship between Church and world. In this connection one fundamental question arises for eschatology, namely, how to conceive of first the relationship between the Church on the one hand and the world on the other (or, more precisely, the mission and task of the Church to the world) and, secondly, the relationship between the immanent consummation of the world (its intramundane utopias and achievements) and its transcendent consummation (the Kingdom of God as the Absolute Future).

To answer both of these questions, Rahner must first provide a more precise description of what he means by *world* and related terms such as *humanism* and *culture*. By *world* Rahner understands "the whole of creation as a unity (in origin, destiny, goal, general structure, interdependence of part on part)."[15] This world, which necessarily includes human beings and serves them as their environment and as the stage of their history, is characterized by three features: it is the good created world, the sinful world, and the world redeemed by God.[16] These three connotations—creation, sin, and redemption—are not disparate but linked together by the fact that this world is a history still in progress whose outcome is still hidden.

Another facet of the world is its 'worldliness'. Rahner speaks frequently of *die Weltlichkeit der Welt* and *die weltliche Welt*. An equivalent term for *worldliness* is *secularization*. By it he means the growing influence of 'world' (as the outcome of human ingenuity) and the process by which it becomes increasingly autonomous and separates itself more and more from the Church considered as a social entity in the world. This 'secularization' or 'worldliness' of the world in relation to the Church must not simply be identified with an atheistic profanization of the world (i.e., secularism), because the world even as secularized still falls under God's universal will to save and is permeated by his grace. This means that the world is actually playing a positive role in the history of salvation and revelation, whether it consciously realizes and accepts this or not. In one important passage Rahner spells out this 'worldliness' of the world and its relevance for the Church and salvation:

> Of her very nature the Church constantly leaves the world free to be itself in its 'worldliness' and to have its own responsibility (and this not only in the execution of its decisions but in the actual process of arriving at the imperative underlying these also) even though this worldly element as such still precisely does *not* cease to have a 'moral' relevance and to have a *significance for salvation*. This worldly element is not merely the secular 'material', in itself indifferent, 'in which' Christian action is to be made real, but also includes (though it is not co-extensive with) Christian activity itself, since not every aspect of this can be controlled by the Church. In this process of 'secularization' of the world which she herself promotes, the Church supplies the grace of God, the principles of the process and its boundaries. But the human and Christian conduct desired is something that is achieved by the world itself on its own ground and its own responsibility.[17]

This phenomenon of secularization of the world would entail new tasks for the Church to perform vis-à-vis the world. But before examining the nature of these tasks, let us see how Rahner understands two other terms, *humanism* and *culture*. He takes *humanism* to mean "the unconditional respect for every human person."[18] Authentic humanism is predicated upon the radical acceptance of the personal uniqueness of each human being and of his or her definitive validity before God. This acceptance of the human person is not contradictory to a positive attitude toward the world since the latter is the environment for humans who must realize themselves in the world and since the world can find its meaning only in and through humans. By *culture* Rahner means "an element of tradition which helps to determine humanity's surroundings and which humans themselves not only receive but also develop through their free creative work as something which is specifically human."[19] In other words, it is the result of the human activities of shaping ourselves and our world through the exercise of our intellect and freedom.

3. The Responsibility of the Official Church and Christians for the World

Now that we have established Rahner's understanding of Church and world, it is possible to examine his view of the relationship between them and, more specifically, of the tasks that the Church and individual Christians have to perform for the world.

Philip Keane, in his thorough study of Rahner's theology of the world, suggests that Rahner's basic approach to the world is characterized by two dialectical tendencies. For Rahner, Christianity upholds and affirms the world in its totality. It proclaims a radical humanism and a genuine openness to human culture. At the same time, Christianity radically questions the world; it questions every concrete form of humanism and human culture.[20] These two apparently opposing tendencies of Rahner's world view, i.e., world-affirmation and world-questioning, do not cancel each other out but are brought together in a unity-in-tension with the world-affirming pole accorded priority and providing the unifying substratum for his view of the relationship between Church and world.

Synthetically, it may be said that Rahner's Christian world view is essentially a *critical affirmation* of the world. It contains both the moment of affirming the values of the world and the moment of questioning them, but with the latter subsumed under and sublimated into the higher affirming synthesis. If one recalls that for Rahner the world is characterized by a triple dimension (creation, sin, and redemption), then it would be apparent that whereas the questioning-negating element is necessitated by the sinfulness of the world, the affirming element is based upon both the goodness of creation and its redemption. Indeed, to be more precise, it is redemption that constitutes the meaning and purpose of creation, and as the eschatological goal it is the most centrally meaningful and unifying of the three dimensions of the world. Redemption is the ultimate reason why Rahner's stance of critical affirmation of the world is more an affirmation than a negation.

This positive attitude toward the world is implied in Rahner's description of the two fundamental ways of misconceiving the relation between Church and world, which he calls "integrism" and "esotericism." Integrism is that attitude, whether at the theoretical or at the practical (although unreflecting) level, according to which human life can be unambiguously mapped out and manipulated in conformity with certain universal principles proclaimed by the Church and developed and applied under its supervision. It regards the world as mere material for the action and self-manifestation of the Church and wants to integrate the world into the Church. It ignores the legitimate autonomy of the secular sphere from ecclesiastical control and overlooks the Catholic doctrine that humankind's intrinsic pluralism can never be fully overcome.[21]

On the opposite side, esotericism regards the secular as a matter of indifference for the Church or so sinful that it must be entirely rejected on the presumption that closeness to God requires distance from the world. In this way, says Rahner, "a Christian considers flight from the world as the only genuinely Christian attitude, and therefore regards affirmation of the world, its values, enjoyment, achievement and success as in principle suspect from a Christian point of view, unless it is already directly or explicitly inspired and commanded by a 'supernatural', 'religious' intention."[22] Neither integrism nor esotericism is a critical affirmation of the world, the former uncritically affirming it and the latter uncritically negating it.

The true relation of the Kingdom of God with the Church on the one hand and with the world on the other lies, Rahner suggests, in the mean between these two extremes. This mean, however, is not constituted by a facile compromise between the extremes but, rather, "lies above the two extremes as a radical unity, combining on its own basis both the unity and the difference of what is explicitly Christian and ecclesiastical on the one hand and the world and secular action on the other."[23]

In practice, there are according to Rahner two ways in which the Church exercises its responsibility for the world, namely, the Church in its official capacity, especially through its hierarchy, and the Church in its individual Christians. In his affirmation (against esotericism) of the Church's responsibility for the world, Rahner repeatedly makes it clear (against integrism) that the Church's competence is severely limited in the exercise this responsibility. These limitations are most clearly evident in the case of the official Church when it attempts to offer solutions to worldly problems such as the state, politics, economics, and culture. But even individual Christians *as* Christians can influence the world only in a limited way. They do not have ready-made answers deducible from the Gospel or from general moral principles. A strong and healthy sense of limitation is, therefore, basic to Rahner's total attitude on Church and Christian responsibility for the world.[24]

Nevertheless, despite the Church's restricted competency, Rahner insists that the Church, both in its official capacity and in its individual Christians, has a definite mission to perform in the service of the world. As far as the official Church is concerned, the task is threefold: First, it should proclaim Christian social principles, moral maxims, and regulative principles that are meaningful for social life, even though they are of restricted validity.[25] Secondly, it should function as a critic of society, judging on the basis of the Gospel which social plans and activities are morally wrong even if it cannot determine which ones are right.[26] Thirdly, it should proclaim 'charismatic social directives', that is, concrete imperatives (*Weisungen*) in the social field that are midway between absolutely binding principles and mere options. These middle-ground directives are counsels to make a concrete decision that in a given situation actualizes some universal principle even though the decision cannot be adequately and conclusively deduced from the universal, either in its content or in its binding force.[27]

To discharge these functions, especially the second and the third, the Church, Rahner believes, needs to develop a new discipline in the field of 'practical theology'. Within the compass of practical theology, which is different from systematic theology, ecclesiology, and the social sciences and whose task is to determine how the Church can accomplish its present tasks, there must be a special branch aimed precisely at the question of how the Church can relate responsibly to the world here and now. Rahner calls this new theological discipline "practical ecclesiological cosmology." (*praktisch-ekklesiologische Kosmologie*).[28] This practical discipline is different from and in a sense goes beyond, Rahner claims, Metz's "political theology," for the latter is concerned with the social implications and the social relevance of Christian revelation in its formal aspect, whereas the former deals with the responsibilities of the Church in the concrete in the face of pressing and immediate social problems of the contemporary world scene. In other words, Rahner holds that Metz's political theology, although it has a valid role in theology, falls short of the goal of his own practical and ecclesiological cosmology, namely, immediate relevance to the Church's role in society and culture.

But it is not only the official Church that has to perform its social responsibilities of issuing principles, prohibitions, charismatic imperatives, and practical judgments but also the individual Christians. Of course, as Rahner points out, the relationship of individual Christians to the world is not the same as that of the official Church, although there are limits in both cases. In performing their social responsibilities, individual Christians are less restricted than the official Church. Indeed, there are instances in which they can and should perform tasks that the official Church cannot and should not. This social responsibility of the individual Christian is grounded in the fact that the world has been accepted by God, above all in the Incarnation of the Logos, who liberated the world into independence, intrinsic significance, and autonomy. Hence, the Christian must accept this world precisely in its concupiscent secular nature and therefore as enduring and growing in this form. Consequently, the individual Christian must avoid the erroneous attitudes toward the world described above, namely, integrism and esotericism. Against integrism they must fulfill their earthly task and can also calmly be secular, having earthly desires and goals and enjoying the material world without religious mediation. Against esotericism they must not flee from the world toward their heavenly home as if the world were evil or indifferent to salvation, even though there are rightly and necessarily found in the Church asceticism, flight from the world, the life of the evangelical counsels as imitation of Christ the Crucified and as inchoative advance toward the renunciation of the world that is demanded of everyone in death.

This mention of asceticism and ultimate renunciation of the world in death brings us to the second issue of this chapter, namely, the relationship between the fulfillment of immanent, intramundane goals and utopias and the transcendent, eschatological consummation of human history. How does Rahner view this relationship?

II. The Immanent and Transcendent Consummation of the World

The point at issue here cannot be more clearly and pointedly formulated than by Rahner himself. He takes his cue from Vatican II's injunction, in the Pastoral Constitution on the Church in the Modern World, that Christians must impress the framework of secular life with the stamp of their eschatological hope so that a 'new earth' and a 'new heaven' may come, even though this new earth and new heaven should not be identified with earthly progress.[29] Rahner asks:

> . . . is the world which humans themselves fashion only the 'material' in which they have morally to prove themselves, and which in itself remains indifferent? And when the final consummation of the Kingdom of God comes, will the world simply be done away with? . . . Can we . . . compare the world . . . with the rush-baskets which the ancient monks of the Scythian desert wove by day and unravelled once more in the evening in order that they might fill up without sinning the interval of waiting for the eternity of this future which still lay wholly before them? Or does this . . . world itself pass, albeit inconceivably 'transformed', into the *eschaton* properly so-called? Does the 'new earth' come down from heaven. . . ? Or alternatively will this world be constructed here in time by man himself?[30]

In other words, the question concerns the precise relationship between the hope of Christian eschatology and the present-day ideology of the future or of the future utopia. That this question is of paramount importance for an understanding of Christian eschatology is obvious; but it is no less clear that it has a direct bearing on the dialogue between Christianity and Marxism. Christians have to face up to the Marxist question of whether they take with due seriousness the world in which they live, the world that they achieve, that is, of whether or not this world constitutes merely the material, ultimately speaking indifferent, upon which they exercise their virtues and will therefore cease to exist once they have reached 'heaven'. In order to grasp Rahner's answer to this question we will first of all examine whether according to him Christianity is an ideology; secondly, how Christianity relates to the Marxist utopia; and, finally, whether the consummation of human history is immanent or transcendent or both.

1. Christianity and Ideology

Rahner understands ideology to be doctrine that converts a partial aspect of reality into an absolute with a view to sociopolitical action and to impose itself as the norm for the whole life of a society. He distinguishes three kinds of ideology. The ideology of immanence converts certain finite areas of our experience into absolutes and regards their structures as the law of reality itself. Examples of this sort of ideology are nationalism, the German idea of 'blood and soil', racialism, Americanism, technicism, sociologism, and materialism. The opposite of this ideology of immanence is the ideology of transmanence in which the ultimate and infinite is turned into a totalitarian absolute in such a way that the relative and finite realities are robbed of their autonomy and value. Examples of this form of ideology include supernaturalism, quietism, utopianism, and chiliasm. The last kind of ideology, that of transcendence, refuses to accept or commit itself to any reality whatsoever, whether finite or infinite, but maintains an attitude of openness for everything and anything; it consists in the empty formal process of overcoming any given reality for its own sake.[31]

Rahner concedes that Christianity may have appeared to be and at times has actually functioned as an ideology of any of the three above-mentioned kinds. It appears as an ideology to those of an empiricist frame of mind for whom anything that cannot be empirically verified is an ideological superstructure. Christianity has also been used by both liberals and conservatives to justify social, economic, political, cultural, and scientific conditions that cannot claim permanent validity and has been in this way turned into an ideology. Further, Christianity has found it necessary to objectify its nature in doctrines and in historical, institutional, sacramental, and juridical forms; and the temptation is to regard these finite objectifications as having absolute validity. Finally, within the contemporary pluralism of world views, any religion such as Christianity that lays claim to absoluteness is likely to be regarded as ideological.[32]

Nevertheless, Rahner firmly rejects the contention that Christianity is an ideology. First of all, it cannot be regarded as an ideology simply because it makes absolute declarations with the claim to truth, in other words, simply because it makes metaphysical statements. Metaphysics must not and cannot be suspected from the outset and in every case of being an ideology since the proposition claiming that every metaphysics is in the last analysis a nonbinding ideology is itself a metaphysical proposition. There is a kind of metaphysics that is inescapably given together with human existence, namely, the transcendental reflection on and systematization of the conditions of possibility for the human experience of knowledge and freedom. If there can be a metaphysics, at least in principle, that cannot be disposed of as an ideology from the start, then, Rahner argues, Christianity cannot be rejected as being an ideology simply because the horizons of its declara-

professes, Rahner claims, a genuine and radical humanism since it upholds the ultimate and radical dignity of humankind. Rahner challenges the non-Christian to come up with a more radical form of humanism and asks whether, comparing theory with theory and not unfairly comparing humanist theory with the miserable practice of Christians, the humanist is certain that his or her humanism is better practically, i.e., more effective. In particular, he asks whether the Marxist can discover in this form of Christian humanism any "opium for the people" and whether it is necessary for a politically powerful Marxism to persecute this Christianity in order to free humankind from servitude and self-alienation.[37] Christianity does not espouse a particular concrete humanism but refuses to grant humanism an absolute value. It accepts the experience of its own humanism as one that is constantly questionable. So affirms Rahner: "For Christianity as such—and this is the decisive point—cancels every concrete humanism by revealing its questionable nature before the incomprehensibility of God. Christianity's *concretissimum*, for which alone it stands, is Jesus Christ, who, in accepting death and suffering *for us* (and in no other way) has created our relationship of immediacy before God, and the Church, which looks for the Kingdom which is yet to be fulfilled and which is *not* identical with the humanism we ourselves have produced or shall produce in the near future. Christianity renders every concrete humanism contingent, i.e. dispensable in favor of another, future humanism, by situating every one within God's open future. In its conviction of man's freedom, *rooted in* and *oriented toward* God, Christianity opens up the permanent possibility of an inhuman 'humanism'."[38]

In this connection it is appropriate to point out that not only does Rahner urge Christians to join with humanists—whether theistic or atheistic—in their work for justice, freedom, dignity, unity, and diversity in society, but he also recognized in 1970 the existence of a global revolutionary situation due to the extremely explosive tension between the northern hemisphere and the southern one, between the developed nations and the underdeveloped ones. Consequently, he argued that the Church, although it cannot be the primary or proper subject of that revolution, nevertheless must recognize the justification for a revolution of this kind at least in general terms, for this revolution is necessary if the underdeveloped world is really to obtain a share in the benefits they justifiably demand. "The Church," says Rahner, "must exhort and arouse Christians to take part in this global revolution in a way appropriate to their position in society and the possibilities open to them as a duty of Christian conscience. . . ."[39]

Rahner is aware, however, that humanism and other utopias with their accomplishments are not identical with the final consummation of human history or the Kingdom of God. Speaking of the achievements of humankind's technological self-manipulation, he remarks that death is not only the "zero hour" through which individuals must pass on their way to the Absolute Future, but also the zero hour for humankind as a whole. Human self-manipulation and all our concrete and utopian aims are constantly subject to the law of death. There is always the threat of total annihilation inflicted by human beings upon humanity itself. Rahner reminds us that the development of the world does not simply move "in an evolutionary way toward its integration into the love of God, into his epiphany in the world and into the Kingdom of God. It moves to this goal through collapse, futility, the zero of death."[40] The question is then raised of how to conceive of the relationship between human achievement (including that of Christians) and the transcendent consummation in the Kingdom of God.

3. Immanent and Transcendent Consummation

Rahner finds the very concept of 'consummation', let alone 'immanent' and 'transcendent', exceedingly complicated. In fact, it can be applied to five different things: (1) to a particular material event of a purely physical or biological kind; (2) to the sum total of all such particular events, i.e., the material world considered as a whole; (3) to the spiritual and personal history of an individual; (4) to all such spiritual and personal histories considered as constituting a unity, this unity being something more than a final collection of all such histories; and (5) to the real unity of the material world together wth the history of the spirit at both the individual and the collective levels, i.e., the unity and totality of the temporal creation.[41] It is obvious that concepts of 'consummation', 'immanent', and 'transcendent' consummation assume different meanings as they are applied to each of five cases.

On closer analysis Rahner finds that the concept of consummation is totally inapplicable in any meaningful way to the first two cases, that is, to purely physical and biological entities and the sum total thereof. The reason is that these realities have no will as it were to achieve their own consummation, but rather tend to go on forever. Consummation implies genuine time and temporality. It requires, in Rahner's judgment, three characteristics: (1) the temporal event must have an end, whether this end is caused by an external agent or by some intrinsic element to the event itself; (2) this event must not merely 'cease' but in time produce some definitive and lasting result, however this result is related to time; and (3) the result must be something for which the event is intended and in which it achieves meaning and finds justification.[42] In other words, the concept of consummation, as opposed to mere end, can be meaningfully applied only to that kind of history which is worked out in personal freedom and in which time has a genuine beginning and a definitive end. The material world can be said to be 'consummated' only to the extent that it has an intrinsic referrence to the free spirit. The same is to be said of biological life as such. It is consummated insofar as it forms a single history of a person in the individual or the collective sense as endowed with knowledge and freedom. Of course the consummation of a person can result in a positive fulfillment or a negative self-loss, that is, a final and definitive state of *non*consummation. In short, the concept of consummation can be applied only to the last three cases mentioned above.

By 'immanent' consummation Rahner means "that which arises from the 'immanent' essential composition of the being which is in process of achieving its consummation, i.e. from the resources proper to it and through the intrinsic tendency of what is taking place toward a future goal."[43] It is the final outcome that has been worked out in time purely from within the event itself: the definitive finality of the freely posited event itself. On the other hand, by 'transcendent' consummation is meant "a consummation which comes *ab externo*, being conferred upon the agent independently of the action he himself posits."[44] It is therefore something that cannot be discerned from the process itself; it goes beyong it and exists in its own right prior to the actual process as its goal, which it can attain to but cannot produce.

If one applies these concepts of immanent and transcendent consummation to the free persons working out their historical destinies in time, then, on the basis of Rahner's metaphysical anthropology, it is clear that their immanence *is* precisely transcendence. Spirit is transcendence to the Absolute Being. This transcendence imparts an orientation to the beginning of the personal existence that is not simply left behind as the person reaches his or her consummation. It also imparts an orientation of the person toward the Absolute Future. Hence, Rahner states: *"The immanent consummation of a history worked out in freedom by a being endowed with spiritual faculties is its transcendent consummation* because the immanence is the transcendence; or: *a spiritual being, acting out of its knowledge and freedom, has of its very nature no immanent consummation* because the immanent transcendentality rises up to that which is truly transcendent. . . . The transcendent consummation of a personal freedom is the only true immanent consummation."*[45] Indeed, the distinction between 'immanent' and 'transcendent' becomes quite blurred when these two terms are applied to the human spirit whose very essence is transcendence to the Absolute Being, the incalculable and uncontrollable future.

This identity between the immanent and transcendent consummation of the spiritual creature is further demonstrated if one takes into consideration the relationship between nature and grace. For Rahner, as we have seen, God is not only the creator of a world distinct from himself; of his own initiative, and in that act of immediate self-bestowal which we call grace, he has made himself an intrinsic principle of this world in the free personal spirits. 'Nature' is in the real order willed by God from the outset for the sake of 'grace' and 'creation' for the sake of the covenant of personal love. God in his gratuitous self-bestowal to finite spirits, while remaining the absolute transcendent, becomes their innermost principle and goal. Hence, God is not only their *causa efficiens* but also their *causa quasi formalis*. The self-bestowal of God, in which God gives himself precisely as the absolute transcendent, is the most immanent factor in the creature. Consequently, God in his absolute immediacy is, in the concrete order of reality, not only the consummation, the goal (*beatitudo objectiva*) of the spiritual creature, but the principle in the movement that is most proper and necessary to it, the sole really connatural principle by which it is impelled toward the consummation of this goal. For human beings, then, the immanent and transcendent consummation is the same; it is one consummation in which the one aspect implies the other.

Can the same thing be said of the consummation of the world *as a whole*, including the basic material element in it? As has been observed above, the material world as such, so long as it remains confined to itself, has no consummation. However, as Rahner has repeatedly argued in his metaphysical anthropology, there is a real unity and mutual interrelationship between spirit and matter. Matter is that other necessary factor in which alone a finite and creaturely spirit can be precisely that which it is of its nature and can enact itself into awareness, transcendence, and freedom. Spirit and matter are essentially different precisely in that they constitute the metaphysical principles of the one single spiritual-material being. Matter, by virtue of its active self-transcendence, tends toward the spirit and shares in the destiny of the spirit. Consequently, as regards the consummation of the material world, Rahner maintains that the material world, by reason of its essential orientation toward the spirit, is sustained from the outset by that creative impetus, implanted by God, by which it strives toward the spirit as its goal.

This impetus, furthermore, is the divine self-bestowal that manifests itself in history and found final expression in the Incarnation of the Logos. Since this history is tainted by sin, the immanent development of matter into personal spirit in the process of redemption and divinization should not be conceived of in the pattern of mechanical or evolutionary growth. Nevertheless, it is the history in which the material world itself arrives at its goal and the fullness of its consummation. Matter is not a transitory or superfluous stage of the spirit's progress toward its consummation. Rather, it endures as an intrinsic element of the spirit and of its history even in its consummation. In sum, even for the material world, the immanent consummation is the same as the transcendent one.

One can now come to Rahner's answer to the question of the relationship between the intramundane utopias achieved through human endeavors and the Absolute Future, the Kingdom of God. "The Kingdom of God," says Rahner, "the final consummation which brings history to an end and 'raises' it, is that which is coming of itself."[46] It is not the final outcome of the history planned and accomplished by human work. Rather it is the deed and gift of God. But this deed of God is to be conceived of as the act of *self*-transcendence of history the innermost principle of which is the self-bestowal of God himself. It is true that the intramundane history and utopias as planned and realized by humans must be radically transformed into that which is unknown and into an openness to the Absolute Future that is God himself. Nevertheless, that history will endure not only in its spiritual aspect but in its material element as well. Of course, it is not possible to depict and imagine how this history will endure in the concrete. To attempt to do so is to produce a false "apocalyptic" and not a genuine eschatology. Two statements, then, must be dialectically affirmed: Everything is transformed, and everything endures. Says Rahner:

> So far as we are concerned in the here and now there is a basic dialectical tension between the two statements, on the one hand that human history will finally endure, and on the other hand that it will be radically transformed. This tension maintains us in an openness to the future while still according a radical importance to the present. Both statements are hermeneutic principles and at the same time statements of fact. Bearing these points in mind as provisos we can positively say: history itself constructs its own final and definitive state. That which endures is the *work* of love as expressed in the concrete in human history. It remains itself as something achieved by humankind, and not merely a moral distillation of this, something which history leaves behind it as though it were the 'grapes' from which the wine had been pressed. History itself passes into the definitive consummation of God. . . .[47]

III. Summary and Critical Questions

This chapter concludes our exposition of Rahner's eschatology. It is appropriate that it should deal with his theology of the relationship between inner-worldly utopias and the Christian hope for transcendent fulfillment. For it is here that Rahner on the one hand makes a decisive advance beyond traditional eschatology which focused primarily on the destiny of the individual, and on the other hand it is also here that his shift from a personal, existential outlook to a more sociopolitical perspective is made most manifest. As he puts it eloquently in one of his later essays: ". . . love of neighbor . . . is not merely a private relationship between individuals within the static, existing structures of society. Love of neighbor has as its concrete object the changing of these sociological conditions under which love of neighbor as a private activity has to be practised. Changing society in order to provide more opportunities of love of neighbor, humanity's socio-political and socio-critical task, the struggle for greater freedom and justice: all these are requirements and tasks of love of neighbor, if the latter is understood rightly, in this rapidly changing but planned society."[48]

In explicating the relationship between the achievements of inner-worldly utopias and the Kingdom of God, Rahner skillfully charts a middle course between the Scylla of sociological horizontalism and the Charybdis of spiritualistic verticalism. On the one hand he refuses to identify earthly progress with the Kingdom of God, and on the other hand he urges the offical Church and individual Christians to commit themselves, together with believing and nonbelieving humanists, to ameliorating the conditions of the world for greater peace and justice. Further, his theology of the world is not a facile reconciliation of horizontalism and verticalism but is characterized by a critical affirmation of the secularity and autonomy of the world on the basis of its created goodness and redemption.

It is this balanced view of the relationship between earthly progress and the Kingdom of God that enables Rahner to build a much-needed bridge between secular utopias, Marxist and humanistic, and Christian eschatology. Again here he convincingly demonstrates how Christianity can render an invaluable service to these intramundane utopias. With its hope in the Absolute Future it prevents them from absolutizing any particular achievement or goal, and with its teaching on the unity of love of God and love of neighbor it lends them radical seriousness and significance. At the same time Rahner does not capitulate to these vociferous and at times violent utopias, nor does he surrender the transcendence of Christian eschatology. Rather, he shows that immanence and transcendence of human and cosmic consummation are ultimately the same thing.

Again and again one marvels at the vitality and coherence of Rahner's theological vision. Stimulated by the sociopolitical and economic problems of the contemporary world, he never ceased to reformulate his theology in response to them. Nevertheless, these later developments are deeply rooted in his original, basic stance embodied in his philosophical and theological anthropology, his view of the relationship between nature and grace, and his theology of time and eternity.

There are, however, a few questions that may be raised with regard to Rahner's view of the immanent and transcendent consummation of the world. First, Rahner's insistence on the necessity of developing a "practical ecclesiological cosmology" is very welcome, and his suggestions on how to devise one are quite tantalizing, but they amount to no more than programmatic essays. If his theology of the world is to issue forth in some concrete norms for action and lead to some practical sociopolitical and economic agenda, there is needed a detailed and highly scientific analysis of the situation of the contemporary world in all its aspects. Such a mammoth task cannot of course be carried out single-handedly by any individual; but unless such an analysis is available to guide concrete actions, Christian eschatology cannot but remain abstract and unable to enter into effective dialogue and collaboration with intramundane utopias.

Secondly, Rahner's repeated admonitions regarding the limitations of the official Church in issuing concrete directives and carrying out sociopolitical and economic programs may unwittingly have a paralyzing effect on the Church's exercise of its mission towards the world. Perhaps this emphasis on the Church's severe limitations is linked to the absence of a well-formulated "practical ecclesiological cosmology." In any case, recent magisterial interventions, especially at the level of national conferences of bishops, e.g., the American bishops' pastoral letters on war and peace and on the economy, demonstrate that the official Church is not as limited in its competency in dealing with worldly affairs as Rahner tends to think.

Thirdly, and more importantly, Rahner's use of the category of the future to reconceptualize God is challenging and places him in the company of the foremost contemporary expositors of the new political and liberationist theologies. God is here interpreted *eschatologically*. This means first of all that God is not the God of the present; rather, God's full being and sovereignty are promises to be hoped for in the future. Secondly, this also means that God is, as Pannenberg says, "the power of the future"[49] effecting and transforming the present *from* the future in a kind of "reverse causality." Finally, the eschatological interpretation of God means that God's being is intrinsically related to history, that therefore his being and his actualized sovereignty (i.e., his Kingdom) are one, and, consequently, that only in the future *eschaton* when God's power and glory are manifest will God's being 'be' or 'be realized' in the fullest sense.[50]

There is no doubt that such eschatological interpretation of God is extremely attractive, especially in view of a possible collaboration with intramundane utopias. Since God is conceived as the future transforming the present, his Kingdom appears as the negation of the dominant structures of the present and thus implies a political stance of radical social reform and possibly of revolution. The Church is then seen as the 'sacrament of history' making visible the presence of grace within history and so history's future and ultimate meaning.

Nevertheless the eschatological conception of God as the Absolute Future is not free from difficulties. First, it runs the risk of divesting present experience of any relation to the divine, much as Barthian dialectical theology did, only now on a temporal axis into the future rather than on the vertical axis into the transcendent. Of course, Rahner's position on the identity of immanent and transcendent consummation may in the long run obviate such a risk; this risk, however, is inherent in such a position and is quite real.

Secondly, political actions of any sort, in order to be effective, must take into account and realize the latent possibilities of the present situation. Unless possibilities are there in the structures of the present, no new social reality can be established by political actions. If, however, God is understood exclusively as the Absolute Future negating the present and transforming the present solely from the future, it is impossible to unite political actions with theological interpretation in an intelligible way. Is this perhaps one of the reasons why Rahner is so skeptical about the Church's competence for social transformation?[51]

Finally, the conception of God as the Absolute Future implies a processive, rather than classical, metaphysics of the nature of God. As we have seen, Rahner insists that the Christian God, although 'immutable' and 'eternal' in himself, has *himself*, in the otherness of the world, undergone change, history, and time. He derives this dynamic understanding of God from the Incarnation of the Logos. It remains, however, in a rather embryonic stage in Rahner's theology that continues to be informed by the transcendental conception of God as the horizon of being, knowledge, and love. It is true that he attempts to transform the vertical dialectic between immanence and transcendence into the horizontal temporal axis of present and future. Similarly, his dialectic of time and eternity, which is primarily one of immanence and transcendence, is gradually understood in terms of the temporal tension between the present and the future. Nevertheless, these attempts have not produced a full-fledged integration of these polarities, and there remains an unresolved ambiguity between a transcendental and a processive understanding of God.

9

Retrospect and Prospect

It is not my intention in this concluding chapter to provide a point-by-point summary of Rahner's eschatology. Rather I will bring this study to a close by first high-lighting some of Rahner's most significant and distinctive contributions to Christian eschatology and secondly by examining whether and how these insights concerning Rahner's eschatology are susceptible of further development.

I. Retrospect: From "Physics" through Anthropology to Pneumatology

The study was undertaken with the conviction that eschatology is one of the fundamental themes not only of Christian theology in general but also of Rahner's total theological vision. While it is true that Rahner has not written a complete treatise on eschatology, the doctrine of the Last Things occupied his earliest attention and remained a constant theme throughout his theological career. He was invariably sharply critical of the textbook version of eschatology. However, he was not prepared to jettison the achievement of neo-scholasticism but attempted to revitalize and enrich it by means of a *ressourcement* in the original founts of Christian faith, an appropriate hermeneutics, and an integral philosophical and theological anthropology.

Like any living theology, Rahner's eschatology evolved and developed, although without any radical reversal, often in response to the signs of the times and to the criticisms of his fellow theologians. Operating initially within the narrow epistemological framework of transcendental Thomism, he gradually expanded his existentialist and interpersonal eschatology to include sociopolitical and economic dimensions of human existence and attempted to relate Christian transcendent fulfillment to inner-worldly utopias.

My presentation of Rahner's eschatology discussed the themes traditionally associated with individual and collective eschatologies: death, the intermediate state, purgatory, heaven, hell, the resurrection of the dead, the Parousia, the last judgment, and the consummation of the world. Preparatory to this account of Rahner's eschatology an effort was made to compare and contrast it with nine other models of eschatology as well as to outline Rahner's basic principles of interpretation with specific application to eschatological assertions. And since one of these principles affirms that eschatology is anthropology projected into its mode of future fulfillment, it was necessary to consider those aspects of Rahnerian anthropology which constitute the unity, the conditions of possibility, and the anticipation of eschatological fulfillment in the Kingdom of God.

It is doubtless here that Rahner's first momentous contribution to eschatology lies.[1] Rather than a detailed description of the future events at the end of the world and an anticipated report of the 'next world', eschatology is conceived as a reflection on what God's creative power has brought about in humanity and in the world and a 'projection' of this achievement into its mode of final fulfillment on the basis of what has occurred in Jesus Christ.

With this radical reenvisioning of the nature and scope of eschatology, Rahner not only rescued it from the irrelevancy and frivolity to which it had been condemned since the late Middle Ages but also formulated a hermeneutics of eschatological assertions of far-reaching consequences and a new understanding of the intrinsic unity and interrelatedness of various Christian mysteries. As far as hermeneutics is concerned, and here lies Rahner's second major contribution, Rahner's seven theses have exercised a widespread influence on contemporary eschatology. There is simply no recent discussion of the hermeneutics of eschatology that does not betray the powerful impact of Rahner's ideas.[2] This does not of course mean that all of Rahner's principles are universally and peacefully accepted, but there is no dispute about the fact that their fundamental validity has been recognized by theologians, Catholic and Protestant alike.

Rahner's basic understanding of eschatology as an 'extrapolation' of anthropology into its mode of future fulfillment on the basis of christology provides a framework for constructing a much-needed unitary vision of Christian theology and imparts cohesiveness and unity to his own theological achievement. Eschatology, and this is Rahner's third significant contribution, is transformed into an integral part of the Christian theological system. As is well known, Rahner, on the basis of his transcendental analysis of human existence and history, maintains that theology is anthropology and vice versa. Theology deals with God as the absolutely mysterious term of human transcendence who has communicated himself in forgiving love to humans both 'existentielly' (as Spirit) and historically (as Logos) as their ultimate fulfillment. This divine self-communication reached its historical, irreversible, and victorious climax in Jesus of Nazareth. Anthropology, on the other hand, discusses the possibility and nature of a person who, by the act of radical love for the neighbor, grasps this God as the horizon and object of his or her love. This love, moreover, is indissolubly interpersonal and social and constitutes the essence of the Church. Lastly, eschatology transforms Christianity into a religion that keeps open the question about the Absolute Future who has bestowed himself irreversibly in Jesus Christ but is still the outstanding future of humankind and remains forever as an absolute mystery even in the final consummation of all things, that is, in the Kingdom of God.

Theology, anthropology, and eschatology form the three pivotal points around which Rahner chisels a new formulation of the Christian creed. The "Father" is represented as the incomprehensible term of human transcendence, the *principium inprincipiatum* of all conceivable reality. The "Son," the incarnate God, is the realm within which the radical unity of love of God and love of neighbor is made visible, particularly in the Church. The Absolute Future of humankind and history is in a special way the "Spirit" of God insofar as the Spirit is characterized as love and freedom and as ever new and surprising. Thus eschatology moves from "physics" through anthropology into the heart of the Christian mystery, namely, the Trinity (especially pneumatology), and therein regains its rightful place.

Rahner's fourth contribution to eschatology consists in his amazing ability to hold in fruitful tension the opposing polarities of human existence and hence of the eschatological fulfillment of humankind and history. To use Geoffrey Wainwright's expressions, his eschatology contains a polarity of the 'already' and the 'not yet'", concerns the individual in community, implies both a divine gift and its human appropriation, embraces the material as well as the spiritual, is universal in scope, allows progress in the establishment of the Kingdom of God, and includes a moment of judgment and renewal.[3] Only an eschatology that integrates these diverse dimensions, not laying them side by side as aggregates but unifying them into an organic whole on the basis of a comprehensive anthropology, can do justice to the richness and diversity of the Christian understanding of humankind and our consummation and at the same time achieve some measure of credibility in our present world.

Last but not least, Rahner has greatly advanced the progress of theological reflections on particular *eschata*, in some instances by retrieving and deepening certain traditional but misunderstood or forgotten doctrines, in others by boldly venturing into a dialogue with non-Christian religions and non-Thomistic philosophical traditions. Among the latter are to be included his theory of the pancosmicity of the soul, his hypothesis regarding the compatibility of the doctrine of reincarnation with the Christian faith, his proposal of *apocatastasis* as an object of prayer and hope, and his hypothesis of an immediate resurrection after death. Among the former are to be mentioned, inter alia, his transcendental anthropology in general (in particular, his understanding of the unity of humankind, freedom, history, time, eternity, and grace); his interpretation of death as a personal act, of death as the consequence of sin, of the death of Christ as a redemptive act qua death; his opinion regarding the intermediate state as a cultural amalgam; his justification of purgatory on the basis of the multileveled ontology of the human being and his explication of purgation as integration and transformation; his emphasis on the permanent significance of Christ's humanity for heavenly blessedness; his retrieval of the beatific vision as union in love with the Trinity and as contemplation of the abiding incomprehensibility of the Divine Mystery; his understanding of hell as a serious *possibility* for human freedom; his development of a transcendental hope for the resurrection as the condition of possibility for the belief in Jesus' Resurrection and the general resurrection of the flesh; his rapprochement of the doctrine of the resurrection of the body and that of the immortality of the soul; and, finally, his unification of Christian transcendent consummation and secular, inner-worldly utopias.

By any standard Rahner's achievements in eschatology are monumental and impressive. The above summary can hardly do justice to the depth, originality, and boldness of his thought. Future theology, and eschatology in particular, will certainly exploit to great advantage the insights of this theologian who, ironically but honestly and with conviction, described himself on several occasions as a nonphilosopher and an amateur theologian whose interests were never scholarship and erudition but pastoral concerns.[4] This mention of the course of future theology naturally brings us to the second part of this chapter with the question of whether these Rahnerian insights are susceptible of further development.

II. Prospect: Historical Experience, Freedom, and the Future of God

At the ends of chapters 3 through 8 I have raised a large number of critical questions regarding particular themes of Rahner's eschatology. It is not my intention nor is it feasible to take all of them up again here. This would mean writing another book on eschatology along Rahnerian lines with more or less significant modifications. Rather, in the remaining pages, I will focus on a few select key themes of Rahner's eschatology that are, in my judgment, capable of greater refinement and precision.

Any fundamental critique of Rahner's theology will have to deal with at least three basic issues: the strategy with which it seeks to understand the Christian faith, its basic tenet in the light of which any other theological theme is grasped and interpreted, and the matrix underlying the entire system. The strategy is Rahner's transcendental method and, in our context, his hermeneutics of eschatological assertions. The basic tenet is Rahner's doctrine of the supernatural existential and, in our context, his theological anthropology 'extrapolated' into its mode of future fulfillment. Its underlying matrix is his doctrine of the experience of grace, that is, of the mediated immediacy of God, and, in our context, God as the Absolute Future to every human person. Something will therefore be said about each of these three issues and their implications for eschatology.

1. Method and Hermeneutics

The transcendental method with its mutually conditioning moments of transcendental reflections on the conditions of possibility of knowledge and freedom and the consideration of the historical event itself has proved to be a powerful tool in Rahner's hand for articulating the Christian faith. He used it to great advantage in his theology of the Trinity, christology, theological anthropology, and other parts of theology. In his eschatology, too, the transcendental method is consistently applied with much benefit. Two areas may be singled out as examples, namely, death and resurrection. In Rahner's theology of death, the transcendental reflections on the nature of death, i.e., death as a personal act, lead to a better understanding of the salvific efficacy of Christ's death qua death. In his theology of the resurrection, the transcendental reflections on hope as humanity's inescapable existential desire for the definitive meaning and validity of our lives provide a useful apologetics for the belief in the Resurrection of Jesus and the universal resurrection of the dead.

But the weakness of the transcendental method is also glaring. Transcendental reflections, however profound, will not be able to give an adequate account of the contingency and concreteness of historical events. A theology of the death of Christ cannot be based primarily on a transcendental analysis of death as a personal act; it has to be grounded in a careful analysis of the biblical account of this historical, unique event. Again, the transcendental hope for the permanent validity of one's free decisions in history cannot exhaust the meaning of the reality of Jesus' Resurrection and the resurrection of the dead, especially their bodily dimension.

Of course, Rahner is aware that historical events cannot be deduced from transcendental analysis and repeatedly insists that the two moments of his theological method—transcendental and historical considerations—mutually condition each other. The fact, however, is that in Rahner's theology the historical experience is often left in the background to the detriment of a fuller understanding of the faith. A more extended and closer analysis of the historical events as they actually occur would enrich many themes of Rahner's eschatology. To return to the problem of Christ's death as an example, Rahner's theology of death, which is contructed primarily on his transcendental philosophy of freedom as the capacity for definitive self-determination, will be greatly enhanced if it considers more carefully Jesus' death as a death *on the cross* in obedience and love to his Father. Similarly, his elaboration on the beatific vision, which relies heavily on his analysis of human knowing as transcendence into mystery, will be less abstract if it draws more of its inspiration and substance from the mystical experience of the saints.

The need for Rahner's eschatology to be more rooted in historical experience brings us to his hermeneutics of eschatological assertions. Of his seven theses, the fourth and the fifth are of capital importance and yet are quite problematical. The fifth thesis describes the nature of eschatology in contrast to apocalyptic. For Rahner, to read from the present out into the future (*Aussage*) is eschatology; to read from the future back into the present (*Einsage*) is apocalyptic. We will critically examine Rahner's definition of eschatology when we come back to his fourth thesis, but it must be noted here that his usage of the term *apocalyptic* is, to say the least, confusing. Of course, there are not a few contemporary preachers and writers, often of a fundamentalist persuasion, who do precisely what Rahner describes as apocalyptic. But recent biblical studies have revealed a body of writings that can be defined as "a genre of revelatory literature with a narrative framework, in which a revelation is mediated by an otherworldly being to a human recipient, disclosing a transcendent reality which is both temporal, insofar as it envisages eschatological salvation, and spatial insofar as it involves another, supernatural world."[5] To regard these writings as apocalyptic in Rahner's pejorative sense of the word is unfair, and not to label them as apocalyptic is an arbitrary restriction of the common usage of the term.

Apart from terminology, however, there is a more serious theological issue. Is eschatology a reading of the present out into the future? As Rahner's fourth thesis states more bluntly, eschatological knowledge is knowledge of the eschatological present. For him, Christian eschatology is nothing but Christian anthropology conjugated in the future sense.[6] Here is a clear instance of the *anthropologische Wende* for which Rahner is justly famous. Is such an anthropological reduction of eschatology warranted? No doubt it brings with it several advantages: it shows clearly that eschatological assertions are not reports on the other world but etiological accounts of the present situation of salvation and sin; it integrates eschatology into the whole fabric of theology; and it rejects the existential demythologization of history.

Nevertheless, this anthropological reduction inevitably brings in its wake an impoverishment of Christian eschatology, especially if the anthropolgy at its base is predominantly, if not exclusively, transcendental. We will examine some of the fundamental features of this anthropology in the next section; let it simply be noted here for instance that Rahner's treatment of the resurrection of the flesh might have given a greater prominence to the

Abbreviations

Works of Karl Rahner

DT   *Dictionary of Theology*. This is the second edition of *Kleines Theologisches Wörterbuch*, published in Great Britain under the title *Concise Theological Dictionary* and in the United States under the title *Theological Dictionary* in the first edition.

FCF   *Foundations of Christian Faith.*

HW   *Hearers of the Word.*

KRIG   *Karl Rahner in Gespräch*, 2 vols., ed. Paul Imhof and Hubert Biallowons. Vol. 1 (1964–77); Vol. 2 (1978–82).

LThK   *Lexikon für Theologie und Kirche*, 2d edition.

SM   *Sacramentum Mundi: An Encyclopedia of Theology*, 6 vols.

ST   *Schriften zur Theologie*, 16 vols.

SW   *Spirit in the World.*

TD   *On the Theology of Death.*

TI   *Theological Investigations*, 20 vols.

Other Works

CD   *Christian Dogmatic*, vols. 1–2, ed. Carl E. Braaten and Robert W. Jenson (Philadelphia: Fortress Press, 1984).

CF   *The Christian Faith in the Doctrinal Documents of the Catholic Church*, rev. ed., ed. Joseph Neuner and Joseph Dupuis (Staten Island, N.Y.: Alba House, 1982). The numbers given after this abbreviation refer to the marginal numbers and not the pages as in other cases.

CHFM   Stephen H. Travis, *Christian Hope and the Future of Man* (Leicester: Inter-Varsity Press, 1980).

DBT   *Dictionary of Biblical Theology*, new rev. ed., ed. Xavier Léon-Dufour (New York: The Seabury Press, 1973).

DCG   Gerhard Ebeling, *Dogmatik des Christlichen Glaubens*, vols. 1–3 (Tübingen: J. C. B. Mohr, 1979).

DHI   *Dictionary of the History of Ideas*, vols. 1–4, ed. Philip P. Wiener (New York: Charles Scribner's Sons, 1968).

211

DID   Fritz Buri, Jan M. Lochman and Heinrich Ott, *Dogmatik im Dialog*, vol. 1: *Die Kirche und die Letzten Dinge* (Gütersloh: Gütersloher Verlaghaus, 1973).

Dogma 6   Michael Schmaus, *Dogma 6: Justification and the Last Things* (Kansas City and London: Sheed and Ward, 1977).

DS   *Enchiridion Symbolorum Definitionum et Declarationum*, 36th ed. ed. Henricus Denzinger and Adolfus Schönmetzer (Freiburg: Herder, 1973). The numbers given after this abbreviation refer to the marginal numbers and not to the pages as in other cases.

DTI   *Dizionario Teologico Interdisciplinare*, vols. 1–3, ed. Franco Ardusso et al. (Rome: Marietti, 1977).

EBT   *Encyclopedia of Biblical Theology. The Complete "Sacramentum Verbi,"* ed. Johannes B. Bauer (New York: Crossroad, 1981).

EL   Hans Küng, *Eternal Life? Life After Death as a Medical, Philosophical, and Theological Problem* (Garden City, N.Y.: Doubleday, 1984).

EP   *The Encyclopedia of Philosophy*, vols. 1–6, ed. Paul Edwards (New York: Macmillan Publishing Co., 1967).

Eschatologie Joseph Ratzinger, *Eschatologie. Tod und Ewiges Leben* (Regensburg: F. Pustet, 1978).

HAV   Herbert Vorgrimler, *Hoffnung auf Vollendung. Aufriss der Eschatologie* (Freiburg: Herder, 1980).

KD   Michael Schmaus, *Katholische Dogmatik*, vol. 4, pt. 2 (Munich: Max Hueber, 1959).

MDA   *Il Mistero dell'Aldilà*, ed. Eraldo Quarello (Rome: Libreria Ateneo Salesiano, 1979).

MS   *Mysterium Salutis. Grundriss heilsgeschichtlicher Dogmatik*, vols. 1–5, ed. Johannes Feiner and Magnus Löhrer (Einsiedeln: Benziger, 1955).

NAU   Grisbert Greshake and Gerhard Lohfink, *Naherwartung, Auferstehung, Untersblichkeit. Untersuchung zur christlichen Eschatologie*, 4th ed. (Freiburg: Herder, 1984).

NCE   *New Catholic Encyclopedia*, ed. William J. McDonald (New York: McGraw-Hill Book Co., 1967).

NDT   *Nuovo Dizionario di Teologia*, ed. Giuseppe Barbaglio and Severino Dianich (Alba: Edizione Paolina, 1976).

ST   Thomas Aquinas, *Summa Theologica*, vols. 1–3 (New York: Benziger Brothers, 1948).

TRE   *Theologische Realenzyclopädie*, vols. 1–10, ed. Gerhard Krause and Gerhard Müller (Berlin: Walter de Gruyter, 1977 ff).

Vat. II 1   *Vatican Council II. The Conciliar and Post-Conciliar Documents*, ed. Austin Flannery (Northport, N.Y.: Costello Publishing Co., 1975).

Vat. II 2   *Vatican Council II. More Post-Conciliar Documents*, ed. Austin Flannery (Collegeville, Minn.: The Liturgical Press, 1982).

WG   *A World of Grace. An Introduction to the Themes and Foundations* of *Karl Rahner's Theology*, ed. Leo O'Donovan (New York: The Seabury Press, 1980).

WT   *Wagnis Theologie.Erfahrung mit der Theologie Karl Rahners*, ed. Herbert Vorgrimler (Freiburg: Herder, 1979).

Abbreviations of biblical books are adopted from *The New American Bible* while those of Vatican II's documents are taken from *Vat. II, 1* and *Vat. II, 2*.

Notes

Preface

1. See, for example, Adoff Tanquerey, *A Manual of Dogmatic Theology* (New York: Desclée Co., 1959), 2:409–62. Even a more recent work by Edmund J. Fortman, *Everlasting Life After Death* (New York: Alba House, 1976) still provides fantastic details on heaven. The blessed will have, says Fortman, "telepathic powers . . . clairvoyant powers . . . precognitive powers . . . retro-cognitive powers . . . psycho-kinetic powers . . . projective powers. . . . And very likely they will have still other powers, paranormal powers, perhaps paranormal linguistic powers, perhaps other paranormal communicatory powers. . . ." (312). The author goes on to say that the blessed "could use their minds to grow in knowledge—both speculative and practical. They could learn more, grow more in any area of knowledge that interested them. In Science. In Art. In Philosophy. In Theology. In Languages. In Music. In Astronomy. In Cosmology. In Anthropology. In Scripture. In History. In Geography. In Literature. In Engineering. In Sociology. And so on and so on. . . . They could have Halls of Science, of Art, of Literature, Mathematics, . . . Halls of Music . . . Halls of Psychology. . . . They can have Halls of Travel, of Interplanetary Travel, of Interstellar Travel, Intergalactic Travel. . . ." (315–16). This long quotation in which "heaven" is transformed into an open university and a travel agency, written by a scholar of Fortman's stature, can serve as a reminder of the importance of Rahner's transcendental eschatology.

2. See Hans Küng's *EL*. Küng dismisses almost entirely individual eschatology. Dietrich Wiederkehr in his *Perspektiven der Eschatologie* (Einsiedeln: Benziger Verlag, 1974) gives scant attention to individual eschatology and devotes the major part of his book to collective eschatology. Protestant eschatologies, too, generally speaking remain silent on individual eschatology. See *DCG* 3:385–471 and *CD* 2:475–587. As far as the contents of eschatology are concerned, both Gerhard Ebeling in *DCG* and Hans Schwarz discuss only death and resurrection, the last judgment, the Parousia, and the Kingdom of God. See, however, *DID*, in which Fritz Buri, Jan M. Lochman, and Heinrich Ott discuss under the title "Spezielle Fragen" the question of the fate of the individual after death (264–277).

3. See n. 14 of the Introduction.

4. See "The Hermeneutics of Eschatological Assertions," *TI* 4:340–42, 343.

5. *FCF*, 432: "Because Christian eschatology makes statements about the future of the single and total person as he actually is, there is necessarily an eschatology which makes assertions about man insofar as he is a free person, insofar as he is a concrete, corporeal being in time and space, and insofar as he is an even unique individual who cannot be deduced. And there is an eschatology which makes assertions about the same person insofar as he is a member of a community and an

214

individual within a collective history. This is a collective eschatology which makes assertions about the future of mankind and of the world insofar as this world is understood by Christianity to begin with as the milieu and environment of transcendental spirit."

6. *FCF*, 436.

7. Michael Schmaus's justification for inverting the order is that the Scripture places a greater emphasis on universal eschatology than on particular eschatology and that the final life of the individual can only be understood as a life within the perfected community. See *KD* Vol. 4, pt. 2, 1–3 and *Dogma 6*, 215–16.

Introduction: Eschatology and Rahner's Theology

1. For a brief exposition of the meaning of this term and its use in the Bible, see the excellent article "Kingdom of God" by Rudolf Schnackenburg in *EBT*, 455–70. See also *DBT*, 292–95; *NDT*, 1235–50.

2. For a short overview of Old Testament messianism and eschatology, see *EBT*, 575–82; *DBT*, 354–57; *TRE*, 256–70; *HAV*, 18–32; *MS*, 5:701–21. See also a helpful discussion by John L. McKenzie in *The Jerome Biblical Commentary*, ed. Raymond E. Brown, Joseph A. Fitzmyer, and Roland E. Murphy (Englewood Cliffs, N.J.: Prentice-Hall, 1968), 762–67.

3. John L. McKenzie, *Jerome Biblical Commentary*, distinguishes three stages of development. The first stage, found in the oracle of Nathan, preserved in three forms (2 Sam 7; Ps 89; 1 Chr 17), in the blessing of Judah by Jacob (Gn 49:9–12) and in the royal psalms (in particular Pss 2, 72, 110) emphasizes the political salvation to be accomplished by David and his dynasty. The second stage, found predominantly in the preexilic prophets, highlights a future inbreak of the power of Yahweh to revive the decadent dynasty of David and to insure its permanence under a new ideal ruler. The third stage, spanning the postexilic period, places the national hope in the emergence in an indefinite future of one supreme king who would represent Yahweh's definitive intervention to save his people. It is in this period that we may begin to speak of the Messiah in the strict sense.

4. For studies in apocalyptic literature, see two most recent books, one by Christopher Rowland, *The Open Heaven. A Study of Apocalyptic in Judaism and Early Christianity* (New York: Crossroad, 1982) and the other by John J. Collins, *The Apocalyptic Imagination. An Introduction of the Jewish Matrix of Christianity* (New York: Crossroad, 1984). We will come back to this latter work in our last chapter in our discussion of Rahner's distinction between eschatology and apocalyptic.

5. *EBT,* 462. In chap. 1, various contemporary theological interpretations of the eschatological nature of the Kingdom of God will be discussed. For further discussions of New Testament eschatologies, see *TRE*, 270–99; *MS* 5:722–78; *NAU*, 38–81; *HAV*, 32–70.

6. There is no doubt that a great number of early Christians (Mk 9:1, 13:30; 1 Pet 4:7; Rev 1:3), including for a time even Paul (Rom 13:11; 1 Thess 4:15–18; 1 Cor 7:26) hoped for an early Parousia. But the fact that its evident delay did not lead to any crisis of faith—the scoffers of 2 Pet 3:1–10 are heretical teachers—is proof enough that there can be no question of a so-called postponement of the Parousia. When the imminence of the Parousia is emphasized in the New Testament (e.g., Mk 13:32) this refers not so much to a definite point in time laid down for it to arrive as to the urgency for conversion and watchfulness on the part of the disciples and the irreversibility of the course of history approaching its definitive

fulfillment. See Elpidius Pax, "Parousia," *EBT*, 636–37.

7. For a summary of patristic eschatology, see *MS* 5:567–89; *TRE*, 299–305. See also John N. D. Kelly, *Early Christian Doctrines* (New York: Harper & Row, 1960), 459–89.

8. The doctrine of *apocatastasis* is shared also by Clement of Alexandria and Gregory of Nyssa. It was strongly attacked by Augustine and formally condemned in the first anathema against Origenism probably formulated by the Council of Constantinople in 543.

9. See the constitution *Benedictus Deus* in *DS*, 1000–1002 and *CF*, 684–85.

10. One example among thousands: It was disputed how long the souls are detained in purgatory. Some theologians think that they are kept there for a long time; others, that the period of purgation is brief. Dominic Soto and Maldonatus even ventured to opine that no one remains in purgatory longer than ten years!

11. *SM* 2:242.

12. "The Prospects for Dogmatic Theology," *TI* 1:11–12. In this essay, published in 1954, Rahner first raised the problem of eschatology.

13. See ibid., 14 n. 1. Although the scheme was worked out in close collaboration with von Balthasar, Rahner claimed sole responsibility for the published version. This claim is to be noted since von Balthasar was to become one of Rahner's most outspoken critics, especially of what he regarded as an excessively anthropocentric approach to theology. See his *Cordula oder der Ernstfall*, 3d ed. (Einsiedein: Johannes, 1968) where he criticized in particular Rahner's theories of the supernatural existential, anonymous Christianity, and transcendental method.

14. See *TI* 1:35–37. For the convenience of readers, I will reproduce here the scheme proposed by Rahner:

E. *The Theological Anthropology of the Redeemed*
  VI. The Theology of Death.
    1. The supernatural dimensions of death.
      a. The supernatural character of death in general in the present dispensation.
      b. Death as punishment. First and second death and their relationship.
      c. Death as dying with Christ and redemption.
      d. Death as supernatural consummation and as supernatural separation from this world.
    2. The sacramentality of dying: extreme unction.
    3. Individual death as the beginning of the Last Things, as judgment.
      a. The possibility of eternal reprobation.
      b. Hell as private destiny.
      c. The definitive character of union with God.

F. *Eschatology*
  I. The theological gnoseology of eschatological statememts considered in their possibility and their limits.
  II. The Eschata.
    1. The New Aion as a whole.
      a. The transformation of time.
      b. The transformation of matter.
      c. The transformation of spirit.
      d. The transformation of the new aion.
    2. The relation between individual eschatology and collective eschatology.

3. The relation between the present and the future aion.
4. The individual elements of Eschatology.
   a. The Return of Christ.
   b. The Resurrection of the body.
   c. The General Judgment.
   d. Hell as the collective destiny of the "Corpus diaboli."
   e. Heaven as the eternal Kingdom of God the Father.

15. As Rahner explained in *TI* 1:35 n. 1: ". . . death must first of all be seen as something which takes place in this Christian world here and now, as a part of the Christian life. . . . Death must not be left out of account by looking forward to what properly comes *after* it." He had already essayed a reinterpretation of death in "Zur Theologie des Todes," *Zeitschrift für Katholische Theologie* 79 (1957): 1–44.

16. *TI* 1:36 n. 1: "'Individual' eschatology is intentionally introduced here, before Eschatology, so as to make it clear in this way too that Eschatology is fundamentally 'general' eschatology and thus that something essential remains to be said over and above 'special' eschatology."

17. *LThK* 3:1094–98. This article, which can be regarded as Rahner's programmatic essay on eschatology, is reprinted in *SM* 2:242–46. The fact that it was reproduced here without any alteration some ten years later (1967) might suggest that in Rahner's estimation the theological situation had not improved appreciably in the intervening years. This is confirmed by his assessment of post-Vatican II theology, as will be shown later.

18. See *SM* 2:243–44. For Rahner's description of this new situation and its implications for faith in general, see "Christianity and the 'New Man'," *TI* 5:135–53; "The Man of Today and Religion," *TI* 6:3–20; "Christian Living Formerly and Today," *TI* 7:3–24; "The Experience of God Today," *TI* 11:149–65; "On the Situation of Faith," *TI* 20:13–32.

19. See *SM* 2:244–45. Briefly, for Rahner genuine eschatology, in contrast to false apocalyptic, is not an advance report of events taking place in the future but a "forward look which is necessary to man for his spiritual decision in freedom, and it is made from the standpoint of his situation in saving history as this is determined by the Christ-event." This question of the nature of eschatology and the hermeneutics of eschatological assertions will be discussed at length in chap. 3 when Rahner's other foundational article, "The Hermeneutics of Eschatological Assertions," *TI* 4:323–46, will be studied.

20. "Reflections on Methodology in Theology," *TI* 11:98.

21. See *SM* 2:245; *TD* 151.

22. See *SM* 2:246.

23. See ibid.

24. See ibid.

25. On Rahner's own admission, the relatively complete one-volume *Foundations of Christian Faith* should not be regarded as the synthesis of his thought. See *FCF*, xv: "If what is being offered here is an introduction, then neither should the reader expect that this book is a final summary of the previous theological work of the author. It is not that and does not intend to be."

As to the genre that Rahner adopted, see his own explanations in his foreword to Peter Eicher, *Die anthropologische Wende. K. Rahners philosophischer Weg vom Wesen des Menschen zur personalen Existenz* (Freiburg, Switzerland: Universität-verlag, 1970), x–xvii, 243–48 and his letter to Klaus P. Fischer, *Der Mensch als Geheimnis. Die Anthropologie Karl Rahners* (Freiburg: Herder, 1974), 400–410.

The genre can be best described as "theology of the first-level of reflection" (*Theologie der ersten Reflexionsstufe*) on the personal experience of Christian living and is meant to serve the purpose of witness. *Foundations of Christian Faith* belongs precisely to this genre. In any case, the seventeen pages found in *FCF*, 431–47 cannot be regarded as a summary of Rahner's eschatology.

26. See *Theology of Death* (New York: Herder and Herder, 1961); for articles published in *TI*, see Bibliography, I, C. These writings will of course be examined in detail in the course of this study.

27. "The Second Vatican Council's Challenge to Theology." *TI* 9:19–20. The article was first delivered as a lecture at the International Theological Congress of the University of Notre Dame (U.S.A.) on 23 March 1966.

28. We will discuss this development in detail in the next chapter.

29. *TI* 9:45.

30. See "The Need for a 'Short Formula' of Christian Faith," Ibid. 117–22. On pages 122–26 Rahner suggests in a general way the doctrinal contents that such brief creedal formulas should proclaim. In this article, which was first published in 1967, Rahner has not yet offered an example of such brief creedal formulas. This he did in 1970 in his article "Reflections on the Problems Involved in Devising a Short Formula of the Faith," Ibid. 11:238–44. The three-part formula was reprinted in 1967 in *FCF*, 454–59 with a minor change of the title of the second part; instead of "soziologische" we have a more precise "anthropologische." See also his "In Search of a Short Formula for the Christian Faith," *Concilium* 3 (March 1967): 36–42. For a critique of Rahner's attempts at formulating creedal formulas, see George Vass, *A Theologian in Search of a Philosophy* (London: Sheed & Ward, 1985), 1–17.

31. *FCF*, 457. The German original is: "Das Christentum ist die offenhaltung der Frage nach der absoluten Zukunft, die sich als solche selbst in Selbstmitteilung geben will, diesen ihren Willen in Jesus Christus eschatologisch irreversibel festgemacht hat und Gott heist" (*ST* 9:254).

32. *FCF*, 454.

33. Ibid., 456.

34. See ibid., 431: "It [eschatology] is the doctrine about man insofar as he is a being who is open to the absolute future of God himself." See also "Theology and Anthropology," *TI* 9:45: "In order to be equal to today's demands *eschatology* needs the foundation provided by a transcendental anthropology, in which man is comprehended as the being who plans himself, looking forward to an open future, as the being who *hopes*, empowered by God to embrace an absolute future."

35. See "Theology and Anthropology," *TI* 9:28: ". . . dogmatic theology today must be theological anthropology. . . . As soon as man is understood as the being who is absolutely transcendent in respect to God, 'anthropocentricity' and 'theocentricity' in theology are not opposites but strictly one and the same thing, seen from two sides."

36. See *SM* 194–95; *FCF*, 295–98; 318–21.

37. See, for example, Albert Raffelt, "Karl Rahner. Bibliographie der Secundärliteratur 1948–1978," in *Wagnis Theologie*, ed. H. Vorgrimler (Freibury: Herder, 1979), 598–622.

38. In the following notes (38–44) I will list only some of the most significant studies. For studies on Rahner's philosophical presuppositions, see Denis J. M. Bradley, "Rahner's *Spirit in the World*: Aquinas or Hegel?" *The Thomist* 41 (1977): 167–99; James J. Buckley, "On Being a Symbol: An Appraisal of Karl Rahner," *Theological Studies* 40, no. 3 (1979): 285–98; Robert Masson, "Rahner

and Heidegger: Being, Hearing and God," *The Thomist* 37 (1973): 455–88; Gerald A. McCool, "The Philosophical Theology of Rahner and Lonergan," in *God, Knowable and Unknowable,* ed. Robert J. Roth (New York: Fordham University Press, 1973), 123–57; idem, "Philosophical Pluralism and an Evolving Thomism," *Continuum* 2 (1964): 3–16; idem, "Karl Rahner and the Christian Philosophy of St. Thomas Aquinas," in *Theology and Discovery: Essays in Honor of Karl Rahner,* ed. William Kelly, (Milwaukee, Wis.: Marquette University Press, 1980), 63–93; Joseph Donceel, *The Philosophy of Karl Rahner* (Albany: Magi Books, 1969); idem, "Transcendental Thomism," *Monist* 58 (1974): 67–68; also published in *Listening* 9 (1974): 157–64; idem, "A Thomistic Misapprehension?" *Thought* 32 (1958): 189–98; Andrew Tallon, "Rahner and Personization," *Philosophy Today* 14 (1970): 44–56; Vincent Branick, *An Ontology of Understanding. Karl Rahner's Metaphysics of Knowledge in the Context of Modern German Hermeneutics* (St. Louis: Marianist Communications Center, 1971).

39. See Ann Carr, *The Theological Method of Karl Rahner* (Missoula, Mont.: Scholar's Press, 1977); idem, "Theology and Experience in the Thought of Karl Rahner," *Journal of Religion* 13 (1973): 359–76; Otto Muck, *The Transcendental Method* (New York: Herder & Herder, 1967); William V. Dych, "Method in Theology According to Karl Rahner," in *Theology and Discovery: Essays in Honor of Karl Rahner,* ed. William Kelly (Milwaukee, Wis.: Marquette University Press, 1980), 39–53; idem, "Theology in a New Key," *WG,* 1–16; Matthew Lamb, ed., *Creativity and Method* (Milwaukee, Wis.: Marquette University Press, 1981); Leo J. O'Donovan, "Orthopraxis and Theological Method in Karl Rahner," *Proceedings of the Catholic Theological Society of America* 35 (1980): 47–65; James B. Reichmann, "Transcendental Method and Psychogenesis of Being," *The Thomist* 32 (1968): 449–508; Cornelio Fabro, *La svolta antropologica di Karl Rahner* (Milan: Rusconi Editore, 1974).

40. See Joseph A. Bracken, "The Holy Trinity as a Community of Divine Persons, II. Person and Nature in the Doctrine of God," *Heythrop Journal* 15, no. 3 (1974): 257–70; Ann Carr, "The God Who Is Involved," *Theology Today* 38 (1981): 314–28; Joseph Donceel, "Second Thoughts on the Nature of God," *Thought* 48 (1971): 346–70; Anthony J. Kelly, "Trinity and Process. Relevance of the Basic Christian Confession of God," *Theological Studies* 31 (1970): 393–414; Lawrence B. Porter, "On Keeping 'Persons' in the Trinity: A Linguistic Approach to Trinitarian Thought," *Theological Studies* 41 (1980): 530–48.

41. See Joseph H. P. Wong, *Logos-Symbol in the Christology of Karl Rahner* (Rome: LAS, 1984); Robert E. Doud, "Rahner's Christology. A Whiteheadian Critique," *Journal of Religion* 57 (1977): 144–55; Anselm Grün, *Erlösung durch das Kreuz. Karl Rahners Beitrag an einem heutigen Erlösungsverständnis* (Vier Törin: Münsterschwarzach, 1978); Thomas Pearl, "Dialectical Panentheism: On the Hegelian Character of Karl Rahner's Key Christological Writings," *Irish Theological Quarterly* 42 (1970): 119–37; David A. Taylor, *"Unio Hypostatica in the Christology of Karl Rahner"* (diss., Oxford University, 1976); John B. Galvin, "Jesus' Approach to Death: An Examination of Some Recent Studies," *Theological Studies* 41, no. 4 (1980): 713–44; I. Sanna, *La cristologia antropologica di K. Rahner* (Rome: Edizioni Paoline, 1970).

42. See Fischer, *Der Mensch als Geheimnis. Die Anthropologie Karl Rahners;* William C. Shepherd, *Man's Condition. God in the World Process* (New York: Herder & Herder, 1964); Andrew Tallon, "Personal Becoming: Karl Rahner's Christian Anthropology," *Thomist* 43 (1979): 1–177; Gerald A. McCool, "The Philosophy of the Human Person in Karl Rahner's Theology," *Theological*

Studies 22 (1961): 537–62; Peter Eicher, *Die anthropologische Wende. Karl Rahners philosophischer Weg vom Wesen des Menschen zur personalen Existenz* (Freiburg, Switzerland: Universitätverlag, 1970); Josef Speck, *Karl Rahners theologische Anthropologie. Eine Einführung* (Munich: Kösel Verlag, 1967).

43. See Nicolaus Schwerdtfeger, *Gnade und Welt. Zum Grundgefüge von Karl Rahners Theorie der "Anonymen Christen"* (Freiburg: Herder, 1982); Peter Hebblethwaite, "The Status of 'Anonymous Christians', " *Heythrop Journal* 18 (1977): 47–55; Anita Roper, *The Anonymous Christian* (New York: Sheed and Ward, 1966); Paul Stassen, "The Anonymous Christian," *Christ to the World* 13 (1967): 246–47; Eugene Hillman, "'Anonymous Christianity' and the Missions," *Downside Review* 85 (1966): 361–79; Karl-Heinz Weger, "Überlegungen zum 'anonymen Christen'," *Wagnis Theologie,* ed. Herbert Vorgrimler (Freiburg: Herder, 1979), 499–519; Klaus Riesenhuber, "Karl Rahner's Anonymous Christian," *Theology Digest* 13 (1965): 163–71; Hans Kruse, "Die 'Anonymen Christen' exegetisch gesehen," *Münchener theologische Zeitschrift* 18 (1967): 2–29.

44. See John Carmody, "Karl Rahner's Theology of the Spiritual Life," *Chicago Studies* 8 (1969): 71–86; Harvey Egan, "Rahner's Mystical Theology," in *Theology and Discovery: Essays in Honor of Karl Rahner,* ed. William Kelly (Milwaukee, Wis.: Marquette University Press, 1980), 139–58; Michael J. Walsh, *The Heart of Christ in the Writings of Karl Rahner. An Investigation of Its Christological Foundation as an Example of the Relationship Between Theology and Spirituality* (Rome: Univ. Gregoriana, 1977); David B. Knight, *"The Implications for Spiritual Theology of Karl Rahner's Theology of Renunciation Studied in the Light of His Concept of Man"* (Ph. D. diss., The Catholic University of America, 1971).

45. "Theology of Death," *Clergy Review* 44 (1959): 588–602.

46. "Zur Theologie des Todes," *Freiburger Zeitschrift für Philosophie und Theologie* 7 (1960): 56–63.

47. "The Paschal Character of the Christian Death," *Liturgy* 33 (1964): 87–90.

48. "Karl Rahner y el sentido teológico de la muerte," *Stromata* 21 (1965): 515–23.

49. "Sentido teológico de la muerte," *Franciscanum* 8 (1966): 99–101.

50. *Interview sur la mort avec Karl Rahner* (Paris: Lethielleux, 1967).

51. "The Meaning of Death. Paul and Modern Theologians," *Bible Today* 41 (1969): 2856–61.

52. "La muerte en la antropología de K. Rahner," *Revista Española de Teologia* 31 (1971): 189–212; 335–60.

53. "II Mistero della morte. 'Anima separata' o 'cessata animazione'?" *Salesianum* 34 (1972): 97–115.

54. "A halál teologiája Karl Rahnernél [The Theology of Death According to Karl Rahner]," *Vigilia* (Budapest) 37 (1973): 737–44.

55. *Der Tod des Menschen. Zur Deutung des Todes in der gegenwärtigen Philosophie und Theologie* (Bern: Peter Lang, 1977), 70–80.

56. *Hoffnung angesichts des Todes. Das Todesproblem bei Karl Barth und in der zeitgenössischen Theologie des deutschen Sprachraums.* (Munich: Verlag Ferdinand Schöningh, 1977), 202–99.

57. *Der Tod im Denken und Leben des Christen* (Düsseldorf: Patmos Verlag, 1978), 76–79.

58. "Der Tod. 'Trennung von Seele und Leib'?," in *Wagnis Theologie,* ed. Herbert Vorgrimler (Freiburg: Herder, 1979), 311–38.

59. "Tod und Auferstehung in der Sicht christlicher Dogmatik," *Kerygma und Dogma* 20 (1974): 167–80.

60. "Theology of the Darkness of Death," *Theological Studies* 39 (1978): 22–54.

61. "The Hope for Humanity: Rahner's Eschatology," in *The World of Grace,* ed. Leo J. O'Donovan (New York: The Seabury Press, 1980), 153–68.

62. "Conception de la mort et conception de l'homme. La conception de la mort chez K. Rahner et L. Boros," *Nova et Vetera* 56, no. 3 (1981): 195–213.

63. "De Mysterio Mortis," in *Glaube im Prozess,* ed. Elmar Klinger and Klaus Wittstadt (Freiburg: Herder, 1984), 492–513.

64. *La teologia della morte in K. Rahner* (Bologna: Edizione Dehoniana, 1983).

65. *The Death in Every Now* (New York: Sheed and Ward, 1969); "Time, Death and the Sacred. An Essay on Rahner's Theology of Death and the Unmanageable" (diss., Institut Catholique, Paris, 1969); "Death as an Act: An Interpretation of Karl Rahner," in *The Mystery of Suffering and Death,* ed. Michael J. Taylor (New York: Alba House, 1973), 119–36.

66. "Incarnation and Eschatology," *Cord* 14 (1964): 211–16.

67. "Dimensión escatológica de la vida cristiana según K. Rahner. Aportación a la teología de la esperanza," *Ephemerides Carmeliticae* 22 (1971): 38–94.

68. "Zukunft und Hoffnung in der gegenwärtige Theologie," in *Eschatologie und geschichtliche Zukunft,* ed. Georg Scherer (Essen: Verlag Fredebeul & Koenen, 1972), 66–88.

69. See Andrew Tallon, "Personal Becoming," *The Thomist* 43 (1979): 1–177. This development will be discussed at greater length in the next chapter.

Chapter 1. Karl Rahner's Eschatology in Context

1. See "Umrisse der Eschatologie," *Verbum Caro* (Einsiedeln: Johannes Verlag, 1960), 276.

2. See, for instance, *DTI* 2:94–101; *NDT*, 398–406; *MS* 5:617–26; *Eschatologie*, 49–64; *NAU*, 11–37. *CHFM* is an excellent discussion of contemporary eschatologies. See also Jürgen Moltmann, *The Future of Creation*, trans. Margaret Kohl (Philadelphia: Fortress Press, 1979), 18–40. For general historical surveys of eschatology, see *TRE* 10:254–361; Timotheus Rast, "Die Eschatologie in der Theologie des 20. Jahrhunderts," in *Bilanz der Theologie im 20. Jahrhundert*, ed. Herbert Vorgrimler and Robert van der Gucht (Freiburg-Basel and Vienna: Herder, 1970) 3:294–315; Peter Müller-Goldkuhle, "Post-Biblical Developments in Eschatological Thought," *Concilium* 41 (1969): 24–41; Erhard Kunz, *Protestantische Eschatologie. Von der Reformation bis zur Aufklärung*, vol. 4 of *Handbuch der Dogmengeschichte* (Freiburg: Herder, 1980), fasc. 7c, pt. 1; Philip Schäfer, *Eschatologie. Trient und Gegenreformation*, vol. 4 of *Handbuch der Dogmengeschichte* (Freiburg: Herder, 1984), fasc. 7c. pt. 2; Brian Daley, *Eschatologie in der Schrift und Patristik*, vol. 4 of *Handbuch der Dogmengeschichte*, fasc. 7a. Other volumes in the same collection on the eschatology in Scholasticism, and from the Enlightenment to the present times have been announced but have not yet appeared. Rahner himself has written short overviews of the historical development of eschatology. See *LThK* 3:1094–96; *SM* 2:242–4.

3. See his *Das Messianitäts—und Leidengeheimnis* (1901) and his famous *Von Reimarus zu Wrede* (1906), recast and completed under the title *Geschichte der Leben-Jesu-Forschung* (1913).

4. See his *The Formation of Christian Dogma* (Boston: Beacon Press, 1985).

5. *Der Römerbrief* (Munich: Kaiser Verlag, 1918), 298: "Christentum, das nicht ganz und gar und restlos Eschatologie ist, hat mit Christus ganz und gar und

restlos nichts zu tun." Supratemporal eschatology is also espoused by Emil Brunner, Barth's ardent supporter, for whom time and eternity are given contemporaneously side by side and only eternity has value.

6. See in particular his *Jesus Christ and Mythology* (London: SCM Press, 1958) and *Jesus and the Word* (London: Collins/Fontana, 1958).

7. See his *The Parables of the Kingdom* (London: Charles Scribner's Sons, 1935).

8. See his *Christ and Time* (Philadelphia: Westminster Press, 1947) and *Salvation in History* (New York: Harper & Row, 1967).

9. See his *The Parables of Jesus*, 2d ed. (New York: Charles Scribner's Sons, 1963).

10. See his *Offenbarung als Geschichte* (Göttingen: Vamdenbroeck & Ruprecht, 1961) and "Heilsgeschichte und Geschichte," *Kerygma und Dogma* 5 (1959): 218–37.

11. *Theology of Hope*, trans. James W. Leitch (London: SCM Press, 1967), 16. See also his influential essay "Theology as Eschatology," in *The Future of Hope*, ed. Frederick Herzog (New York: Herder and Herder, 1970), 1–50.

12. *Theology of Hope*, 84. Theology is therefore *intellectus spei*.

13. Ibid., 329. See also *The Future of Hope*, ed. Frederick Herzog (New York: Herder and Herder, 1970), 34–50. The influence of the Frankfurt School of Theodor Adorno and Max Horkheimer is evident in Moltmann's critique of modern society. In his later works, e.g., *The Crucified God* (New York: Harper and Row, 1974), without abandoning his theology of hope, Moltmann developed his dialectic of contradiction more systematically in the elaborate treatment given to the theology of the cross.

14. See Metz's most important works: *Theology of the World*, ed. and trans. William Glen-Doepel (New York: Herder and Herder, 1969); *Faith in History and Society*, English translation by David Smith (New York: The Seabury Press, 1980); *The Emergent Church. The Future of Christianity in a Postbourgeois World*, English translation by Peter Mann (New York: Crossroad, 1981).

15. See Rahner's letter to James J. Bacik, printed as introduction to the latter's book, *Apologetics and the Eclipse of Mystery. Mystagogy according to Karl Rahner* (Notre Dame, Ind.: University of Notre Dame Press, 1980), ix: "Metz's critique of my theology (which he calls transcendental theology) is the only criticism which I take seriously."

16. Tallon, "Personal Becoming," 3.

17. "The Peace of God and the Peace of the World," *TI* 10:388 n. 36. Albert Schweitzer's book referred to by Rahner is *Friede oder Atomkrieg?* (Munich: C. H. Beck, 1958).

18. See "Dogmatic Reflections on the Knowledge and Self-Consciousness of Christ," *TI* 5:199–205.

19. "The Hermeneutics of Eschatological Assertions," ibid. 4:338 n. 13.

20. See "Remarks on the Dogmatic Treatise 'De Trinitate'," *TI*, ibid., 101; "What Is a Dogmatic Statement?" ibid. 5:56, 60.

21. See "The Sinful Church in the Decrees of Vatican II," ibid. 6:280 n. 24; 290 n. 52.

22. See "Theological Reflections on the Problem of Secularization," ibid. 10:320.

23. See "Nature and Grace," ibid. 4:163; "Questions of Controversial Theology on Justification," ibid. 4:189–218; "Pluralism in Theology," ibid. 11:9.

24. "Possible Courses for the Theology of the Future," ibid. 13:42.

25. For Rahner's distinction between "Historie" and "Geschichte," see *FCF*, 240–41. Rahner has spelled out the difference between him and Barth and Bultmann in an interview with Joachim Schickel in *KRIG* 2:233–36.

26. See "Marriage as a Sacrament," *TI* 10:219 n. 36.

27. See ibid. 4:149 n. 46; 6:289 n. 50, 293; 9:170 n. 9; 11:186 n. 2.

28. *CHFM*, 88–89. In comparing Cullmann's eschatology with those of Bultmann, Dodd, and Robinson, Travis comes out in favor of Cullmann's. Ratzinger, too, comparing and contrasting Cullmann with Barth, Bultmann, and Dodd, prefers Cullmann. See *Eschatologie*, 56: "Obgleich die gegenwärtige Stimmung in der Theologie dem Ansatz von 'Heilsgeschichte' her nicht günstig ist, muss man sagen, dass hier konkreter und schriftnäher gesprochen wird als in den Entwürfen, die uns bisher begegneten."

29. See his "Personal Becoming," 20–29 and above all 30–71.

30. See *HW*, chaps. 6–8. In the introduction to *HW*, Metz explicitly mentions this new attempt to complement the Thomistic concept of the world of things (*Gegenstandswelt*) by means of that of the world of persons (*Mitwelt*). See *HW*, ix. In editing *HW*, Metz has added five notes to emphasize the dimensions of freedom, love, and community in the human person. See in particular *HW*, 133 n. 2; 138 n. 6; 142 n. 2; 146 n. 3.

31. *HW*, 89. The emphasis is mine.

32. This important quotation is unaccountably dropped from the English text of *HW* on p. 116. The German text, found in the second German edition, p. 143, runs as follows: "Der Mensch ist als *geschichtliches* Wesen Geist. Der Ort seiner Transzendenz ist immer auch ein geschichtlicher Ort. Und damit ist der Ort einer möglichen Offenbarung immer und notwendig die Geschichte des Menschen."

33. Ibid., 134.

34. I can only cite a few early representative articles: "Theological Reflections on Monogenism," *TI* 1:229–96; "Concerning the Relationship between Nature and Grace," ibid., 297–317; "The Theological Concept of Concupiscentia," ibid., 347–82; "The Dignity and Freedom of Man," ibid., 2:235–63; "Guilt and Its Remission: The Borderland between Theology and Psychotherapy," ibid., 265–81; "The Theology of the Symbol," ibid. 4:221–52. For a detailed account of Rahner's later development, especially in his understanding of personization, see Tallon, "Personal Becoming," 95–177.

35. See "Zur Theologie des Todes," *Synopsis* 3 (1949): 87–112, reprinted in 1957 by Herder, Freiburg.

36. See "The Dignity and Freedom of Man," *TI* 2:235–63, first published in 1952.

37. Ibid., 1:347–82.

38. Ibid., 2:175–201.

39. Ibid., 203–16,

40. Ibid., 3:35–46.

41. Ibid., 141–57.

42. Ibid., 4:347–54.

43. See especially ibid. 2:272–74. For an excellent analysis of this long text, see Tallon, "Personal Becoming," 120–29. Tallon carefully distinguishes two "othernesses" in interaction with which human beings become persons. First, our own bodies (individuals as spirits incarnated in matter) and second, our world of things and above all persons. It is the second "otherness" that obtains primacy of place.

44. "The 'Commandment' of Love in Relation to the Other Commandments," *TI* 5:439–59.

45. "Reflections on the Unity of the Love of Neighbor and the Love of God," ibid. 6:231–49. Other later significant essays on this theme include: "Theology of Freedom," ibid., 178–96; "Experience of Self and Experience of God," ibid. 13:122–32; "The Theological Dimension of the Question about Man," ibid. 17:53–70; "The Human Question of Meaning in Face of the Absolute Mystery of God," ibid. 18:89–104; "Experience of Transcendence from the Standpoint of Catholic Dogmatics," ibid., 173–88; "Experience of the Holy Spirit," ibid., 189–210.

46. See "Ideology and Christianity," ibid. 6:43–58; "Marxist Utopia and the Christian Future of Man," ibid, 59–68.

47. See "A Fragmentary Aspect of a Theological Evaluation of the Concept of the Future," ibid. 10:235–41; "Theological Observations on the Concept of Time," ibid. 11:288–308; "The Question of the Future," ibid. 12:181–201; "Eternity from Time," ibid. 19:169–77; "The Inexhaustible Transcendence of God and our Concern for the Future," ibid. 20:173–86.

48. See "On the Theology of Hope," ibid. 10:242–59.

49. See "Christian Humanism," ibid. 9:187–204.

50. See "The Church and the Parousia of Christ," ibid. 6:295–312; "The Experiment with Man," ibid. 9:205–24; "The Theological Problems Entailed in the Idea of the 'New Earth'," ibid. 10:260–72; "Immanent and Transcendent Consummation of the World," ibid., 273–89; "Theological Reflections on the Problem of Secularization," ibid., 318–48; "The Peace of God and the Peace of the World," ibid., 271–88; "The Function of the Church as a Critic of Society" ibid. 12:229–49; "The Church's Commission to Bring Salvation and the Humanization of the World," ibid. 14:295–313; "Justification and World Development," ibid. 18:259–73; "Profangeschichte und Heilsgeschichte," *ST*, 15:11–23; "Naturwissenschaft und Vernünftiger Glaube," ibid., 24–62.

51. See "On the Theology of Revolution," *TI* 14:314–30.

52. See *Befreiende Theologie, der Beitrag Lateinamerikas zur Theologie der Gegenwart* (Stuttgart: Verlag W. Kohlhammer, 1977).

53. See "Christian Humanism," *TI* 9:197 n. 26, and "On the Theology of Hope," ibid. 10:242. See also *KRIG* 1:282–83; 2:49, 124. For a discussion of the influence of Bloch on Moltmann and Metz, see Walter H. Capps, *Time Invades the Cathedral. Tensions in the School of Hope* (Philadelphia: Fortress Press, 1972), in particular 91–109.

54. "Christian Humanism," *TI* 9:189.

55. Ibid., 199.

56. "Perspectives for the Future of the Church," ibid. 12:213.

57. "Possible Courses for the Theology of the Future," ibid. 13:56.

58. Ibid., 57.

Chapter 2. Anthropology as Eschatology

1. For excellent critical studies of Rahner's anthropology, see Peter Eicher, *Die Anthropologische Wende: Karl Rahners philosophischer Weg vom Wesen des Menschen zur personalen Existenz* (Freiburg, Switzerland: Universitätsverlag, 1970); Fischer, *Der Mensch als Geheimnis*; Brennan Hill, "Karl Rahner's Metaphysical Anthropology," *Carmelus* 18 (1971): 181–94; James H. John, "Karl Rahner: Man as the Being Who Must Question Being," in *Thomist Spectrum* (New York: Fordham University Press, 1966), 167–179; Thomas D. Logan, "Karl Rahner's Trans-

cendental Anthropology" (diss., Leeds University, 1978); Thomas J. Sheehan, *Subjectivity and Transcendental Method as the Fundamental Groundwork of Karl Rahner's Theological Anthropology* (Ph. D. diss., Fordham University, 1971); William C. Shepherd, *Man's Condition. God and the World Process* (New York: Herder and Herder, 1969).

2. See *SW*, 57–77.

3. *Hominization: The Evolutionary Origin of Man as a Theological Problem*, 53. This position is consistent with Rahner's view that 'nature' is a *"Restbegriff"* and that sensibility is emanated by the (possible) intellect.

4. See *SW*, 60.

5. For Rahner's explanations of the act of abstraction as return to oneself, see ibid., 117–20, 226–36; of the act of judging, see ibid., 120.

6. For Rahner's identification of the power for self-presence with the agent intellect, see ibid., 135–42.

7. See ibid., 143–202. This *Vorgriff* is the act of the agent intellect (ibid., 202–26).

8. See *SW*, 248–53 in which Rahner shows how this line of thought is present in Thomas.

9. See *Hominization*, 93–101.

10. "The Unity of Spirit and Matter in the Christian Understanding of Faith," *TI* 6:168. One can readily see the implications of this position for Rahner's transcendental christology. See "Christology Within an Evolutionary View of the World," ibid. 5:157–92.

11. See his important article "The Theology of the Symbol," ibid. 6:221–52. For studies on Rahner's theology of the symbol, see C. Annice Callahan, "Karl Rahner's Theology of the Symbol: Basis for His Theology of the Church and the Sacraments," *Irish Theological Quarterly* 49, no. 3 (1982): 195–205; Maria E. Motzko, *Karl Rahner's Theology: A Theology of the Symbol* (Ph. D. diss., Fordham University, 1976). James J. Buckley, "On Being a Symbol: An Appraisal of Karl Rahner," *Theological Studies* 40 (1979): 453–73; George E. Tracy, *On the Nature of the Symbol as Set Out in the Theology of Karl Rahner, S. J.* (Ph. D. diss., Boston College, 1976); Joseph H. P. Wong, *Logos-Symbol in the Christology of Karl Rahner* (Rome: Libreria Ateneo Salesiano, 1984). Because most scholars often trace Rahner's theory of symbol back to his metaphysics of knowledge and to Heidegger's philosophy of being, it is perhaps opportune to point out that Rahner derived his theory of symbol no less from spiritual writings, especially those of Ignatius of Loyola. See his theological dissertation, *E latere Christi: Der Ursprung der Kirche als zweiter Eva aus der Seite Christi des Zweiten Adam. Eine Untersuchung über den typologischen Sinn Von Jo 19*, 34, his early publications on spirituality and his writings on the "Spiritual Exercises."

12. "The Theology of the Symbol," *TI* 4:225. Note that the German word for *representation* here is *Repräsentanz* and not *Vertretung* which is used for *derivative symbols*.

13. Ibid., 224.

14. Ibid., 225. The English translation is emended to express more accurately Rahner's thesis that any moment of a being which is essentially plural can be the expression of another moment in the plural unity of the *same* being. The German original reads: ". . . dass ein Seiendes (d.h. jedes) in sich plural ist und in dieser Einheit des Pluralen—eines in dieser Pluralität wesentlish Ausdruck eines anderen in dieser pluralen Einheit ist oder sein kann." (*ST* 4:279–80). This notion of being as at once one and plural is applied not only to finite beings composed of essence

and existence but to God himself. Rahner claimed that this assertion can be deduced from the Christian doctrine of the Trinity, a deduction he regarded as a legitimate form of 'theological ontology'.

15. Ibid., 234.

16. Ibid., 247.

17. I am adopting the terms *first otherness, second otherness, first gap, second gap* from Tallon, "Personal Becoming," 51–71.

18. See *HW*, 130–33. In these first pages of the chapter on human historicity Rahner summarizes his view of the human being as material. Matter is the ground of human spatiality and temporality.

19. Metz's notes are found in *HW*, 133 n. 2; 138 n. 6; 142 n. 2; 146 n. 3; 149 n. 6. Metz suggests that Rahner's cosmocentric approach to human sociality could be complemented by a more anthropocentric one. Rather than speaking simply of *"das" Andere, Welt, Dingwelt,* and *Gegenstandwelt,* Metz adds *"der" Andere* and *Mitwelt.*

20. *HW*, 132–33.

21. "Theological Reflexions on Monogenism," *TI* 1:286.

22. See his later writings on the subject of monogenism, "Monogenism," *SM* 4:105–7. *"Erbsünde und Monogenismus,"* in *Theologie der Erbsünde,* ed. Karl-Heinz Weger, Questiones Disputatae 44 (Freiburg, 1970), 176–223; *Hominization;* "The Sin of Adam," *TI* 11:247–62; "Evolution and Original Sin," *Concilium* 6, no. 3 (June 1967). Basically, for Rahner, Pius XII's *Humani Generis* in 1950 rejected polygenism because and insofar as it was not at all clear how it could be reconciled with the doctrine of original sin. Now, however, Catholic theology has developed a doctrine of original sin that is compatible with polygenism.

23. "Guilt and its Remission: The Borderland Between Theology and Psychotherapy," *TI* 2:272–74. The text starts with "Man is a being constructed, as it were, from the interior towards the outside" and ends with ". . . into the very medium belonging to the person as sphere of his self-fulfillment."

24. Ibid., 272.

25. See ibid. 5:441. For a study of the implications of Rahner's anthropology for ethics, see Ronald Modras, "Implications of Rahner's Anthropology for Fundamental Moral Theology," *Horizons* 12 (1985): 70–90.

26. *TI* 6:231–49.

27. Ibid. 13:122–32.

28. See *SW*, 291–99.

29. See "The Theological Concept of Concupiscentia," *TI* 1:347–82; "Guilt-Responsibility-Punishment within the View of Catholic Theology," ibid. 6:197–217; *FCF*, 106–15.

30. See "Freedom in the Church," *TI* 2:89–107; "The Dignity and Freedom of Man," ibid., 255–63; "Institution and Freedom," ibid. 13:105–21; "Theology of Freedom," ibid. 6:178–96. *Grace in Freedom,* 203–61; "The Church's Responsibility for the Freedom of the Individual," *TI* 20:51–64; *Free Speech in the Church* (New York: Sheed and Ward, 1959).

31. "The Liberty of the Sick, Theologically Considered," *TI* 17:100–113. For studies on the theology of freedom in Rahner, see Robert L. Hurd, "The Conception of Freedom in Rahner," *Listening* 17 (1982): 138–52; Brian O. McDermott, "The Bonds of Freedom," *WG,* 50–63.

32. "The Theology of Freedom," *TI* 6:184.

33. See "The Theological Concept of Concupiscentia," ibid. 1:346–82.

34. Ibid., 181.

35. See *FCF*, 106–15.

36. See *HW*, 130–33, 136–39.

37. Adoff Darlap calls this time "external time" in which every moment is of equal importance and each lives by the annulment of the previous one and to which the human being is exposed and made a slave as to a cosmic power. It is time as understood by Aristotle ("the numbering of motion with respect to before and after," *Physics* 4. 11, 219b). This concept of time was adopted by medieval schoolmen such as Albertus Magnus (*Summa Theologica* 1:21,2) and Thomas Aquinas (*Summa Theologiae* 1, q. 10, aa. 1–6; *Summa Contra Gentiles* 1:15, 55; *In octo libros physicorum Aristotelis* 4:15–23), even though these authors, following the teaching of the Christian faith, maintain that time has a beginning. See "Time," *SM* 6:258–59.

38. See Darlap, "Time," 259.

39. See *DT*, 147–48.

40. "The Comfort of Time," *TI* 3:147–48.

41. *FCF*, 437. See also "The Life of the Dead," *TI* 4:348.

42. For all these hints of how eternity manifests itself in time, see "Eternity From Time," *TI* 19:172–75.

43. "Theological Observations on the Concept of Time," ibid. 11:307. It is to be noted that for Rahner God's eternity is not merely a metaphysical 'attribute' denoting immutability but a 'disposition', an 'attitude' God freely adopts toward his creatures. See "*Theos* in the New Testament," ibid. 1:104–17; "Gott," *LTK* 4:1080–87; "Gotteslehre," ibid., 1119–24; and "Observations on the Doctrine of God in Catholic Dogmatics," *TI* 9:127–45.

44. Ibid., 221–22.

45. See "Christianity and the 'New Man'," ibid. 6:135–53; "Marxist Utopia and the Christian Future of Man," ibid., 59–68; "The Festival of the Future of the World," ibid. 7:181–85; "A Fragmentary Aspect of a Theological Evaluation of the Concept of the Future," ibid. 10:235–41; "On the Theology of Hope," ibid., 242–59; "The Theological Problems Entailed in the Idea of the 'New Earth'," ibid., 260–72; "The Experiment with Man," ibid. 11:205–24; "The Problem of Genetic Manipulation," ibid., 225–52; "The Question of the Future," ibid. 12:181–201; "The Inexhaustible Transcendence of God and our Concern for the Future," ibid. 20:173–86.

46. "The Question of the Future," ibid. 12:185. It is obvious that Rahner's distinction between Absolute Future and the intramundane future is parallel to Moltmann's distinctions between *Adventus* and *Futurum*, *Zukunft* and *Futur*.

47. "The Question of the Future," *TI* 12:190.

48. "Marxist Utopia and the Christian Future of Man," ibid. 7:60–61.

49. "The Question of the Future," ibid. 12:188.

50. Rahner's writings on grace and related topics are prolific. See especially "Concerning the Relationship between Nature and Grace," ibid. 1:297–317; "Some Implications of the Scholastic Concept of Uncreated Grace," ibid., 319–46; "Reflections on the Experience of Grace," ibid. 3:86–90; "Nature and Grace," ibid. 4:165–88; "Justified and Sinner at the Same Time," ibid. 6:218–30; "The Experience of God Today," ibid. 11:149–65; "Religious Enthusiasm and the Experience of Grace," ibid. 16:35–51; "Grace, Theological," *SM* 2:412–22; "Grace, Structure of *De Gratia*," ibid., 422–24; "Grace and Freedom," ibid., 424–27; *FCF*, 116–137.

51. Note that Rahner is referring to concrete, historical human beings, and not human 'nature' in the abstract.

52. That in revelation and grace God gives *himself* to humankind and not some created reality other than himself is the cornerstone of Rahner's theological anthropology.

53. For Rahner's discussion of grace as Uncreated Grace see "Some Implications of the Scholastic Concept of Uncreated Grace," *TI* 1:319–46. Note the date of the first publication of this article, 1939, in *Zeitschrift für Katholische Theologie* 63 (1939): 137–57. If the theology of grace is the core of Rahner's theology, then it was already well formed at the beginning of his theological career and underwent no substantial change thereafter.

54. "The Theological Concept of Concupiscentia," *TI* 1:350.

55. Ibid., 360.

56. See ibid., 360–62.

57. "Reflections on Methodology in Theology," ibid. 11:98.

58. Ibid., 99.

59. *FCF*, 431.

Chapter 3. The Hermeneutics of Eschatological Statements

1. See Richard Palmer, *Hermeneutics* (Evanston: Northwestern University Press, 1969), 33–35, for a brief survey of these hermeneutical issues. There is little point in providing here a bibliography on hermeneutics in general or on theological hermeneutics in particular. For a general bibliography on the history and theory of modern hermeneutics, see Norbert Henrichs, *Bibliographie der Hermeneutik und ihrer Anwendungsbereiche seit Schleiermacher* (Düsseldorf: Philosophia-Verlag, 1968). Palmer, *Hermeneutics*, 255–74 also provides a good bibliography. For general helpful articles on hermeneutics, see Pier A. Sequeri, "Ermeneutica e filosofia," *DTI* 2:60–73; Carlo Molari, "Ermeneutica e linguaggio," ibid., 74–94; Italo Mancini, "Ermeneutica," *NDT*, 370–82; Karl Lehman, "Hermeneutics," *SM* 3:23–27.

2. *SW*, 1. The same point was made in an earlier essay of 1938, published later in *ST* 10, "Thomas Aquinas on Truth," (*TI* 13:13–31).

3. See *Belief Today*, 13–43 and *Everyday Faith*, 193–204.

4. See *FCF*, 75–81. Note that 'creatureliness' for Rahner does not signify a particular instance of a universal causal relationship between God and the created realities; it cannot be understood on the analogy of the relationship of one thing being grounded on or in another thing alongside of it or of the functional relationship between one phenomenon and another in our empirical experience. Rather it is an absolutely unique relationship mediated to us only in the transcendental experience in which we experience our radical difference from and utter dependence on God.

5. For Rahner's writings on religious experience as sources for theology, see "Reflections on the Experience of Grace," *TI* 3:86–90; "Being Open to God as Ever Greater," ibid. 7:25–46; "The Experience of God Today," ibid. 11:149–65; "Experience of Self and Experience of God," ibid. 13:122–32; "Experience of the Spirit and Existential Commitment," ibid. 16:24–34; "Religious Enthusiasm and the Experience of Grace," ibid., 35–51; "Religious Feeling Inside and Outside the Church," ibid. 17:228–42; "Experience of Transcendence from the Standpoint of Christian Dogmatics," ibid. 18:173–88; *The Spirit in the Church*, 3–21. For Rahner's interpretation of Ignatius's "consolación sin causa," see his *The Dynamic Element in the Church*, chap. 3 entitled "The Logic of Concrete Individual Knowledge in Ignatius of Loyola," 84–170.

6. "Mysticism and Karl Rahner's Theology," *Theology and Discovery*, ed. William J. Kelly (Milwaukee, Wis.: Marquette University Press, 1970), 142.

7. See "Priest and Poet," *TI* 3:296. For Rahner's extended reflections on "primary words," see in particular "'Behold this Heart!': Preliminaries to a Theology of Devotion to the Sacred Heart," ibid., 321–30.

8. See Rahner's early essay on the philosophy of Heidegger written in 1940, "Introduction au concept de philosophie existentiale chez Heidegger," *Recherches de sciences religieuses* 30 (1940): 152–71, later translated into English by Andrew Tallon and published in *Philosophy Today* 13 (Spring 1969): 126–37. As an indication of the influence of Heidegger's hermeneutics on Rahner, the latter's following autobiographical remark is quite suggestive: "I would definitively consider him [Heidegger] to be a great philosopher. . . . One can distinguish, of course, between what Heidegger meant for his students as a kind of mystagogue in philosophy and what he lectured about in a philosophical and systematic way. For me, Heidegger's first function was important. He taught us how to read texts in a new way, to ask what is behind the text, to see connections between a philosopher's individual texts and his statements that wouldn't immediately strike the ordinary person, and so on." (*I Remember: An Autobiographical Interview* [New York: Crossroad, 1985], 45). This is a translation by Harvey D. Egan of an interview Rahner gave to Meinold Krauss in 1979.

9. See his influential essay, "The Hermeneutics of Eschatological Assertions," *TI* 4:326–46.

10. Ibid., 325.

11. Ibid., 326.

12. Ibid.

13. Ibid., 329.

14. Ibid., 330–31.

15. Ibid., 332.

16. Ibid., 337, translation slightly amended. I intentionally avoid translating *Aussage* and *Einsage* with *extrapolation* and *interpolation* respectively. To interpolate, in functional analysis, is to estimate values of a function between two known values; interpolations are checkable. To extrapolate, on the other hand, is to give a meaning to the descriptive function beyond the sphere of what is measurable and checkable. Interpolation generally presents no problems. But extrapolation becomes all the more problematic the further it is removed from the realm of direct experience and therefore in popular parlance suggests projection of known data into an area not known or experienced so as to arrive at a usually conjectural knowledge of the unknown area. This is certainly not what Rahner means when he says that "Aus-sage von Gegenwart in Zukunft hinein ist Eschatologie, Ein-sage aus der Zukunft heraus in die Gegenwart hinein ist Apokalyptik" (*ST* 4:418). See Moltman's critique of Hendrik Berkhof on this point in *The Future of Creation* (Philadelphia: Fortress Press, 1979), 42–43.

17. "The Hermeneutics of Eschatological Assertions," *TI* 4:336.

18. Ibid., 338–39.

19. Note that Rahner excludes universal *apocatastasis* as *a statement of fact*, not as an object of prayer and hope.

20. *TI* 4:340.

21. Ibid.

22. Ibid., 342.

23. Ibid., 342–43.

24. Ibid., 343–44.

25. Ibid., 344.
26. Ibid., 345.
27. See ibid., 345–56.
28. See *La Svolta antropologica di Karl Rahner* (Milan: Ruscone Editore, 1974), 9: "In questo assunto di soggettivismo radicale, mai finora tentato dopo la crisi modernistica, Rahner non soltanto non teme di capovolgere i principi fondamentali del realismo tomistico. . . . ma mistifica e manipola apertamente i testi e contesti tomistici ovvi e fondamentali." See also ibid., 121: ". . . Rahner, il *deformator thomisticus radicalis* a tutti i livelli: dei testi, dei contesti e dei principi."
29. See his *Die Hermeneutik als allgemeine Methodik der Geisteswissenschaften* (Tübingen: J. C. B. Mohr, 1962) and *Teoria generale della interpretazione* (Milan: A. Giuffrè, 1955).
30. See *The Mystery of Man and the Foundations of a Theological System* (London: Sheed & Ward, 1985), 141–45.
31. See ibid., 149–54.

Chapter 4. Christian Death

1. See "Zur Theologie des Todes," *Synopsis. Studien aus Medizin und Naturwissenschaft* 3 (1949): 87–112, later expanded and published under the same title in *Zeitschrift für Katholische Theologie* 79 (1957): 1–44 and subsequently published as a separate book with an excursus on martyrdom, *Zur Theologie des Todes. Mit einem Exkursus über das Martyrium* (Freiburg: Herder, 1958).
2. *Death. A Bibliographical Guide* (Metuchen, New Jersey: The Scarecrow Press, 1978), vi–420. For excellent general articles on death, see Robert Olson, "Death," *EP* 2:307–9; Jacques Choron, "Death and Immortality," *DHI* 1:634–46; Giampiero Bof, "Morte," *DTI* 2:590–603; Amilcare Giudici, "Morte," *NDT*, 961–75.
3. See "Death," *SM* 2:58.
4. There is a secondary methodological question that must briefly be considered, namely, where to locate the discussion of Christian death in the whole corpus of dogmatic theology. As has already been mentioned, in his proposed outline of dogmatic theology, (cf. *TI* 1:33) Rahner places the topic of death in the section on "The Theological Anthropology of the Redeemed" and not in the section on eschatology. He plans to treat death in two parts, "Dying with Christ" and "The Theology of Death." Rahner's reason for placing the topic of death in theological anthropology is to emphasize the fact that death is something that is occurring here and now, not merely biologically but spiritually, as part of the Christian life and therefore must be treated on its own right, and not as a mere prelude to what follows after death. A Christian anthropology therefore must show that human existence is intrinsically ordained as a whole to death and that "this 'being-for-death' [*sein zum Tode*] co-determines everything in human life and imparts to the latter its uncertainty, its openness to mystery and its ultimate seriousness" ("Christian Dying," *TI* 18:228). The influence of Heidegger here is apparent.
On the other hand this more or less universal presence of death in the whole of human life, which transforms anthropology into a theology of death, can be adequately understood only in the light of the knowledge we have received form revelation about the condition of being dead and the final consummation. The theology of death therefore serves as a link between theological anthropology and eschatology.

5. *TD*, 8.

6. "On Christian Dying," *TI* 7:286. Heidegger's notions of authentic existence are clearly echoed in these words.

7. "On Christian Dying," *TI* 7:287.

8. "Christianity and the 'New Man'," ibid. 5:143. See also "The Experiment with Man," ibid. 9:222–23: "It remains true . . . that self-manipulation and all its concrete and utopian aims are constantly subject to the law of death—which can be neither disposed of nor manipulated. And this experience of death (in this comprehensive sense) arises from the experience of self-manipulation itself. . . . This death is not only the zero hour through which the individual must pass on his way to the absolute future, but also the zero hour for mankind as a whole."

9. "Christianity and the 'New Man'," ibid. 5:142.

10. *TD*, 13.

11. "The Unity of Spirit and Matter in the Christian Understanding of Faith," *TI* 6:160. Emphasis mine.

12. "Theological Considerations Concerning the Moment of Death," ibid. 11:317.

13. See "Ideas for a Theology of Death," ibid. 13:179: "Precisely from the point of view of a Christian theology it would be a failure to recognise the reality of death if we sought to approach it from an attitude of anthropological dichotomy by supposing that death affects only the so-called body of man, while the so-called soul, at least if it boldly resolves upon an attitude of Stoic transcendence will be able to view the fate of its former partner called the body unaffected and undismayed as from above."

14. *TD*, 17.

15. Ibid.

16. Ibid., 18.

17. "Current Problems in Christology," *TI* 1:195.

18. *TD*, 20.

19. Ibid, 21. This doctrine of 'life-entelechies' was proposed by Hans Driesch (1867–1941), German philosopher and biologist. Driesch holds that organic processes, in which the whole is in the part, are characterized by directing and sustaining entelechies, that is, some force or principle not reducible to the categories of physics and chemistry. While mechanical causality is not denied, it is said to be embedded in entelechical causality, which operates in a nonmechanical way, God being the superpersonal entelechy of the world. See his *Philosophie der Organischen*, 4th ed. (Leipzig: Quelle & Meyer, 1928). See also John Russell, "Entelechy," *SM* 2:232–33.

20. In the essay "The Life of the Dead," *TI* 4:353, Rahner explains more clearly the nature of these contacts with the dead: "There is no place in Catholic Christianity for intercourse with the dead as individuals, such as spiritualism aims at. This is not because the dead do not exist, not because they are really separated from us, not because their fidelity and love, made perfect before God, does not watch over us, not as if their existence were not truly embedded by death above all in the silent, secret ground of our own existence. But we are still creatures *in* time. And hence, unless God has wrought the miracle of a special revelation, as in the resurrection of the Lord, if the reality of the living dead as individuals were to be transposed into our concrete world, they could only appear as *we* are, not as *they* are. And in fact spiritualist seances display the spirit of the *earth-bound*, with their crude ideas and manias, not the tranquility of an eternity filled by God. And it is always possible . . . that in such efforts at contact . . . there is a strange shift in the

dimensions of time, where we do not meet *the* dead as they are *now* before God and in the definitive kernel of their being, but their as yet unredeemed and limited, confused and obscure past, which—still perhaps not totally accomplished—is then once more transfused into the categories of our own world." This intriguing explanation of the presence of the dead in the material world obviously does not intend to deny their real relation to the material world but to explain how the dead, if and when they appear to us, do so only as we are, and not as they really are before God.

21. *TD*, 21.

22. See ibid., 21–22.

23. Ibid., 22. The pancosmicity of the soul may find support in the Christian doctrine of the communion of saints according to which each human being, when his or her personal history has been consummated before God, becomes coresponsible for the other human individuals and can exercise a direct influence on the world.

24. Ibid., 24. I will discuss Rahner's theology of purgatory in greater detail in the next chapter.

25. Ibid., 26. The resurrection of the body will receive a more extended treatment in chap. 7.

26. For the traditional teaching on this topic, see *DS*, 839, 854, 926, 1000–1002, 1304.

27. "Ideas for a Theology of Childhood," *TI* 8:34–35.

28. "Dogmatic Questions on Easter" ibid. 4:131. See also "Death," *SM* 2:60.

29. *TD*, 27.

30. Ibid.

31. See "Purgatory," *TI* 19:181–93. First published as "Kleine Bemerkungen zur Fegfeuerlehre," in *Unterwegs zur Einheit, Heinrich Stirnimann zum 60. Geburstag*, ed. Johannes Brantschen and Pedro Selvatico (Freiburg: Herder, 1980), 476–85.

32. *TD*, 27.

33. Ibid., 29. We will return to the topic of the consummation of the world in chap. 8.

34. The fact of the particular judgment is not formally stated in the Church's teachings. It is implied, however, in those statements which affirm that the individual enters upon his or her final destiny immediately after death. See *DS*, 857, 1002, 1304–6.

35. See, for instance, John A. T. Robinson's *In the End, God* (London: Collins Fontana, 1968) and Russell Aldwinckle, *Death in the Secular City* (Grand Rapids, Mich.: W. B. Eerdmans Publishing Co., 1974).

36. *TD*, 29.

37. Ibid., 30. Rahner did not cite the sources in John Damascene and Thomas Aquinas to support his opinion. The following texts may be taken as confirmation of Rahner's position: John Damascene, *De fide orthodoxa* 2, 4, PG 94, col. 877 c: "Hoc enim est hominibus mors quod angelis casus." Thomas Aquinas, *ST* 2, pt. 2, q. 164, a 1, ad 6: "In quantum igitur sancti bene morte utuntur, fit eis mors meritoria."

38. *TD*, 30–31.

39. For this analysis of "passion," see "The Passion and Asceticism," *TI* 3:69–72.

40. Ibid., 72.

41. Ibid., 72–73.

42. Ibid., 73.
43. Ibid.
44. "On Martyrdom," *TD*, 87.
45. The most extensive and critical study of this topic is Nicolaus Schwerdtfeger, *Gnade und Welt. Zum Grundgefüge von Karl Rahner's Theorie der "Anonymen Christen"* (Freiburg: Herder, 1982).
46. *TD*, 88.
47. Ibid., 94. Rahner subscribes to Anton Straub's theory that the readiness to believe in principle, which he calls a "*fides virtualis*," can bring about justification. See Antonius Straub's *De Analysi fidei* (Innsbruck: Feliciani Rausch, 1922). Rahner carefully distinguishes this theory from another that maintains that a *fides late dicta*, that is, a basically philosophical knowledge of God, is sufficient for justification. Whereas this latter theory was condemned by Innocent XI (cf. *DS*, 2133), Straub's has never been subjected to ecclesiastical censure.
48. See "Anonymous Christianity and the Missionary Task of the Church," *TI* 12:161–78. For Rahner the missionary task presupposes the existence of anonymous Christianity for its success; on the other hand, anonymous Christianity, in virtue of its nature and its own intrinsic dynamism, demands to be incarnated in explicit Christianity. It is the task of missionary work to enable anonymous Christianity to come to its explicit level and assume a social and historical form in the Church.
49. *TD*, 96.
50. Ibid., 98.
51. Ibid., 106.
52. Ibid., 108.
53. Ibid., 109.
54. Ibid., 110.
55. Ibid., 111.
56. Among the most important proponents of this hypothesis, the following should be noted: Palémon Glorieux, "Endurcissement final et grâces dernières," *Nouvelle Revue Théologique* 59 (1931): 865–92; idem, "In hora mortis," *Mélanges de Science religieuse* 6 (1949): 185–216; Robert W. Gleason, *The World to Come* (New York: Sheed and Ward, 1958); idem, "Toward a Theology of Death," *Thought* 23 (1957): 39–68; Roger Troisfontaines, "La Mort, épreuve de l'amour, condition de la liberté," *Cahiers Laënnec* 7 (1946): 6–21; idem, *Je ne meurs pas* (Paris: Les Editions universitaires, 1960). Older authors in whose writings the *Endentscheidungshypothese* was adumbrated were Cajetan (1469–1534) who posited that the individual must undertake a fundamental act of love for God in death in order to obtain the forgiveness of venial sins (In *Summa Theologiae*, I, q. 63, a. 5, fin.); Mayerhofer (1951); L. Philibert Machet (1817); Vosen (1815); E. L. Fischer (1833), who all attempted to resolve the problem of the salvation of children who die without baptism by means of a decision in death; Gaston Demaret, *Les morts peu rassurantes, motifs d'espérance et de prière* (Montligéon, 1923); Jean Valéty, "Le dernier péché du croyant. Essai théologique sur l'impénitence finale," *Revue des Sciences religieuses* (1928): 50–68. For discussions of this problem, see Marcello Bordoni, *Dimensioni antropologiche della morte* (Rome: Herder, 1969) and Silvano Zucal, *La teologia della morte in Karl Rahner* (Bologna: Centro editoriale dehoniano, 1982), 239–63.
57. Boros's principal writing on this topic is *Mysterium Mortis. Der Mensch in der letzten Entscheidung* (Olten and Freiburg im Breisgau: Walter-Verlag, 1962) *(The Mystery of Death,* English translation Gregory Bainbridge [New York: Her-

der and Herder, 1965]). This book is the amplified version of an earlier article, "Sacramentum Mortis. Ein Versuch über den Sinn des Todes," *Orientierung* 23 (1959):61–75.

58. *Mysterium Mortis,* ix. The same thesis is repeated with slight variations on pp. 84 and 165.

59. By "clinical death," Boros means "the act of dying in which the cessation of the essential bodily function occurs"; by "relative death," he means "the state obtaining after the cessation of function has lasted for some length of time." By "absolute death" he means "the moment when 'the soul leaves the body'." Depending on the cause of death, the lapse of time needed for the process of death to pass through all these stages may be greater or smaller. See ibid., 172.

60. Ibid., 5.

61. Ibid., 7.

62. See ibid., 76–78.

63. Boros himself offers excellent summaries of the philosophical and theological arguments for his thesis. See ibid., 81–84; 165–69 respectively.

64. Ibid., 165.

65. See Piet Schoonenberg, "Und das Leben der zukünftigen Welt," in *Leben nach dem Tode?*, ed. H. H. Berger, (Cologne, 1962), 64–104; Joseph Pieper, *Tod und Untersblichkeit* (Munich, 1968), 120–33; Eberhard Jüngel, *Tod* (Stuttgart and Berlin: Kreuz-Verlag, 1977), 59 ff.; Amilcare Giudici, "Morte," *NDT,* 972–73; Giampiero Bof, "Morte," *DTI,* 596; Alois Winklhofer, "Zur Frage der Endentscheidung im Tode, *Theologie und Glaube* 3 (1967): 197–209; Alois Spindeler, "Mysterium Mortis. Neue eschatologische Lehren im Lichte der katholischen Dogmen," *Theologie und Glaube* 2 (1966): 144–59; Georg Scheltens, "La mort comme option finale. L'ouvrage de Boros," *Etudes franciscaines* 36 (1965): 23–35; Gisbert Greshake, *NAU,* 121–30; Edmund Fortman, *Everlasting Life After Death* (New York: Alba House, 1976), 78–82.

66. See "Ideas for a Theology of Death," *TI* 13–171. Rahner refers to Boros's article "Strukturen christlicher Vollendung," in *Strukturen christlicher Existenz,* ed. *Heinrich* Schlier et al. (Würzburg: Echter-Verlag, 1968), 251–62 and his famous book, *Mysterium Mortis.*

67. "Experience of the Spirit and Existential Commitment," *TI* 16:25 n. 2.

68. See "The Liberty of the Sick, Theologically Considered," ibid. 17:101 n. 2.

69. "Christian Dying," ibid. 18:229. This charge of mythology Rahner repeats in his foreword to Silvano Zucal's *La Teologia della morte in Karl Rahner* (Bologna: Centro editoriale dehoniano, 1982), where he rejects Greshake's accusation that he concurs with Boros's hypothesis. He further adds that ". . . wenn man Schüller Heideggers war, weiss man, dass der Tod inwendig im ganzen Leben sitzt, und bedarf darum der mythologischen klingenden Aufwertung des medizinischen Exitus bei Boros nicht" (ibid., 6).

70. See Herbert Vorgrimler, "Das Fegfeuer," in *Mysterium Salutis,* ed. Johannes Feiner and Magnus Löhrer (Einsiedeln: Benziger Verlag, 1976), 5:453–57; Juan L. Ruiz de la Peña, "La muerte—acción en la teoría de la opción final y en K. Rahner," in *Teología y mundo contemporaneo. Homenaje a K. Rahner* (Madrid: Libreria Parroquial, 1975), 545–64; Klaus Fischer, "Der Tod—'Trennung von Seele und Leib'?" *WT,* 319–20; Zucal, *La Teologia della morte in Karl Rahner* (Bologna: Centro editoriale dehoniano, 1982), 259–63.

71. *Mysterium Mortis,* 8.

72. See ibid., 9: "Quomodo medici quando inspexerint valetudinem, et mortiferam esse cognoverint, hoc pronuntiant: Moritur, inde non evadit. Ex quo nascitur homo, dicendum est: Non evadit" (*Sermo* 93, 3; 3). Another text is from

Augustine's *De Civitate Dei* 13, 10: "Si ex illo quisque incipit mori, hoc est esse in morte, ex quo in illo agi coeperit ipsa mors, id est vitae detractio . . . : profecto, ex quo esse incipit in hoc corpore, in morte est."

73. *Mysterium Mortis,* 97.

74. Ibid., ix. Emphasis added.

75. See *DS*, 1955 and 1978.

76. *TD*, 36.

77. "Christian Dying," *TI* 18:236.

78. See ibid., 247–48.

79. Ibid., 248. See also *TD*, 38. It is clear then that the hiddenness of death, which constitutes its penal character, is rooted in concupiscence as this is understood by Rahner, namely, the resistance of nature to the free act of the person in favor of either the good or the bad.

80. *TD*, 40–41.

81. Ibid., 41.

82. Ibid., 49. In the same manner, concupiscence, which is the antagonism between nature and the person endowed with grace or at least the supernatural existential, is the manifestation and penalty for original sin.

83. "On Christian Dying," *TI* 7:290.

84. See *TD*, 44–46.

85. Ibid., 56.

86. For Rahner's exposition of the "satisfaction theory," see ibid., 58–59. It is well known that this theory received a classical exposition in Anselm's *Cur Deus Homo.* Christ's death is seen as a sufficient vicarious satisfaction for the sins of the world. Sin, being an infinite offence against God, required an equally infinite satisfaction. Such satisfaction cannot be rendered by a finite being, angel or human, but only by God. On the other hand, since it is humans who have sinned, a human should perform the satisfaction and no one else. Hence the necessity of the Incarnation of God in human flesh to carry out the work of atonement.

87. *TD*, 62. In a felicitous sentence, Rahner expresses the relationship among Christ's obedience, death, and redemption: "Therefore, it is just as correct to say that his obedience is redemption, because it is death, as it is to say that his death effects our redemption, because it is obedience" (ibid., 63).

88. Ibid., 63.

89. Ibid., 66.

90. "On Christian Dying," *TI* 7:290–91.

91. *TD*, 69.

92. Ibid., 70.

93. Ibid., 71–72. See also "Ideas for a Theology of Death," *TI* 13:176–84 and "Christian Dying," ibid. 18:252–56.

94. *TD*, 72. See also "Christian Dying," *TI* 18:230–34.

95. *TD*, 74.

96. Ibid., 75.

97. Ibid., 76.

98. See ibid., 77. See also "The Eucharist and our Daily Lives," *TI* 7:211–26. "When we receive the Lord in the Eucharist as him who died on the Cross, then we receive the innermost governing factor of the everyday, because the crucified Lord in his Cross and in his death only expresses in visible terms the lot that is imparted to us in the 'prolixitas mortis' of everyday, as it were piecemeal and drop by drop, or as though we were gradually habituating ourselves to death by practising it again and again" (ibid., 219).

99. *TD*, 77–78.

100. "Proving Oneself in Time of Sickness," *TI* 7:278–79.

101. *TD,* 78. See also "The Liberty of the Sick, Theologically Considered," *TI* 17:104–9.

102. For example, in his long treatise on death prepared for the monumental series *Mysterium Salutis,* ed. Johannes Feiner and Magnus Löhrer (Einsiedeln: Benziger Verlag, 1976), 5:463–92 and reprinted in *TI* 18:226–56, Rahner did not mention this hypothesis. In this foreword to Zucal's *La Teologia delle Morte in Karl Rahner,* 6, Rahner explicitly said that he had abandoned the theory of pancosmicity of the soul and adopted rather the view proposed by Gisbert Greshake in hiſ book, *Naherwartung, Auferstehung, Untersblichkeit* (Freiburg in Breisgau, 1982). See also "'The Intermediate State'," *TI* 17:119–20.

Chapter 5. The Intermediate State

1. See *DS,* 1000–1002; 2305–7. The doctrine of purification, which is connected with that of the intermediate state, had already been taught earlier in the "Profession of Faith of Michael Palaeologus" proposed by Pope Clement VI to the emperor on 4 March 1267. However, this profession of faith, later read at the General Council of Lyons (1274), was not discussed or promulgated by the council nor accepted by the Greeks as a basis for a doctrinal agreement with the Latins. For the "Profession of Faith of Michael Palaeologus," see *DS,* 851–61; *CF,* 22–29.

2. The bibliography on this subject is immense. For a convenient summary of current opinions on the intermediate state, see Edmund J. Fortman, *Everlasting Life After Death* (New York: Alba House, 1976), 95–117.

3. "'The Intermediate State'," *TI* 17:115.

4. Rahner's interpretation of *Benedictus Deus* meets the agreement of most scholars today. See Giuseppe Barbaglio, "Risurrezione e Immortalità," *DTI* 3:135: "Il testo magisteriale suppone con tutta evidenza l'anima separata dopo morte, ma questo non constituisce la sua intenzione didattica, volta invece a definire l'immediata beatitudine e visione di Dio dopo il decesso. . . . La rappresentazione dell'anima separata fa parte di un quadro culturale recepito irriflessamente e non è elemento insegnato dal documento magisteriale."

Rahner points out a parallel between the status of the doctrine of the intermediate state and the teaching on monogenism, which is the cultural framework for the dogma of original sin. See "'The Intermediate State'," *TI* 17:115–16.

5. "'The Intermediate State'," *TI* 17:117.

6. See ibid., 117–18.

7. Ibid., 118.

8. Ibid.

9. For a distinction between time, eternity, and eviternity, see *ST* 1, q. 10, a. 5. While time is the measure of movement and eternity the measure of permanence, eviternity "differs from time and from eternity as the mean between them both." Thomas rejects the notion of eviternity as "having *before* and *after* without innovation and veteration" as self-contradictory. Rather he believes that some things recede from permanence of being (eternity) in such a way that their being is subject to change or consists in change, and these are temporal, while others recede less from permanence of being, so that their being neither consists in change nor is subject to change, and yet have change annexed to them either actually or potentially. These latter are eviternal, for example, the heavenly bodies or the angels and, one might add, the *anima separata.* So Thomas concludes: "In this way time has *before* and *after*; eviternity in itself has no *before* and *after*, which can, however,

be annexed to it; while eternity has neither *before* and *after*, nor is it compatible with such at all."

10. See, for example, Cornelius Ernst, "Theology of Death," *Clergy Review* 44 (1959): 588–93; Hermann Volk, *Das christliche Verständnis des Todes* (Münster: Verlag Regensburg, 1957); Juan L. Ruiz de la Peña, *El hombre y su muerte. Antropología teológica actual* (Burgos: Ediciones Aldecoa, 1971).

11. See the German text in "Über den 'zwischenzustand'," *ST* 12:461: "Doch wird man zugeben, dass sich das ganze Problem wesentlich vereinfacht, wenn man diese bleibende Bezogenheit der Geistseele auf die Materie scholastisch ausgedruckt as bleibende informiertheit des verklärten Leibes durch die vollendete Geistseele denkt."

12. "'The Intermediate State'," *TI* 17:120.

13. Ibid. We will come back to the question of the resurrection of the body in chap. 7.

14. Ibid.

15. Ibid., 121.

16. Ibid.

17. For the text of the definition of the Assumption (*Munificentissimus Deus*), see *DS*, 3900–3904. The definition itself runs: "Immaculatam Deiparam semper Virginem Mariam, expleto terrestris vitae cursu, fuisse *corpore et anima* ad caelestem gloriam assumptam." Emphasis added.

18. Originally published as "Zum Sinn des neuen Dogmas," *Schweizer Rundschau* 50 (1951): 585–96.

19. "The Interpretation of the Dogma of the Assumption," *TI* 1:219.

20. See ibid., 220 n. 2: "The Bull nowhere affirms that Mary's 'privilege' of 'anticipated' resurrection is to be understood as being unique in itself simply, as well as in its cause and title."

21. Ibid., 225.

22. Ibid., 226. In this way Rahner followed Hermann Zeller's interpretation of Mt 27:52–53. ("Corpora Sanctorum. Eine Studie zu Mt 27:52–53," *Zeitschrift für Katholische Theologie* 81 [1949]: 385–465) as referring to the physical resurrection of the dead. It has been pointed out by Rahner that most of the Fathers of the Church had given an eschatological interpretation to this text. Rahner also noted that, significantly enough, most of the Fathers and theologians adduced as witnesses for Mary's Assumption in the Apostolic Constitution had given explicit support to this eschatological interpretation of Mt 27:52–53 as well.

23. "'The Intermediate State'," *TI* 17:123.

24. Ibid.

25. Ibid., 115.

26. "The Life of the Dead," ibid. 4:353. English translation slightly amended.

27. Besides a brief study, "Fegfeuer," *LThK* 4:51–55 and *FCF*, 441–42, see the following articles in their chronological order: "Remarks on the Theology of Indulgences," *TI* 2:197–98 (1948); "A Brief Theological Study on Indulgences," ibid. 10:164–65 (1955); "The Comfort of Time," ibid. 3:153–54 (1956); "The Life of the Dead," ibid. 4:353 (1959); "On the Official Teaching of the Church Today on the Subject of Indulgences," ibid. 10:189 (1967).

28. Briefly, for Rahner, "an indulgence is the sacramental of the remission of sin's temporal punishment before God, and this in conjunction with a jurisdictional remission of an (at least hypothetically) imposed ecclesiastical penance. Being a sacramental, it operates *ex opere operantis* (*orantis*) *Ecclesiae*, and not *ex opere operato* as most theologians teach nowadays, even though, for historical reasons, it is connected with a jurisdictional act of the Church which is concerned with the

remission of an ecclesiastical penance and produces a sure effect in this regard" ("Remarks on the Theology of Indulgences," ibid. 2:200–201). This definition of indulgences Rahner worked out in conjunction with Bernard Poschmann's study on the indulgences from the viewpoint of the sacrament of penance, *Der Ablass im Licht der Bussgeschichte* (Bonn: Hanstein, 1948).

Rahner pointed out in 1964 that in all his writings on indulgences he had never deviated from this basic understanding, except in his conception of the temporal punishments due to sin, his interpretation of the special intercession of the Church, and his understanding of the part played by love as the basic unifying force in the process of human spiritual maturation. See "On the Official Teaching of the Church Today on the Subject of Indulgences," *TI* 10:166 n. 2.

Rahner further claims that contrary to the opinions of their critics, Roberto Masi and Charles Journet, his and Poschmann's understanding of the indulgences is not contradicted by Pope Paul VI's more recent Apostolic Constitution *Indulgentiarum Doctrina* (1 January 1967). For an English text of this document, see *Vat. II* 1:62–79. It would be interesting to compare Rahner's definition of the indulgence given above and the document's definition given in no. 8: "The taking away of the temporal punishments due to sins when their guilt has already been forgiven has been called specifically 'indulgence'. While it has something in common with other ways of eliminating the vestiges of sin, an indulgence is clearly different from them. In fact, in granting an indulgence the Church uses its power as minister of Christ's redemption. It not only prays. It intervenes with its authority to dispense to the faithful [*non tantum orat* sed . . . *auctoritative dispensat*], provided they have the right dispositions, the treasury of satisfaction which Christ and the saints won for the remission of temporal punishment." For a shorter definition see also no. 1 of the Norms contained in the same document. Rahner himself has provided a comparison in his "On the Official Teaching of the Church Today on the Subject of Indulgences," *TI* 10:166–98.

29. "Purgatory," *TI* 19:181–93.

30. Ibid. 3:220–36. Another interesting genre that Rahner employs as a *ballon d'essai* for his experimental ideas is recounting dreams. See "Dream of the Church," ibid. 20:133–42.

31. For excellent surveys, see Elmar Klinger, "Purgatory," *SM* 5:166–68; Ralph J. Bastian, "Purgatory," *NCE* 11:1034–39; and Jacques LeGoff, "Le Purgatoire. Entre l'Enfer et le Paradis," *La Maison-Dieu* 144 (1980): 103–38.

32. The first official teaching on purgatory is found in the "Profession of Faith of Michael Palaeologus" (1267): "Quod si vere paenitentes in caritate decesserint, antequam dignis paenitentiae fructibus de commissis satisfecerint et omissis: eorum animas poenis purgatoriis seu catharteriis, . . . post mortem purgari: et ad poenas huius modi relevandas prodesse eis fidelium vivorum suffragia, missarum scilicet sacrificia, orationes et eleemosynas et alia pietatis officia, quae a fidelibus pro aliis fidelibus fieri consueverunt secundum Ecclesiae instituta" (*DS,* 856–57).

Later magisterial pronouncements do not go beyond the doctrinal points, namely, the necessity of purification after death for those who have died before satisfying for their sins through penance and the usefulness of prayers for the dead. Benedict XII's *Benedictus Deus* (1336) spoke of "purgatio" (*DS,* 1000), and the General Council of Florence (1439), in its Decree for the Greeks, took over almost verbatim the "Profession of Faith of Michael Palaeologus" (*DS,* 1304). Orientals admitted the existence of purgatory as well as the efficacy of prayers offered for the dead. However, whereas the Latins explained the nature of purgatory with the help of the juridical concept of satisfaction, the Orientals conceived it in more personalistic terms, as a process of maturation and spiritual growth. The council refrained from making any allusion to fire and from using images that might depict purgatory as a place.

33. See *DS*, 1820. The distinction between the imputability of guilt and the debt of punishment had been introduced by Peter Lombard (1199–1160). Note that the language of Trent is much more spatial than that of previous councils. Trent also warned that all that does not serve to edify, but only encourages greed, curiosity, and superstition, must be avoided by preachers.

34. Vatican II's teaching on purgatory is extremely brief: "At the present time some of his (Christ's) disciples are pilgrims on earth. Others have died and are being purified, while still others are in glory. . . ." (*LG*, no. 49). Post-Vatican II teaching on purgatory is contained in the "Letter to the Sacred Congregation for the Doctrine of the Faith on Certain Questions Concerning Eschatology" (17 May 1979), of which we will speak later.

35. "Purgatory," *TI* 19:182–83.

36. "A Brief Theological Study on Indulgences," ibid. 10:151.

37. Ibid., 152. See also "Purgatory," ibid. 19;184–85: "Man is perhaps sure that he loves God and yet does not venture to assert that he loves God with all his heart, that his whole existence is integrated into this love: he admits that in him are abysmal depths, a mass of instincts, a subconscious, an 'id,' etc., as realities of which it certainly cannot be said that they are all completely integrated into the personal decision of the subject that has decided or can decide finally for or against God." In this connection one should recall to mind what Rahner has said about the role of concupiscence in the individual's growth from 'nature' to 'person'.

38. "A Brief Theological Study on Indulgences," ibid. 10:153. Rahner suggests that it is because of the necessity of undergoing this process of transformation and integration that the early Church demanded severe and lengthy penance from the baptized Christians who had relapsed into serious sins. See ibid, 154–55 and "Remarks on the Theology of Indulgences," ibid. 2:195–96.

39. Ibid., 198.

40. Ibid., 197.

41. Ibid., 198.

42. "A Brief Theological Study on Indulgence," ibid. 10:157.

43. Ibid. Hence, indulgence, if it is of any use at all, must be an aid toward this perfect love that blots out all the punishments due to sin, and not an easy and cheap way to escape from this painful process of unselfish love. See "On the Official Teaching," ibid., 193: "Indulgence, therefore, is not a *substitute* for the difficulties involved in the exercise of love, and it is not in *this* sense that it is the 'easier' way of blotting out the temporal punishments due to sin. Rather the indulgence is the assistance of the Church which supports the works of love, always difficult as these are, and precisely in *this* sense renders them 'easier'."

44. "Purgatory," ibid. 19:186.

45. Ibid., 187. This thesis was proposed by Boros, *The Mystery of Death* (New York: Herder and Herder, 1965), 136: "On the one hand, therefore, the final decision (i. e. in death) as it turns towards God is the highest act of our love for God and as such capable of effecting the forgiveness of our imputed guilt (*reatus culpae*). On the other hand, it is bound up with suffering and can be included under the concept of the pains of satisfaction (*satispassio*), and even represents a possible means for paying the debt of temporal punishment (*reatus poenae*)."

46. See ibid., 188. Perhaps Rahner is referring to Küng's unfair attack on his theology as "speculative transcendental." See Hans Küng, "Toward a New Con-

sensus in Catholic (and Ecumenical) Theology," *Journal of Ecumenical Studies* 17 (1980): 2.

47. "Purgatory," *TI* 19:189.

48. Ibid., 190.

49. Ibid., 191.

50. Ibid. Rahner suggests that Boros's hypothesis of a final decision in death is making basically the same point insofar as it allows for an opportunity of making a final decision that is opened up through the biological and clinical death and does not precede the latter.

51. See "Christian Dying," *TI* 17:237–38.

52. "Purgatory," ibid. 19:193.

53. See Boros, *Living in Hope* (New York: Doubleday Image, 1970).

54. *ST* 12:461.

55. Pierre Benoit, "Resurrection at the End of Time or Immediately After Death?" *Concilium* no. 60 (1970): 103–14.

56. For the full text of this letter see *Vat. II* 2:500–504.

57. See Elmar Klinger, "Purgatory," *SM* 5:168.

58. See *DS*, 403.

Chapter 6. Heaven and Hell

1. In fact, in his scheme for a treatise of dogmatic theolgoy, Rahner treats of heaven and hell in two different places, first in the section on the anthropology of the redeemed ("Hell as private destiny" and "The definitive character of union with God") and in the section on eschatology ("Hell as the collective destiny of the 'Corpus Diaboli'" and "Heaven as the eternal kingdom of God the Father"). See "A Scheme for a Theology of Dogmatic Theology," *TI* 1:36–37.

For biblical studies on heaven and hell, see Johann Michl, "Heaven," *EBT*, 366–69 and idem., "Hell," *EBT*, 369–71; Jean-Marie Fenasse and Jacques Guillet, "Heaven," *DBT*, 229–322 and idem, "Hell," *DBT*, 233–35. For systematic elaborations of these themes, see Gianni Colzani, "Beatitudine—Damnazione," *DTI* 1:491–503; *KG* 4:2, 452–501, 564–703 (on heaven); Joseph Ratzinger and Joseph Schmid, "Himmel," *LThK* 5:354–58; Joseph Ratzinger, "Hölle," *LThK* 5:445–49.

2. The two essays dealing explicity with heaven are: "Beatific Vision," *SM* 1:151–53 and "The Eternal Significance of the Humanity of Jesus for our Relationship with God," *TI* 3:35–46.

3. For these remarks, see "The Eternal Significance of the Humanity of Jesus for our Relationship with God," *TI* 2:35–37.

4. Ibid., 37–38.

5. *CF*, 2305. Emphasis added. See *DS*, 1000: ". . . et vident divinam essentiam visione intuitiva et etiam faciali, nulla mediante creatura in ratione obiecti visi se habente, sed divina essentia immediate se nude, clare et aperte eis ostendente, quodque sic videntes eadem divina essentia perfruuntur."

6. "The Eternal Significance of the Humanity of Jesus for our Relationship with God," *TI* 3:41.

7. Ibid.

8. Ibid., 43.

9. "Why and How Can We Venerate the Saints?," ibid. 8:12.

10. *FCF*, 84.

11. "Why and How Can We Venerate the Saints?," *TI* 8:16.

12. "The Eternal Significance of the Humanity of Jesus for our Relationship with God," ibid. 3:44.

13. See *Summa Contra Gentiles*, bk. 3, chap. 53, 6: "Therefore, this disposition whereby the created intellect is raised to the intellectual vision of divine substance is fittingly called the light of glory; not because it makes some object actually intelligible, as does the light of the agent intellect, but because it makes the intellect actually powerful enough to understand."

14. See "Beatific Vision," *SM* 1:151–53.

15. Ibid., 151.

16. Ibid., 153.

17. Ibid., 152.

18. See *The Trinity*, 22. See also "Remarks on the Dogmatic Treatise 'De Trinitate,'" *TI* 4:87. Obviously this is not the place to report Rahner's Trinitarian theology in full but only those aspects that illumine the nature of beatific vision. For a synthesis and critique of Rahner's theology of the Trinity, see Walter Kasper, *The God of Jesus Christ*, trans. Matthew J. O'Connell (New York: Crossroad, 1984), 273–77, 300–303.

19. *The Trinity*, 99.

20. "Trinity, Divine," *SM* 6:298–99.

21. "Beatific Vision," ibid. 1:153.

22. For Rahner's theology of mystery, see his classic three-lecture essay "The Concept of Mystery in Catholic Theology," *TI* 4:36–73. Also relevant to our topic are two other essays, "The Hiddenness of God," ibid. 16:227–43 and "An Investigation of the Incomprehensibility of God in St. Thomas Aquinas," Ibid., 244–54.

23. "The Concept of Mystery in Catholic Theology," ibid. 4:41.

24. Ibid., 55.

25. See "The Hiddenness of God," ibid. 16:228–33.

26. Ibid., 236–37.

27. "The Concept of Mystery in Catholic Theology," ibid. 4:56.

28. "The Hiddenness of God," ibid. 16–238.

29. "An Investigation of the Incomprehensibility of God in St. Thomas Aquinas," ibid., 254.

30. See his article on hell in *SM* 3:7–9 and *Herders theologisches Taschen-Lexikon* (Freiburg: Verlag Herder, 1967–69), 3:305–8.

31. See "Hell," *SM* 3:7.

32. See ibid.

33. Ibid.

34. *FCF*, 103.

35. Ibid., 100.

36. Ibid., 101.

37. Ibid., 102.

38. For an excellent survey of the positions of contemporary theologians regarding the possibility of hell and its eternity, see Angelo Amato, "L'inferno eterno: una realtà incompresa e contestata," *MDA*, 65–80.

39. For these difficulties, see Karl Rahner and Karl-Heinz Weger, *Our Christian Faith: Answers for the Future*, translated by Francis McDonagh (New York: Crossroad, 1981), 106–107.

40. See *CF*, 2301 and *DS*, 411, 801, 1002.

41. "Living Into Mystery. Karl Rahner's Reflections at 75," *America*, 10 March 1979, 179. See also *KRIG* 2:56.

42. *FCF*, 435.

43. See "Universal Salvific Will," *SM* 5:406.
44. *Our Christian Faith,* 121.
45. See "Universal Salvific Will," *SM* 5:407.
46. "On the Theology of Hope," *TI* 10:254.
47. "The Experience of a Catholic Theologian," *Communio: International Catholic Review* 11, no. 4 (1984): 409. English translation by Peter Verhalen. See the German text in Karl Lehmann, ed., *Vor dem Geheimnis Gottes den Menschen verstehen. Karl Rahner zum 80. Geburtstag* (Munich: Verlag Schnell und Steiner, 1984), 112.
48. *Church Dogmatics* (Edinburgh: T. & T. Clark, 1967), vol. 2, pt. 2, 477.

Chapter 7. The Resurrection of Jesus and the Resurrection of the Dead

1. *FCF,* 269. This quest for the transcendental hope in the resurrection as the horizon for understanding Jesus' Resurrection and the resurrection of the dead is made urgent today by the fact that the article of faith regarding the resurrection of the body has become largely a forgotten or irrelevant truth, even for orthodox Christians, although it still remains in the official, written catechism. The situation is rendered more difficult by the so-called demythologization theology. See "The Resurrection of the Body," *TI* 2:203–10.
2. "The Resurrection of the Body," *TI* 2:210–11.
3. Ibid., 211.
4. "Resurrection," *SM* 5:323.
5. *Our Christian Faith,* 110.
6. *FCF,* 273–74. In this way, Rahner concludes, the person who truly hopes in his or her own resurrection is an anonymous Christian.
7. For a biblical study of the resurrection in general and the Resurrection of Jesus in particular, see *EBT,* "Resurrection," 754–64; *DBT,* "Resurrection," 494–99. For more systematic studies, see *SM,* "Resurrection," 5:323–33; *DTI,* "Risurrezione di Cristo," 3:102–18; "Risurrezione e immortalità," 3:119–136; *NDT,* "Risurrezione," 1307–32; *CD* 2:556–71; *GCD* 3:464–66; *HAV,* 141–55, 167–68; *MS* 5:864–90; *Eschatologie,* 91–160; *J,* 73–118.
8. *FCF,* 266.
9. See ibid., 267. For Willi Marxsen's interpretation of Jesus' Resurrection, see his *The Resurrection of Jesus of Nazareth* (London: SCM Press, 1970). For Rahner's discussion of Marxsen's thesis, see Karl Rahner and Wilhem Thüsing, *Christologie—systematisch und exegetisch* (Freiburg: Herder, 1972), 36–38 and "Jesus' Resurrection," *TI* 17:21–23.
10. *FCF,* 268.
11. Ibid.
12. *SM* 5:330.
13. Ibid., 331. For Rahner's more extended discussion of the circular structure of faith knowledge, with particular reference to the historical Jesus, see *FCF,* 228–35; 274–76. For his view of how this Easter faith informs Christian spirituality, see "On the Spirituality of the Easter Faith," *TI* 17:8–15.
14. *SM* 5:332.
15. *FCF,* 266.
16. Rahner cites Thomas Aquinas, *ST* 3, q. 56, a. 1 ad 3 as support of this thesis. See *SM* 5:332–33. Rahner reminds us that, according to Thomas, even the resurrection of the damned depends on Jesus' glorified humanity as the efficient cause.
17. See *DT,* 442, and *SM* 5:332–33. On this point, recall Rahner's reflections on

the mediating role of Christ's glorified humanity in our beatific vision given in the last chapter.

18. For biblical studies on Parousia, see *EBT*, "Parousia," 633–38; *SM*, "Parousia," 4:342–44.

19. *SM* 4:345.

20. On the absence of Jesus after the Ascension as a source of consolation and promise, see "He Will Come Again," *ST* 7:177–80.

21. *DT*, 362.

22. "The Church and the Parousia of Christ," *TI* 6:296.

23. See *SM* 4:345 and *DT*, 257–58.

24. See *SM* 5:346.

25. Ibid.

26. See Oscar Cullmann, "Immortality of the Soul or Resurrection of the Dead," in *Immortality and Resurrection,* ed. Krister Stendahl (New York: The Macmillan Co., 1965), 9–53. Originally, Cullmann's essay was an Ingersoll Lecture delivered at Harvard University in 1955.

27. See Harry A. Wolfson, "Immortality and Resurrection in the Philosophy of the Church Fathers, " in ibid., 54–96 and Joseph Ratzinger, "Eschatologie," 119–32 and "Resurrection, B. Theological," *SM* 5:340–42.

28. For the teaching of the Fifth Lateran council regarding the immortality of the soul, see *DS*, 1440 and *CF*, 410: "The intellectual soul is not only truly, of itself and essentially, the form of the body . . . , but it is also immortal . . . ."

29. "'The Intermediate State,'" *TI* 17:116.

30. See "Eternity From Time," ibid. 19:172–75.

31. *DT*, 231.

32. *FCF,* 273.

33. Ibid.

34. "The Life of the Dead," *TI* 4:352.

35. See ibid., 120.

36. Joseph M. Shaw in his *Life After Death* (Toronto : The Ryerson Press, 1945) posited an immediate resurrection and did away with the intermediate state and the general resurrection at the end of the world. Russell Aldwinckle also posited an immediate "embodiment" after death but this embodiment is only a provisional one and therefore does not eliminate the general resurrection. See his *Death in the Secular City* (Grand Rapids, Mich.: W. B. Eerdmans Publishing Co., 1974). Boros speaks of an "initial resurrection" at death followed at the end of time by a final and complete resurrection in a transfigured universe.

37. "'The Intermediate State,'" *TI* 17:120.

38. "The Interpretation of the Dogma of the Assumption," ibid. 1:221.

39. Ibid.

40. "The Resurrection of the Body," ibid. 2:214.

41. "The Interpretation of the Dogma of the Assumption," ibid. 1:222.

42. See ibid., 223.

43. "The Resurrection of the Body," ibid. 2:213.

44. Ibid.

45. For a brilliant description and critique of this neo-scholastic apologetic of the Resurrection of Jesus, see Francis S. Fiorenza, *Foundational Theology* (New York: Crossroad, 1984), 5–12.

46. See "Dogmatische Erwägungen zur Auferstehung Jesu," *Kerygma und Dogma* 14 (1968): 105 n. 2 and "Tod und Auferstehung in der Sicht christlischer Dogmatik," *Kerygma und Dogma* 20 (1974): 175–77.

Chapter 8. The Immanent and Transcendent Consummation of the World

1. See "Immanente und transzendente Vollendung der Welt," *ST* 8:593–609; English translation in *TI* 10:273–89.

2. For an extensive study of this theme, see Philip Keane, *Karl Rahner's Theology of the World* (Washington, D.C.: The Catholic Universtiy of America, 1971).

3. For brief biblical theologies of the Kingdom of God, see *LThK* 8:1109–20; *EBT*, 455–70; *DBT*, 292–95. For a systematic theology of the Kingdom of God, see *DCG*, 477–508; *DID*, 15–23; *CD* 2:243–47; *KG*, 70–114; *NAU*, 41–81; *SM* 5:233–40.

4. *FCF*, 116. In *DT*, 264, 'Kingdom of God' is taken to mean "(a) the validity of God's holy, salvific will (as Creator, conserver, legislator, and bestower of supernatural grace) in all his creation but especially in men and angels, and (b) the actual execution of this will."

5. See, among Rahner's many writings on the subject of the supernatural existential, *FCF*, 126–33 and *SM* 2:304–6. See also "Church, Churches and Religions," *TI* 10:32–38 for a brief and lucid exposition on the supernatural existential.

6. On the necessity of historical mediation of human transcendentality, see *FCF*, 140–42; 151–54.

7. On the general revelation, see ibid., 142–51 and "History of the World and Salvation-History," *TI* 5:97–114.

8. See *FCF*, 158–62.

9. *Our Christian Faith*, 95.

10. Karl Rahner and Wilhem Thüsing, *A New Christology*, (New York: The Seabury Press, 1980), 36.

11. "Reflections on the Problems Involved in Devising a Short Formula of the Faith," *TI* 11:244. Rahner suggests that the first "theological" creedal formula refers to God the Father, the second "anthropological" formula to God the Son, and the third "futurologist" or eschatological formula to God the Spirit. This bold linkage of eschatology with pneumatology has been systematically developed by Gerhard Ebeling in *DCG* 3:3–32. Rahner's suggestion seems to be confirmed by the way the apostolic tradition of Hippolytus (c. 215–217) construes the third question of the baptismal liturgy: "Credis in Spiritu et Sanctam Ecclesiam et carnis resurrectionem?" The object of faith seems to be that the present era of the history of salvation, viz., the Church, lives in the Holy Spirit and that the resurrection of the dead takes places in him. See *CF*, 2.

12. See "The Church of Sinners," *TI* 6:253–69; "The Sinful Church in the Decrees of Vatican II," ibid., 270–94. See also *SM* 1:348: "The Church is not identical with the Kingdom of God in the eschatological phase of sacred history which began with Christ, the phase which brings about the Kingdom God. It is the sacrament of the Kingdom of God. As long as history lasts, the Church will not be identical with the Kingdom of God, for the latter is only definitively present when history ends with the coming of Christ and the last judgment."

13. *The Christian of the Future*, 82.

14. Ibid., 83.

15. *SM* 1:347.

16. See ibid.

17. "Theological Reflections on the Problem of Secularization," *TI* 10:326.

18. *Grace in Freedom*, 260.

19. Ibid., 70. Rahner has written several essays on particular cultural endeavors, e.g., philosophy, the verbal arts (poetry, music, and songs, even two essays on the

songs of the Beatles), and the sciences. He has also written on such daily routines as sleeping, moving around, sitting, seeing, laughing, eating, working, and recreating.

20. See Philip Keane, *Karl Rahner's Theology of the World,* 88–106.

21. See "Theological Reflections on the Problem of Secularization," *TI* 10:322.

22. *SM* 1:350.

23. Ibid., 350–51.

24. Rahner is critical of both "clerical triumphalists" and "lay defeatists" because both expect that the Church must have ready-made answers to all the problems of the world. Of course they differ in their judgment of whether the Church has fulfilled its role. The clerical triumphalists affirm it and attribute in consequence the misery of the world to its wicked disobedience, whereas the lay defeatists deny it and attribute the misery of the world to the failure of the official Church. See *The Christian of the Future,* 49–53.

25. See ibid., 54–62.

26. Rahner distinguishes this criticism of society from political action. To affirm that the Church has the right and duty of social criticism does not mean that the Church may and should act as a higher authority to manipulate or control the autonomous secular society or engage in politics explicitly or behind the scenes. Since the Church cannot offer any universally binding concrete plan of action, this function of the Church as a critic of society can only consist in "opening up ever anew a perspective which transcends the concrete social reality such that within this perspective the social reality concerned appears in its relative value, and so as capable of alteration" ("The Function of the Church as a Critic of Society," *TI* 12:235).

27. Rahner describes this directive-giving task of the Church as "charismatic," "prophetic," as "discernment," and even as "art" and compares this function with the logic of concrete individual knowledge. See *The Dynamic Element in the Church,* 84–170 and "On the Theological Problems Entailed in a 'Pastoral Constitution,'" *TI* 10:293–17.

28. See "Theological Reflections on the Problem of Secularization," *TI* 10:337: "*The relationship of the Church to the secular world as it exists today demands, within the framework of 'practical theology', that a special theological discipline shall be worked out and shall have a constitution of its own.* This constitution we shall call, provisionally and for want of any better term, a '*practical ecclesiological cosmology.*'" See also "Practical Theology and Social Work in the Church" ibid., 350–54.

29. See *Gaudium et Spes,* no. 39: "Far from diminishing our concern to develop this earth, the expectancy of a new earth should spur us on, for it is here that the body of a new human family grows, foreshadowing in some way the age which is to come. That is why, although we must be careful to distinguish earthly progress clearly from the increase of the Kingdom of Christ, such progress is of vital concern to the Kingdom of God, insofar as it can contribute to the better ordering of human society."

30. "The Theological Problems Entailed in the Idea of the 'New Earth,'" *TI* 10:266.

31. See "Ideology and Christianity," ibid. 6:43–45. On these distinctions Rahner follows Jörg Splett, "Ideologie und Toleranz," *Wort und Wahrheit* 20 (1965): 37–49.

32. See "Ideology and Christianity," *TI* 6:45–47.

33. See ibid., 50–55. The fact that Christianity is not an ideology implies, in Rahner's judgment, several consequences. First, although it can certainly devise

general principles and norms for concrete actions, it cannot, in its official capacity, issue binding specific imperatives and prescribe concrete actions to resolve a particular problem in the world. The Church must leave to individual Christians the responsibility and the burden to decide on the concrete course of action for the situation here and now. Secondly, it must cultivate an attitude of tolerance for Christians and non-Christians alike. And, finally, it must be on constant guard against being turned into an ideology, often a reactionary one. See ibid., 55–58.

34. See "Christianity and the 'New Man,'" ibid. 5:135–49 and "Marxist Utopia and the Christian Future of Man," ibid. 6:59–65.

35. Ibid. 6:65.

36. Ibid., 66.

37. See "Christian Humanism," ibid. 9:190–91.

38. Ibid., 195–96.

39. "On the Theology of Revolution," ibid. 14:326.

40. "Church and World," *SM* 1:353.

41. See "Immanent and Transcendent Consummation of the World," *TI* 10:273–74.

42. See ibid., 274–75.

43. Ibid., 277.

44. Ibid.

45. Ibid., 278–79.

46. "The Theological Problems Entailed in the Idea of the 'New Earth,'" ibid., 268.

47. Ibid., 270.

48. "Theological Justification of the Church's Development Work," ibid. 20:69.

49. *Basic Questions in Theology* (Philadelphia: Westminster, 1970–71), 2:242.

50. See ibid., 242–43 and Pannenberg's other book *Theology and the Kingdom of God* (Philadelphia: Westminster, 1969), 55–56.

51. For these remarks I am indebted to Langdon Gilkey's *Reaping the Whirlwind. A Christian Interpretation of History* (New York: The Seabury Press, 1981), 233–36.

Chapter 9. Retrospect and Prospect

1. See Zachary Hayes, *What Are They Saying About the End of the World?* (New York and Ramsey N. J.: Paulist Press, 1983), in particular chap. 2. Of course, Rahner was not the only theologian responsible for this anthropologization of eschatology; other Catholic theologians, in particular Yves Congar, von Balthasar, and Jean Daniélou, also played an important role.

2. See, for instance, Christian Schutz, *MS* 5:626–49; Herbert Vorgrimler, *HAV*, 83–100; Jürgen Moltmann, *The Future of Creation* (Philadelphia: Fortress Press, 1979), 41–48; Edward Schillebeeckx, "The Interpretation of Eschatology," *Concilium* 41 (1969): 42–56; Michael Simpson, *The Theology of Death and Eternal Life* (Cork: Fides Publishers, 1971); and William Dalton, *Salvation and Damnation* (Cork: Fides Publishers, 1977).

3. See Geoffrey Wainwright, *Eucharist and Eschatology* (New York: Oxford University Press, 1981), 147–51 and *Doxology* (New York: Oxford University Press, 1980), 444–62.

4. See *I Remember,* 20–23.

5. John J. Collins, *The Apocalyptic Imagination* (New York: Crossroad, 1984), 4. Collins suggests that apocalyptic literature can be divided into two types. The

first contains the "historical" apocalypses interested in the development of history and characterized by visions such as Daniel and 4 Ezra; the second group includes apocalypses marked by otherwordly journeys with a strong interest in cosmological speculation, such as the apocalypses of Abraham, 1 Enoch, 2 Enoch, testament of Levi, 3 Baruch, testament of Abraham, and apocalypse of Zephaniah. It would seem that Rahner would not object to considering the first group of apocalypses as eschatological in his use of the term since they evince a strong interest in history and its development.

6. This reductionistic language is Rahner's own. See *Grundkurs des Glaubens* (Freiburg: Herder, 1976), 414: "Es zeigt sich, dass eine solche christliche Eschatologie *gar nichts anders* als die Wiederholung all dessen, was bisher gesagt worden ist vom Menschen, insofern er der von Gottes selbstmitteilung begnadete, freie, kreatürliche Geist ist." Emphasis added.

7. For other ways of interpreting the Resurrection of Jesus, see the brief but very helpful book by Gerald O'Collins, *What Are They Saying About the Resurrection?* (New York: Paulist Press, 1978), in particular 7–40.

8. Moltmann, *The Future of Creation*, 48. In this way, hope should not be interpreted only in a transcendental way as Rahner has done but also temporally, with the future dimension clearly in evidence. For further reflections on the hermeneutics of eschatology, see the important collection of essays edited by Enrico Castelli, *Herméneutique et Eschatologie* (Paris: Aubier, 1971).

9. For a critical assessment of contemporary theologies of the cross, see Gerald O'Collins, Robert Faricy and Maurizio Flick, *The Cross Today* (New York: Paulist Press, n.d.).

10. *I remember*, 101.

11. For an excellent exposition and critique of Rahner's anthropology, see Fischer, *Der Mensch als Geheimnis*. See also the more critical but less helpful work of Vass, *The Mystery of Man and the Foundation of a Theological System*.

12. For a transcendental philosophy of freedom similar to Rahner's, see the article by Max Müller, Rahner's fellow student in Heidegger's seminar in Freiburg, "Freedom, Philosophical," *SM* 2 : 352–61.

13. See Gaboriau, *Interview sur la mort avec Karl Rahner* and Eberhard Jüngel, *Tod* (Stuttgart: Kreuz-Verlag, 1971). Gaboriau argues against Rahner that death is the opposite of nonbeing, the *nihil* of which no existential experience can be had, whereas Jüngel maintains that death is the point of the human being's total passivity, and not an act of freedom as Rahner holds.

14. For contemporary theologies of death different from Rahner's, see Michael Simpson, *The Theology of Death and Eternal Life* (Cork: Fides Publishers, 1971), which emphasizes more strongly the symbolic character of traditional statements about death; Monika K. Hellwig, *What Are They Saying About Death and Christian Hope?* (New York: Paulist Press, 1978), a survey of various current theologies of death and life beyond; and John H. Hick, *Death and Eternal Life* (San Francisco: Harper and Row, 1976), an excellent comprehensive discussion of Eastern and Western views on the subjects mentioned in the title of the book. Hick devotes chap. 12 (pp. 228–41) to an exposition and critique of Rahner's and Boros's theologies of death.

15. For a similar view of time and eternity, Aldwinckle, *Death in the Secular City*, 150–65. Aldwinckle asks three questions regarding time: (1) Is time real or unreal? (2) Does it move in one direction only or is it reversible? and (3) Does it have a beginning or an end, or is it infinite, that is, never ending? Aldwinckle opts for the first set of alternatives. See also Hans Küng, *EL*, 220–221.

16. See the suggestion of William H. Thompson in *WG*, 166–67.

17. A philosophical and theological critique of Rahner's basic thesis regarding humanity's unthematic "co-affirmation" (*Mitbejahung*) of God in the act of categorial knowledge (cf. *SW*, 179–85) and love (cf. *HW*, 83–93), of God in *Bewusstheit*, although not in *Gewusstheit*, is out of the question here. Often the critique takes the form of the question of whether Rahner has correctly interpreted Thomas Aquinas's *ST* 1, q. 84, a.7. The answer of traditional and historical Thomists such as Cornelio Fabro is a resounding no. Whether Rahner "is indeed not a *Thomist* and . . . can hardly claim the authority of Aquinas for his own philosophy," (Vass, *A Theologian in Search of a Philosophy* [London: Sheed & Ward, 1985], 43) is an important question for historical scholarship, but it does not yet settle the issue of whether his ideas are not true. For a recent critique of Rahner's doctrine of God as absolute mystery, see William J. Hoye, *Die Verfinsterung des absoluten Geheimnisses* (Düsseldorf: Patmos Verlag, 1979).

18. See *Apologetics and the Eclipse of Mystery* (Notre Dame: University of Notre Dame Press, 1979), 118–20. See also Wong, *Logos-Symbol in the Christology of Karl Rahner*, 244–55.

19. See the attempt by David Tracy in *Blessed Rage for Order* (New York: The Seabury Press, 1975), 146–203 and the volume edited by Ewert H. Cousins, *Hope and the Future of Man* (Philadelphia: Fortress Press, 1972), which collects essays and dialogues among theologians of hope from Germany (Metz, Pannenberg, and Moltmann), American Process theologians (John B. Cobb, Jr., Daniel D. Williams, Shubert M. Ogden, and Lewis S. Ford) and Teilhardians (Philip Hefner, Donald P. Gray, and Christopher F. Mooney).

20. For an attempt at relating theological hermeneutics to critical theory, especially that of Jürgen Habermas and his Frankfurt School of Social Research, see Edward Schillebeeckx, *The Understanding of Faith* (New York: Crossroad, 1974), 102–55.

Bibliography

Comprehensive lists of Karl Rahner's works can be found in the following works: Roman Bleistein and Elmar Klinger, eds., *Bibliographie Karl Rahner 1924–1969*, with an introduction by Herbert Vorgrimler (Freiburg: Herder, 1969); Roman Bleistein, ed., *Bibliographie Karl Rahner 1969–1974* (Freiburg: Herder, 1974); Paul Imhof and Heinrich Treziak, eds., "Bibliographie Karl Rahner 1974–1979," in *Wagnis Theologie: Erfahrungen mit der Theologie Karl Rahners*, ed. Herbert Vorgimler (Freiburg: Herder, 1979), 579–97; and Paul Imhof and Elisabeth Meuser, eds., "Bibliographie Karl Rahner 1979–1984," in *Glaube im Prozess: Christsein nach dem II. Vatikanum*, ed. Elmar Klinger and Klaus Wittstadt (Freiburg: Herder, 1984), 854–71.

Secondary literature on Karl Rahner can be found in the following works: Andrew Tallon, "In Dialog with Karl Rahner: Bibliography of Books, Articles and Selected Reviews, 1939–1978," *Theology Digest* 26, no. 4 (Winter 1978): 365–85; Albert Raffelt, ed., "Karl Rahner: Bibliographie der Sekundärliteratur 1948–1978" in *Wagnis Theologie*, 598–622; Albert Raffelt, "Karl Rahner: Bibliographie der Secundärliteratur 1979–1983," in *Glaube im Prozess*, 873–85.

The Heythrop Journal 25, no. 3 (July 1984): 319–65 offers excellent English primary and secondary bibliographies on Rahner arranged according to topics.

The following bibliography lists only those works of Rahner's and secondary literature that are pertinent to the topics discussed in this book.

I. Works by Karl Rahner

A. Select Basic Books

Allow Yourself to Be Forgiven: Penance Today. Translated by Salvator Attanasio. Denville, N. J.: Dimension Books, 1975. [*Man darf sich vergeben lassen* (Munich: Ars Sacra, 1974).]

Belief Today. Translated by M. H. Heelan, Rosaleen and Ray Ockendon, and William Whitman. New York: Sheed and Ward, 1967. Combines: *Alltägliche Dinge* (Einsiedeln: Benziger, 1964); *Im Heute glauben* (Einsiedeln: Benziger, 1965); "Intellectuelle Redlichkeit und christlicher Glaube," *Stimmen der Zeit* 177 (1966): 401–17.

Christian at the Crossroads. Translated by Verdant Green. London: Burns and Oates, 1975. This translation contains fourteen of the twenty-one articles in *Wagnis des Christen: Geistliche Texte* (Freiburg: Herder, 1974).

The Christian Commitment: Essays in Pastoral Theology. Translated by Cecily

Hastings. New York: Sheed and Ward, 1963. (Part 1 of *Sendung und Gnade*.) In England: *Mission and Grace*, vol. 1 (London: Sheed and Ward, 1963).

Christian in the Market Place. Translated by Cecily Hastings. New York: Sheed and Ward, 1966. (Part 3 of *Sendung und Gnade*.) In England: *Mission and Grace*, vol. 3 (London: Sheed and Ward, 1966).

The Church after the Council. Translated by Davis C. Herron and Rodelinde Albrecht. New York: Herder and Herder, 1966. Includes: *Das Konzil—ein neuer Beginn* (Freiburg: Herder, 1966); "Das neue Bild der Kirche," *Geist und Leben* 39 (1966); *Die Herausforderung der Theologie durch das II. Vatikanische Konzil* (Freiburg: Herder, 1966).

Do You Believe in God? Translated by Richard Strachan. New York: Paulist Press, 1969. [*Glaubst du an Gott?* (Munich: Ars Sacra, 1967).]

Encounters with Silence. Translated by James M. Demske. Westminster, Md.: Newman Press, 1960. [*Wörte ins Schweigen* (Innsbruck: Felizian Rauch, 1938.]

The Eternal Year. Translated by John Shea. Baltimore: Helicon Press, 1964. [*Kleines Kirchenjahr* (Munich: Ars Sacra, 1954).]

Everyday Faith. Translated by William J. O'Hara. New York: Herder and Herder, 1968. [*Glaube, der die Erde liebt* (Freiburg: Herder, 1966).]

Faith Today. Translated by Ray and Rosaleen Ockendon. London: Sheed and Ward, 1967. [*Im Heute glauben* (Einsiedeln: Benzinger, 1965).]

Foundations of Christian Faith: An Introduction to the Idea of Christianity. Translated by William V. Dych. New York: Seabury, 1978. [*Grundkurs des Glaubens: Einführung in den Begriff des Christentums* (Freiburg: Herder, 1976).]

Freiheit und Manipulation in Gesellschaft und Kirche. 2d ed. Munich: Kösel, 1971.

Das freie Wort in der Kirche. Einsiedeln: Johannes, 1953.

Grace in Freedom. Translated by Hilda Graef. New York: Herder and Herder, 1969. [*Gnade als Freiheit: Kleine theologische Beiträge* (Freiburg: Herder, 1968).]

Hearers of the Word. Translated by Michael Richards. New York: Herder and Herder, 1969. [*Hörer des Wortes: Zur Grundlegung einer Religions-philosophie*, 2d ed. revised by J. B. Metz (Freiburg: Herderbücherei, 1971).]

Herausforderung des Christen: Meditationen—Reflexionen (Freiburg: Herder-bücherei, 1975).

Hörer des Wortes: Zur Grundlegung einer Religions-philosophie. Munich: Kösel-Pustet, 1941). Parts of English translation by Joseph Donceel are printed in *A Rahner Reader*, ed. Gerald McCool (New York: Seabury, 1975), 2–65.

Inquiries: Inspiration in the Bible; Visions and Prophecies; The Church and the Sacraments; The Episcopate and the Primacy; On Heresy. New York: Herder and Herder, 1964. This is a collection of five monographs from the *Quaestiones Disputatae* series. In England: *Studies in Modern Theology* (London: Burns & Oates, 1965).

Kritisches Wort: Aktuelle Probleme in Kirche und Welt. Freiburg: Herderbücherei, 1970.

Leading a Christian Life. Translated by Salvator Attanasio, Dorothy White, and James Quigles. Denville, N.J.: Dimension Books, 1970. Comprising six short works originally published by Ars Sacra in Munich: *Ewiges Ja* (1958); *Glaubend und Liebend* (1957); *Die Gnade wird es vollenden* (1957); *Das Geheimnis unseres Christus* (1959); *Bergend und heilend* (1965).

Meditations on Hope and Love. Translated by Verdant Green. London: Burns & Oates, 1976. [*Was sollen wir jetzt tun?* and *Gott ist Mensch geworden* (Freiburg: Herder, 1974–75).]

Meditations on Priestly Life. Translated by Edward Quinn. London: Sheed and Ward, 1973. [*Einübung Priesterlicher Existenz* (Freiburg: Herder, 1970).] In the U.S.A.: *The Priesthood* (New York: Seabury, 1973).

Nature and Grace: Dilemmas in the Modern Church. Translated by Dinah Wharton. New York: Sheed and Ward, 1964. Chapters 1, 2, 3, and 5 are found in *Gefahren im heutigen Katholizismus* (Einsiedeln: Johannes, 1950).

On Prayer. New York: Paulist Deus Books, 1968. [*Von der Not und dem Segen des Gebetes.* 6th ed. Freiburg: Herderbücherei, 1964. In Ireland: *Happiness through Prayer* (Dublin: Clonomore and Reynolds, 1958).]

Opportunities for Faith: Elements of a Modern Spirituality. Translated by Edward Quinn. New York: Seabury, 1974. [*Chancen des Glaubens Fragmente einer modernen Spiritualität* (Freiburg: Herderbücherei, 1971).]

Schriften zur Theologie. 16 vols. Einsiedeln: Benziger, 1954–75. Vols. 15 and 16 have not yet been translated into English.

Sendung und Gnade: Beiträge zur Pastoraltheologie. 3d ed. Innsbruck: Tyrolia, 1961.

Servants of the Lord. Translated by Richard Strachan. New York: Herder and Herder, 1968. [*Knechte Christi: Meditationen zum Priestertum* (Freiburg: Herder, 1967).]

The Shape of the Church to Come. Translated by Edward Quinn. New York: The Seabury Press, 1974. [*Strukturwandel der Kirche als Aufgabe und Chance* (Freiburg: Herderbücherei, 1972).]

Spirit in the World. Translated by William Dych. New York: Herder and Herder, 1968. [*Geist in Welt: zur Metaphysik der endliche Erkenntnis bei Thomas von Aquin,* 2d ed. revised by J. B. Metz (Munich: Kösel, 1957).] The original *Geist in Welt* was published at Innsbruck by F. Rauch in 1939.

Spiritual Exercise. Translated by Kenneth Baker. London: Sheed and Ward, 1967. [*Betrachtungen zum ignatianischen Exerzitienbuch* (Munich: Kösel, 1965).]

Theological Investigations. 20 vols. 1–6 published in Baltimore by Helicon; vols. 7–10 in New York by Herder and Herder; and vols. 11–20 in New York by Seabury; 1961–81. [*Schriften zur Theologie,* vol. 1–14 (Einsiedeln: Benziger, 1954–80).] Hereafter volume numbers appear immediately after the volume title with the abbreviation *TI.*

God, Christ, Mary and Grace, TI 1. Translated by Cornelius Ernst, 1961. [*Gott, Christus, Maria, Gnade,* vol. 1, 1954.]

Man in the Church, TI 2. Translated by Karl H. Kruger, 1963. [*Kirche und Mensch,* vol. 2, 1955.]

The Theology of the Spiritual Life, TI 3. Translated by Karl H. Kruger and Boniface Kruger, 1967. [*Zur Theologie des Geistlichen Lebens,* vol. 3, 1956.]

More Recent Writings, TI 4. Translated by Kevin Smyth, 1966. [*Neuere Schriften,* vol. 4, 1960.]

Later Writings, TI 5. Translated by Karl Kruger, 1966. [*Neuere Schriften,* vol. 5, 1962.]

Concerning Vatican Council II, TI 6. Translated by Karl H. Kruger and Boniface

Kruger, 1969. [*Neuere Schriften*, vol. 6, 1965.] Five articles are missing in the English translation, four of which appear in *The Christian of the Future*.

Further Theology of the Spiritual Life 1, *TI* 7. Translated by David Bourke, 1971. First part of *Ein Grundriss des Geistlichen Lebens*, vol. 7, 1967.

Further Theology of the Spiritual Life 2, *TI* 8. Translated by David Bourke, 1971. Second part of *ST* 7.

Writings of 1965–1967 I, *TI* 9. Translated by Graham Harrison, 1972. First part of *Theologische Vorträge und Abhandlungen*, vol. 8, 1967.

Writings of 1965–1967 II, *TI* 10. Translated by David Bourke, 1974. Second part of *ST* 8.

Confrontations 1, *TI* 11. Translated by David Bourke, 1974. First part of *Konfrontationen*, vol. 9, 1970.

Confrontations 2, *TI* 12. Translated by David Bourke, 1974. Second part of *ST* 9.

Theology, Anthropology, Christology, *TI* 13. Translated by David Bourke, 1975. First part of *Im Gespräch mit der Zukunft*, vol. 10, 1972.

Ecclesiology, Questions in the Church, The Church in the World, *TI* 14. Translated by David Bourke, 1976. Second part of *ST* 10.

Penance in the Early Church, *TI* 15. Translated by Lionel Swain, 1982. [*Frühe Bussgeschichte in Einzeluntersuchungen*, vol. 11, 1973.]

Experience of the Spirit: Source of Theology, *TI* 16. Translated by David Moreland, 1979. First part of *Theologie aus Erfahrung des Geistes*, vol. 12, 1975.

Jesus, Man, and the Church, *TI* 17. Translated by Margaret Kohl, 1981. Second part of *ST* 12.

God and Revelation, *TI* 18. Translated by Edward Quinn, 1983. First part of *Gott und Offenbarung*, vol. 13, 1978.

Faith and Ministry, *TI* 19. Translated by Edward Quinn, 1983. Portions of *ST* 13 and 14.

Concern for the Church, *TI* 20. Translated by Edward Quinn, 1981. Portions of *Sorge um die Kirche*, vol. 14, 1980.

Theology for Renewal: Bishops, Priests, Laity. Translated by Cecily Hastings and Richard Strachan. New York: Sheed and Ward, 1964. Part 2 of *Sendung und Gnade*. In England: *Mission and Grace*, vol. 2 (London: Sheed and Ward, 1964).

Theology of Pastoral Action. Translated by W. J. O'Hara. New York: Herder and Herder, 1968. ["Grundlegung der Pastoraltheologie als praktische Theologie," in *Handbuch der Pastoral-theologie* (Freiburg: Herder, 1964), 1 : 117–215.]

The Trinity. Translated by Joseph Donceel. London: Burns & Oates, 1970. ["Der dreifaltige Gott als transzendenter Urgrund der Heilsgeschichte," in *Mysterium Salutis*, ed. Johannes Feiner and Magnus Löhrer (Einsiedeln: Benziger, 1967), 2 : 317–401.]

Zur Theologie der Zukunft. Munich: Deutscher Taschenbuch, 1971. This is a collection of articles from *Schriften* 4, 5, 6, 8, and 9, which concern the theme of the 'future'.

B. Select Edited Books and Collaborations

Ed. *Concilium: Theology in the Age of Renewal.* vols. New York: Paulist Press, 1965–69. Vol. 3, *The Pastoral Mission of the Church* (1965). Vol. 13, *Re-thinking the Church's Mission* (1966). Vol. 23, *The Pastoral Approach to Atheism* (1967). Vol. 33, *The Renewal of Preaching* (1968).

Ed. *Encyclopedia of Theology: The Concise Sacrementum Mundi.* Translated by John Griffiths, Francis McDonagh, and David Smith. New York: Seabury, 1975. Rahner himself contributed eighty-five of the articles.

Ed. *The Teaching of the Catholic Church: As Contained in Her Documents.* Translated by Geoffrey Stevens. Originally prepared by Joseph Neuner and Heinrich Roos (Staten Island, N.Y.: Alba House, 1967). [*Der Glaube der Kirche in den Urkunden der Lehrverkündigung*, 7th ed. (Regensburg: Pustet, 1965).]

With Franz X. Arnold, Viktor Schurr, and Ferdinand Klostermann, eds. *Handbuch der Pastoraltheologie.* Vols. 1–4. Freiburg: Herder, 1964–69.

With Joseph Höfer, eds. *Lexikon für Theologie und Kirche.* Vols. 1–10. 2d ed. Freiburg: Herder, 1957–67.

With Karl Lehmann. *Kerygma and Dogma.* Translated by William Glen-Doepel and edited by Thomas O'Meara. New York: Herder and Herder, 1969. A section from *Mysterium Salutis*, ed. Johannes Feiner and Magnus Löhrer (Einsiedeln: Benziger, 1965), 1:622–703.

With Heinrich Schlier, eds. *Quaestiones Disputatae.* New York: Herder and Herder, 1961–67. This series was first published in Freiburg by Herder. The volume numbers in the German and English series sometimes differ and in this listing appear immediately after the volume title with the abbreviation *Q.D.*

Inspiration in the Bible, *Q.D.* 1. Translated by Charles Henkey, 1961. [*Über die Schrift-inspiration*, *Q.D.* 1, 1957.]

On the Theology of Death, *Q.D.* 2. Translated by Charles Henkey, 1961. [*Zur Theologie des Todes*, *Q.D.* 2, 1958.]

With Joseph Ratzinger. *The Episcopate and the Primacy*, *Q.D.* 4. Translated by Kenneth Baker et al., 1962. [*Episkopat und Primat*, *Q.D.* 11, 1961.]

Church and the Sacraments, *Q.D.* 9. Translated by William J. O'Hara, 1963. [*Kirche und Sakramente*, *Q.D.* 10, 1961.]

Visions and Prophecies, *Q.D.* 10. Translated by Charles Henkey and Richard Strachan, 1963. [*Visionen und Prophezeiungen*, *Q.D.* 4, 1958.]

On Heresy, *Q.D.* 11. Translated by William J. O'Hara, 1964. ["Was ist Häresie?" in *Häresien der Zeit*, ed. Anton Bohm (Freiburg: Herder, 1961), 9–44.]

Dynamic Element in the Church, *Q.D.* 12. Translated by William J. O'Hara, 1964. [*Das Dynamische in der Kirche*, *Q.D.* 5, 1958.]

Hominization: The Evolutionary Origin of Man as a Theological Problem, *Q.D.* 13. Translated by William J. O'Hara, 1965. ["Die Hominisation als Theologische Frage," in *Das Problem der Hominisation*, by K. Rahner and Paul Overhage (Freiburg: Herder, 1961).]

With Joseph Ratzinger. *Revelation and Tradition*, *Q.D.* 17. Translated by William J. O'Hara, 1966. [*Offenbarung und Überlieferung*, *Q.D.* 25, 1965.]

The Christian of the Future, *Q.D.* 18. Translated by William J. O'Hara, 1967. This is a collection of four articles from *Schriften zur Theologie* 6: "Kirche im Wandel," "Zur 'situationsethik' aus ökumenischer Sicht," "Grenzen der Amtskirche," and "Konzilliare Lehre der kirche und Künftige Wirklichket christlichen Lebens."

Christologie: systematische und exegetische, *Q.D.* 55, 1972 (in collaboration with William Thüsing).

Vorfragen zu einem ökumenischen Amtsverständnis, *Q.D.* 65, 1974.

Et al., eds. *Sacramentum Mundi: An Encyclopedia of Theology*, vols. 1–6. Translated by William J. O'Hara et al. New York: Herder and Herder, 1968–70.

With Herbert Vorgrimler. *Theological Dictionary*. Edited by Cornelius Ernst and translated by Richard Strachan. New York: Herder and Herder, 1965. [*Kleines Theologisches Wörterbuch* (Freiburg: Herderbücherei, 1961).]

C. Articles Relevant for Eschatology from Theological Investigations

"A Scheme for a Treatise of Dogmatic Theology" (1954), *TI* 1:19–37.

"The Interpretation of the Dogma of the Assumption" (1951), *TI* 1:215–27.

"The Theological Concept of Concupiscentia" (1941), *TI* 1:347–81.

"Remarks on the Theology of Indulgences" (1948), *TI* 2:175–201.

"The Resurrection of the Body" (1953), *TI* 2:203–16.

"The Dignity and Freedom of Man" (1952), *TI* 2:235–63.

"The Eternal Significance of the Humanity of Jesus for our Relationship with God" (1953), *TI* 3:35–46.

"The Passion and Asceticism" (1949), *TI* 3:58–85.

"The Comfort of Time" (1955–56), *TI* 3:141–57.

"The Concept of Mystery in Catholic Theology" (1959), *TI* 4:36–73.

"Dogmatic Questions on Easter" (1959), *TI* 4:121–33.

"The Hermeneutics of Eschatological Assertions" (1960), *TI* 4:323–46.

"The Life of the Dead" (1959), *TI* 4:347–54.

"History of the World and Salvation-History" (1962), *TI* 5:97–114.

"Christianity and the 'New Man'" (1961), *TI* 5:135–53.

"Christology within an Evolutionary View of the World" (1962), *TI* 5:157–92.

"The Saving Force and Healing Power of Faith" (1961), *TI* 5:460–67.

"Ideology and Christianity" (1965), *TI* 6:43–58.

"Marxist Utopia and the Christian Future of Man" (1965), *TI* 6:59–68.

"The Secret of Life" (1965), *TI* 6:141–52.

"The Unity of Spirit and Matter in the Christian Understanding of Faith" (1963), *TI* 6:153–77.

"Theology of Freedom" (1965), *TI* 6:178–96.

"The Church and the Parousia of Christ" (1963), *TI* 6:295–312.

"The Scandal of Death" (1966), *TI* 7:140–44.

"He Descended into Hell" (1957), *TI* 7:145–50.

"Hidden Victory" (1966), *TI* 7:151–58.

"Experiencing Easter" (1965), *TI* 7:159–68.

"Encounters with the Risen Christ" (1955), *TI* 7:169–76.

"He Will Come Again" (1959), *TI* 7:177–80.

"The Festival of the Future of the World" (1961), *TI* 7:181–85.

"The Church as the Subject of the Sending of the Spirit" (1956), *TI* 7:186–92.

"The Spirit That is Over all Life" (1960), *TI* 7:192–201.

"Proving Oneself in Time of Sickness" (1956), *TI* 7:275–84.

"On Christian Dying" (1959), *TI* 7:285–93.

"Why and How Can We Venerate the Saints" (1964), *TI* 8:3–23.

"All Saints" (1956), *TI* 8:24–29.

"Ideas for a Theology of Childhood" (1963), *TI* 8:33–50.

"Christian Humanism" (1966), *TI* 9:187–204.

"The Experience with Man" (1966), *TI* 9:205–24.

"Self-Realization and Taking up One's Cross" (1968), *TI* 9:253–57.

"A Brief Theological Study on Indulgence" (1955), *TI* 10:150–65.

"On the Official Teaching of the Church Today on the Subject of Indulgences" (1964), *TI* 10:166–98.

"A Fragmentary Aspect of a Theological Evaluation of the Concept of the Future" (1966), *TI* 10:235–41.

"On the Theology of Hope" (1967), *TI* 10:242–59.

"The Theological Problems Entailed in the Idea of the 'New Earth'" (1968), *TI* 10:260–72.

"Immanent and Transcendent Consummation of the World" (1966), *TI* 10:273–89.

"Theological Reflections on the Problem of Secularization" (1967), *TI* 10:318–48.

"The Peace of God and the Peace of the World" (1966), *TI* 10:371–88.

"Theological Observations on the Concept of Time" (1967), *TI* 10:288–308.

"Theological Considerations on the Moment of Death" (1968), *TI* 11:309–21.

"The Question of the Future" (1969), *TI* 12:181–201.

"The Function of the Church as a Critic of Society" (1968), *TI* 12:229–49.

"Ideas for a Theology of Death" (1970), *TI* 13:169–86.

"The Quest for Approaches Leading to an Understanding of the Mystery of the God-Man Jesus" (1971), *TI* 13:195–207.

"The Church's Commission to Bring Salvation and the Humanization of the World" (1970), *TI* 14:295–313.

"On the Theology of Revolution" (1970), *TI* 14:314–30.

"The Hiddenness of God" (1974), *TI* 16:227–43.

"An Investigation of the Incomprehensibility of God in St. Thomas Aquinas" (1974), *TI* 16:244–54.

"Jesus' Resurrection" (1975), *TI* 17:16–23.

"The Body in the Order of Salvation" (1967), *TI* 17:71–89.

"The Liberty of the Sick, Theologically Considered" (1975), *TI* 17:100–113.

"The 'Intermediate State'" (1975), *TI* 17:114–24.

"The Human Question of Meaning in Face of the Absolute Mystery of God" (1977), *TI* 18:89–104.

"Following the Crucified" (1978), *TI* 18:157–70.

"Christian Dying" (1976), *TI* 18:226–56.

"Justification and World Development" (1977), *TI* 18:259–73.

"Eternity from Time" (1979), *TI* 19:169–77.

"Purgatory" (1980), *TI* 19:181–93.

"Why Does God Allow us to Suffer" (1980), *TI* 19:194–208.

"On Angels" (1978), *TI* 19:235–74.

"The Inexhaustible Transcendence of God and our Concern for the Future" (1978), *TI* 20:173–86.

"Profangeschichte und Heilsgeschichte" (1982), *ST* 15:11–23.

"Naturwissenschaft und Vernünftiger Glaube" (1981), *ST* 15:24–62.

II. Select Secondary Literature

Aldwinckle, Russell *Death in the Secular City. Life After Death in Contemporary Theology and Philosophy*. Grand Rapids, Mich.: William B. Eerdmans Publishing Co., 1972.

Bacik, James J. *Apologetics and the Eclipse of Mystery. Mystagogy According to Karl Rahner*. Notre Dame, Ind.: University of Norte Dame Press, 1980.

Boros, Ladislaus *The Mystery of Death*. Translated by Gregory Bainbridge. New York: Herder and Herder, 1965.

Buckley, James J. "Karl Rahner as a Dogmatic Theologian." *The Thomist* 47, no. 3 (1983): 364–94.

Callahan, C. Annice "Karl Rahner's Theology of Symbol. Basis for his Theology of the Church and the Sacraments," *Irish Theological Quarterly* 49 (1982): 195–205.

Camilleri, Nazareno "Il Mistero della morte. 'Anima separata' o 'cessata animazione?'" *Salesianum* 34 (1972): 97–115.

Capps, Walter *Time Invades the Cathedral. Tensions in the School of Hope*. Philadelphia: Fortress Press, 1972.

Carr, Ann *The Theological Method of Karl Rahner*. Missoula, Mont.: Scholars Press, 1977.

Castelli, Enrico, ed. *Herméneutique et Eschatologie*. Paris: Aubier, 1971.

Cirne-Lima, Carlos *Personal Faith* Translated by G. Richard Dimler. New York: Herder and Herder, 1964.

Collins, John J. *The Apocalyptic Imagination. An Introduction to the Jewish Matrix of Christianity*. New York: Crossroad, 1984.

Collopy, Bartholomew J. "Theology and the Darkness of Death," *Theological Studies* 39 (1978): 22–54.

Cousins, Ewert H., ed. *Hope and the Future of Man*. Philadelphia: Fortress Press, 1972.

Cullmann, Oscar *Christ and Time*. Translated by Floyd V. Filson. London: SCM Press, 1967.

————. *Salvation in History*, Translated by Sidney G. Sowers. New York and Evanston: Harper and Row, 1967.

Dalton, William J. *Salvation and Damnation*. Cork: Fides, 1977.

Edwards, Denis "Experience of God and Explicit Faith: A Comparison of John of the Cross and Karl Rahner," *The Thomist* 46, no. 1 (1982): 33–74.

Ernst, Cornelius "The Theology of Death," *The Clergy Review* 49, no. 10 (1959): 588–602.

Fabro, Cornelio *La Svolta antropologica di Karl Rahner*. Milan: Rusconi Editore, 1974.

Fahey, Michael A. "1904–1984, Karl Rahner, Theologian." In *Proceedings of the Thirty-Ninth Annual Convention,* 84–98. The Catholic Theological Society of America, Washington, D.C., 1984.

Feiner, Johannes, J. Trutsch, and Franz Böckle, eds. *Fragen der Theologie heute*. Einsiedeln: Benzinger Verlag, 1957.

Fiorenza, Francis S. *Foundational Theology. Jesus and the Church*. New York: Crossroad, 1984.

Fischer, Klaus P. *Der Mensch als Geheimnis. Die Anthropologie Karl Rahners*. Freiburg: Herder, 1974.

Fortman, Edmund T. *Everlasting Life After Death*. New York: Alba House, 1976.

Gadamer, Hans-Georg *Truth and Method*. Translated by Garrett Barden and John Cumming. New York: Continuum, 1975.

Galli, P. Alberto "Perchè Karl Rahner nega la visione beatifica in Cristo." *Divinitas* 13 (1969): 417–56.

Gaboriau, Florent *Interview sur la mort avec Karl Rahner*. Paris: Editions P. Lethielleux, 1967.

Galvin, John P. "Jesus' Approach to Death. An Examination of Some Recent Studies." *Theological Studies* 41 (1980): 713–44.

Gelpi, Donald L. *Life and Light. A Guide to the Theology of Karl Rahner*. New York: Sheed and Ward, 1966.

Gervais, Pierre "Les énoncés de la foi de l'Eglise aux prises avec la contingence de l'histoire selon Karl Rahner." *Nouvelle revue théologique* 103 (1981): 431–511.

Gilkey, Langdon *Reaping the Whirlwind. A Christian Interpretation of History*. New York: The Seabury Press, 1981.

Greshake, Gisbert and Gerhard Lohfink. *Naherwartung, Auferstehung, Unsterblichkeit. Untersuchung zur christlichen Eschatologie*. Freiburg: Herder, 1982.

Görres, Anton and Karl Rahner. *Das Böse. Wege zu seiner Bewaltigung in Psychotherapie und Christentum*. Freiburg: Herder, 1982.

Gutierrez, Gustavo *A Theology of Liberation*. Translated by Caritas Inda and John Eagleson. Maryknoll, N.Y.: Orbis Books, 1971.

Hayes, Zachary *What are They Saying About the End of the World?* New York: Paulist Press, 1983.

Hellwig, Monika K. *What are They Saying About Death and Christian Hope?* New York: Paulist Press, 1978.

Herzog, Frederick, ed. *The Future of Hope. Theology as Eschatology.* New York: Herder and Herder, 1970.

Hick, John H. *Death and Eternal Life.* San Francisco: Harper & Row, 1976.

Hoye, William L. *Die Verfinsterung absoluter Geheimnis. Eine Kritik der Gotteslehre Karl Rahners.* Düsseldorf: Patmos Verlag, 1979.

Hurd, Robert L. "The Conception of Freedom in Rahner." *Listening* 17 (1982): 138–52.

Imhof, Paul and H. Biallowons, eds. *Karl Rahner im Gespräch,* vol. 1 (1964–77). Munich: Kösel-Verlag, 1982.

———. *Karl Rahner im Gespräch,* vol. 2 (1979–82). Munich: Kösel-Verlag, 1983.

Kasper, Walter *The God of Jesus Christ.* Translated by Matthew J. O'Connell. New York: Crossroad, 1984.

Keane, Philip S. *Karl Rahner's Theology of the World.* Washington, D.C.: The Catholic University of America, 1971.

Kelly, William J. *Theology and Discovery: Essays in Honor of Karl Rahner, S. J.* Milwaukee, Wis.: Marquette University Press, 1980.

King, J. Norman *The God of Forgiveness and Healing in the Theology of Karl Rahner.* Washington, D.C.: University Press of America, 1982.

King, J. Norman and B. L. Whitney. "Rahner and Hartshorne on Divine Immutability." *International Philosophical Quarterly* 22 (1982): 195–209.

Kress, Robert *A Rahner Handbook.* Atlanta: John Knox Press, 1982.

Kümmel, Werner G. *Promise and Fulfillment. The Eschatological Message of Jesus.* Translated by Dorothea Barton. London: SCM Press, 1981.

Küng, Hans *Eternal Life? Life After Death as a Medical, Philosophical, and Theological Problem.* Translated by Edward Quinn. Garden City, N.Y.: Doubleday, 1984.

Lamb, Matthew L. "Orthopraxis and Theological Method in Bernard Lonergan." In *Proceedings of the Thirty-Fifth Annual Convention,* 66–87. The Catholic Theological Society of America, Washington, D.C., 1980.

———. *Solidarity with Victims. Toward a Theology of Social Transformation.* New York: Crossroad, 1982.

Lehmann, Karl and Albert Raffelt, eds. *Rechenschaft des Glaubens: Karl Rahner-Lesebuch.* 2d ed. Freiburg: Verlag Herder, 1982.

Lonergan, Bernard *Method in Theology.* New York: Herder and Herder, 1972.

Luyten, Norbert A. "Conception de la mort et conception de l'homme. La conception de la mort chez K. Rahner et L. Boros." *Nova et Vetera* 56 (1981): 195–213.

McCool, Gerald A., ed. *A Rahner Reader.* New York: The Seabury Press, 1975.

———. *The Theology of Karl Rahner.* Albany, N.Y.: Magi Books, 1961.

Macquarrie, John *Christian Hope.* New York: The Seabury Press, 1978.

Manser, Josef *Der Tod des Menschen. Zur Deutung des Todes in der gegenwärtigen Philosophie und Theologie.* Bern: Peter Lang, 1977.

Marshall, I. Howard "Slippery Words: 1. Eschatology." *Expository Times* 89 (1977–78): 264–69.

Mesa, Bernardo A. "Sentido teológico de las muerte." *Franciscanum* 8 (1966): 99–101.

Metz, Johannes B. *Christliche Anthropozentrik. Zur Denkform des Thomas von Aquin.* Munich: Kösel Verlag, 1962.

———. *The Emergent Church.* Translated by P. Mann. New York: Crossroad, 1981.

———. *Faith in History and Society. Toward a Practical Fundamental Theology.* Translated by David Smith. New York: The Seabury Press, 1980.

———. et al., eds. *Gott in Welt. Festgabe für Karl Rahner zum 60. Geburstag.* 2 vols. Freiburg: Herder, 1964.

———. *Theology of the World.* Translated by William Glenn-Doepel. New York: Herder and Herder, 1969.

Modras, Ronald "Implications of Rahner's Anthropology for Fundamental Moral Theology." *Horizons* 12, no. 1 (1985): 70–90.

Moioli, Giovanni "Dal 'De Novissimis' all'Escatologia." *La Scuola Cattolica* 101 (1973): 553–76.

———. *Lezioni sull' "escatologico" cristiano.* Veneto: Venegono Inferiore, 1973.

Moltmann, Jürgen *The Future of Creation.* Translated by Margaret Kohl. Philadelphia: Fortress Press, 1979.

———. *Theology of Hope.* Translated by James W. Leitch. New York and Evanston: Harper and Row, 1967.

Muck, Otto *The Transcendental Method.* Translated by William D. Seidensticker. New York: Herder and Herder, 1968.

Murillo, José S. de. "Dimensión escatológica de la vida cristiana según Karl Rahner. Aportación a la teología de la esperanza." *Ephemerides Carmeliticae* 22, no. 1 (1971): 38–94.

Ochs, Robert *The Death in Every Now.* New York: Sheed and Ward, 1969.

O'Collins, Gerald, Robert and Faricy, and Maurizio Flick. *The Cross Today.* New York: Paulist Press, 1977.

O'Collins, Gerald. *What are They Saying About the Resurrection?* New York: Paulist Press, 1978.

O'Donovan, Leo "De Mysterio Mortis." In *Glaube im Prozess. Christsein nach dem II. Vatikanum,* edited by Elmar Klinger and Klaus Wittstadt, 492–513. Freiburg: Herder, 1984.

———. "Orthopraxis and Theological Method: Rahner." In *Proceedings of the Thirty-Fifth Annual Convention.* 47–65. The Catholic Theological Society of America, Washington, D.C., 1980.

———. *A World of Grace. An Introduction to the Themes and Foundations of Karl Rahner's Theology.* New York: The Seabury Press, 1980.

Palmer, Richard E. *Hermeneutics.* Evanston, Ill.: Northwestern University Press, 1969.

Pannenberg, Wolfhart "Tod und Auferstehung in der Sicht christlicher Dogmatick." *Kerygma und Dogma* 20 (1974): 167–80.

Phan, Peter C. *Culture and Eschatology. The Iconographical Vision of Paul Evdokimov.* New York: Peter Lang, 1985.

Pohle-Preuss. *Eschatology.* St. Louis, Mo.: Herder, 1950.

Pozo, Candido *Teologia dell'aldilà.* Rome: Edizioni Paoline, 1970.

Quarello, Eraldo, ed. *Il Mistero dell'aldilà*. Rome: Libreria Ateneo Salesiano, 1979.

Rast, Timotheus "Die Eschatologie in der Theologie des 20. Jahrhunderts." in *Bilanz der Theologie im 20. Jahrhundert,* edited by Herbert Vorgrimler and Robert van der Gucht, 3:294–315. Freiburg-Basel and Vienna: Herder, 1970.

Ratzinger, Joseph *Eschatologie. Tod und ewiges Leben*. Regensburg: F. Pustet Verlag, 1978.

Roberts, Louis *The Achievement of Karl Rahner*. New York: Herder and Herder, 1967.

Robinson, John A. T. *In the End God*. New York: Harper & Row, 1968.

Rowling, Richard J. *A Philosophy of Revelation According to Karl Rahner*. Washington, D.C.: University Press of America, 1978.

Rondet, Henri *Fins de l'homme et fin du monde*. Paris: Fayard, 1965.

Rowland, Christopher *The Open Heaven. A Study of Apocalyptic in Judaism and Early Christianity*. New York: Crossroad, 1982.

Ruiz de la Peña, Juan L. *El hombre ye su muerte. Antropología teológica actual*. Burgos: Ediciones Aldecoa, 1971.

———. "La muerte en la antropología de K. Rahner." *Revista Española de la Teología* 31 (1971): 189–212, 335–60.

Scanlon, Michael J. "Karl Rahner: A Neo-Augustinian Thomist." *The Thomist* 43, no. 1 (1979): 178–85.

———. "Systematic Theology and the World Church." *Proceeding of the Thirty-Ninth Annual Convention,* 13–34. The Catholic Theological Society of America, Washington, D.C., 1984.

Schillebeeckx, Edward "The Interpretation of Eschatology." *Concilium* 41 (1969): 42–56.

———. *The Understanding of Faith. Interpretation and Criticism*. Translated by N. David Smith. New York: The Seabury Press, 1974.

Schmaus, Michael *Katholische Dogmatik,* vol. 4, pt. 2. *Von den Letzten Dinge*. Munich: Max Hueber Verlag, 1959.

Schutz, Christian, Henrich Gross, Karl H. Schelkle, and Wilhelm Breuning. "Die Vollendung der Geschichte," *Mysterium Salutis* 5:553–890. Einsiedeln: Benziger, 1976.

Schwerdtfeger, Nikolaus *Gnade und Welt. Zum Grundgefüge von Karl Rahner's Theorie der "anonymen Christen."* Freiburg: Herder, 1982.

Shepherd, William C. *Man's Condition. God and the World Process*. New York: Herder and Herder, 1969.

Simpson, Michael *The Theology of Death and Eternal Life*. Cork: Fides, 1971.

Smith, Wilfred C. "The World Church and the World History of Religion: The Theological Issue." In *Proceedings of the Thirty-Ninth Annual Convention*. 52–68. The Catholic Theological Society of America, Washington, D.C., 1984.

Stampa, Lorenz "Zur Theologie des Todes." *Freiburger Zeitschrift für Philosophie und Theologie* 7 (1960): 56–63.

Stendahl, Krister, ed. *Immortality and Resurrection*. New York: The Macmillan Co., 1965.

Stinson, Linda L. *Process and Conscience. Toward a Theology of Human Emergence.* Washington, D.C.: American University Press, 1986.

Tallon, Andrew "Personal Becoming." *The Thomist* 43 no. 1 (1979): 1–177.

Toinet, Paul "Théologie et eschatologie." *Revue Thomiste* 79 (1979): 181–222.

Tracy, David *The Analogical Imagination. Christian Theology and the Culture of Pluralism.* New York: Crossroad, 1981.

———. *Blessed Rage for Order. The New Pluralism in Theology.* New York: The Seabury Press, 1975.

Travis, Stephen T. *Christian Hope and the Future of Man.* Leicester, England: Inter-Varsity Press, 1980.

Vahanian, Gabriel *God and Utopia. The Church in a Technological Civilization.* New York: The Seabury Press, 1977. Translated by Paul Lachance, Paul Schwartz, Roman D. Kozk, and the author, from the French *Dieu et l'utopie, L'Eglise et la technique* (Paris: Les Editions du Cerf, 1976).

Van der Heijden, Bert. *Karl Rahner. Darstellung under Kritik seiner Grundpositionen.* Einsiedeln: Johannes Verlag, 1973.

Vass, George *The Mystery of Man and the Foundations of a Theological System.* London: Sheed and Ward, 1985.

———. *A Theologian in Search of a Philosophy.* London: Sheed and Ward, 1985.

Vorgrimler, Herbert *Der Tod im Denken und Leben des Christen.* Düsseldorf: Patmos Verlag, 1978.

———. *Hoffnung auf Vollendung. Aufriss der Eschatologie.* Freiburg: Herder, 1980.

———. ed. *Wagnis Theologie. Erfahrung mit der Theologie Karl Rahners.* Freiburg: Herder, 1979.

Wainwright, Geoffrey *Doxology. The Praise of God in Worship, Doctrine, and Life.* New York: Oxford University Press, 1980.

———. *Eucharist and Eschatology.* New York: Oxford University Press, 1981.

Weger, Karl-Heinz. *Karl Rahner. An Introduction to His Theology.* Translated by D. Smith. New York: The Seabury Press, 1980.

Wiedekehr, Dietrich *Perspektiven der Eschatologie.* Zürich: Benziger Verlag, 1974.

Winklhofer, Alois *The Coming of His Kingdom. A Theology of the Last Thing.* Translated by A. V. Littledale. New York: Herder and Herder, 1963.

Wong, Joseph H. P. *Logos-Symbol in the Christology of Karl Rahner.* Rome: Libreria Ateneo Salesiano, 1984.

Zucal, Silvano *La Teologia della morte in Karl Rahner.* Bologna: Centro editoriale dehoniano, 1982.

Name Index

Acri, Michael J., 80
Adorno, Theodor, 222 n.13
Albertus Magnus, St., 227 n.37
Aldwinckle, Russell, 173, 232 n.35, 243 n.36, 247 n.15
Alexander VII, 132
Anselm, St., 235 n.86
Aristotle, 227 n.37
Augustine, St., 17, 18, 131, 216 n.8, 234 n.72

Bacik, James, 209
Barbaglio, Giuseppe, 236 n.4
Barth, Karl, 27, 32, 223 n.25
Bastian, Ralph, 238 n.31
Benedict XII, 18, 116, 117, 118, 135, 138, 140, 142, 238 n.32
Benoit, Pierre, 133, 240 n.55
Bergson, Henri, 100
Betti, Emilio, 64, 76
Bloch, Ernst, 29, 38
Blondel, Maurice, 100
Bof, Giampiero, 101, 234 n.65
Bordoni, Marcello, 233 n.56
Boros, Ladilaus, 24, 99, 100, 101, 102, 103, 114, 133, 173, 233 n.56, 234 nn. 59, 66, and 69; 239 n.45, 240 n. 53, 247 n.14
Bracken, Joseph A., 219 n.40
Bradley, Denis, 218 n.38
Branick, Vincent, 219 n.38
Brown, Raymond, 215 n.2
Buckley, James J., 218 n.38, 225 n.11
Bultmann, Rudolf, 27, 28, 29, 33, 179, 223 n.25
Buri, Fritz, 214 n.2

Cajetan, Thomas, 233 n.56
Callahan, C. Annice, 225 n.11

Callopy, Bartholomew J., 24
Camilleri, Nazareno, 24
Carmody, John, 220 n.44
Carr, Ann, 219 nn. 39 and 40
Castelli, Enrico, 247 n.8
Clement of Alexandria, 216 n.8
Cobb, Jr., John, 248 n.19
Collins, John, 215 n.4, 246 n.5
Colzani, Gianni, 240 n.1
Congar, Yves, 246 n.1
Cullmann, Oscar, 28, 29, 33, 170, 172, 243 n.26

Daley, Brian, 221 n.2
Dalton, William, 246 n.2
Daniélou, Jean, 246 n.1
Darlap, Adoff, 227 n.37
Demaret, Gaston, 233 n.56
Didymus the Blind, 153
Dilthey, Wilhelm, 64, 65, 67, 75
Diodore of Tarsus, 153
Dodd, Charles H., 28, 33
Donceel, Joseph, 219 nn. 38 and 40
Doud, Robert, 219 n.40
Driesch, Hans, 231 n.19
Dych, William, 219 n.39

Ebeling, Gerhard, 214 n.2
Egan, Harvey, 66, 220 n.44
Eicher, Peter, 217 n.25, 220 n.42, 224 n.1
Erigena, John Scotus, 153
Ernst, Cornelius, 24, 237 n.10
Evagrius, Ponticus, 153

Fabro, Cornelio, 76, 219 n.39, 248 n.17
Faricy, Robert, 247 n.9
Fenasse, Jean-Marie, 240 n.1
Fiorenza, Francis, 243 n.45

263

Subject Index

Absolute Future, the: as God, 57–58, 200, 209–10

Angels: and the 'pancosmicity' of the soul, 87

Anointing of the sick: and death, 112–13

Anonymous Christianity: and death, 94–96

Anthropology: critique of, 207–9; Rahner's transcendental, 43–63

Apocalyptic: and eschatology, 70–72, 76, 246–47

Apocatastasis: doctrines of, 216 n.8; and hermeneutics of eschatological assertions, 72; as an object of hope and prayer, 154–56

Assumption of Mary: definition of, 237 n.17; and the intermediate state, 120–22

Baptism: and death, 112

Body: humans as unity-in-distinction of body and soul, 46–47; the risen body and its location, 173–76

Christ: and the death of the Christian, 110–13; eschatological consciousness, 32; as the hermeneutical principle of eschatological assertions, 73; his humanity and heaven, 138–42; possession of *visio immediata*, 32

Christology: Chalcedonian christology, 66; as the criterion for interpreting eschatological statements, 73; "Searching Christology," 23

Church: as sinful, 244 n.12; and social criticism, 245 n.26; and world, 183–89

Concupiscence, 60–61, 235 n.82

Consummation of the world: immanent and transcendent, 189–97, 194–97

Creatureliness, 66, 228 n.4

Creed: Rahner's formulations of, 23, 244 n.11

Culture, 185

Dead: contact with the dead, 231 n.20

Death: as action and passion, 91–94; affecting the whole person, 83; and anonymous Christianity, 94–96; of Christ, 108–10; "clinical death," "relative death," "absolute death," 234 n.59; consequence of sin, 103–8; as the definitive and final act of human freedom, 88–90; as a dying with Christ, 110–11; as the end of the human pilgrimage, 88–99; and the hypothesis of a final decision, 99–103; and martyrdom, 96–99; the natural essence of, 103–4; and original sin, 105–6; and the pancosmic dimension of the soul, 85–88; and the particular judgment, 90–91; as a personal mortal sin, 107–8; and the sacraments, 112–13; as a separation of body and soul, 83–88; as a theological topic, 230 n.4

Endentscheidungshypothese: Boros's theory, 99–101; and Rahner, 101–2

Eschatology: anthropology and, 43–63; anticipated, 28; and apocalyptic, 70–72, 76; in Christian theology, 15–18; consequent, 27; contents of, 73–74; development of Rahner's, 31–39; existential, 27–28; as hope, 30–31; individual and collective, 9–11, 17–18, 20–21; neo-scholastic, 19, 21–22; place in Rahner's theology, 19–23; in